Preventing Mass Human-Rights Violations and Atrocity Crimes

STUDIES IN POLITICS, SECURITY AND SOCIETY

Edited by Stanisław Sulowski
Faculty of Political Science and International Studies
University of Warsaw

VOLUME 42

PETER LANG

Angieszka Bieńczyk-Missala

Preventing Mass Human-Rights Violations and Atrocity Crimes

Translated by Joanna Torzewska and James Richards

PETER LANG

Bibliographic Information published by the Deutsche Nationalbibliothek
The Deutsche Nationalbibliothek lists this publication in the Deutsche Nationalbibliografie; detailed bibliographic data is available in the internet at http://dnb.d-nb.de.

Library of Congress Cataloging-in-Publication Data
A CIP catalog record for this book has been applied for at the Library of Congress.

The funding for this project was granted by the National Science Centre, based on decision DEC-2012/07/B/HS5/03776. This publication was financially supported by the Faculty of Political Science and International Studies University of Warsaw.

Cover illustration: Courtesy of Benjamin Ben Chaim.

ISSN 2199-028X
ISBN 978-3-631-86135-6 (Print)
E-ISBN 978-3-631-86810-2 (E-PDF)
E-ISBN 978-3-631-86811-9 (EPUB)
DOI 10.3726/b19087

Peter Lang – Berlin · Bern · Bruxelles · New York · Oxford · Warszawa · Wien

This publication has been peer reviewed.

www.peterlang.com

Table of Contents

Preliminary Remarks 9

Conceptualisation of the terms 11

Assumptions and research hypotheses 14

Research methods and techniques 17

Part One: States, International Institutions and Instruments ... 21

I. The United Nations as a Universal Institution for The Prevention of Mass Human-Rights Violations and Atrocity Crimes 23

1.1. The issue of prevention in universal human-rights instruments of the UN 25

1.2. Prevention as the foundation of Responsibility to Protect (R2P) 29

1.3. Main UN bodies and institutions competent to prevent mass human-rights violations and atrocity crimes 32

1.3.1. The crucial role of the Security Council in the operational prevention 32

1.3.2. The General Assembly as a debate forum on the prevention 36

1.3.3. The UN Secretary General – the *spiritus movens* 38

1.3.4. The Office on Genocide Prevention and the Responsibility to Protect: institutionalisation of prevention 43

1.4. The role of UN human rights institutions in the prevention of mass human-rights violations and atrocity crimes 46

1.4.1. The UN Human Rights Council's contribution 46

1.4.2. Treaty bodies: expert work at the base 49

1.4.3. The High Commissioner's for Human Rights activities towards prevention 51

II. Competence of Regional European Institutions in the Prevention of Mass Human-Rights Violations and Atrocity Crimes 53

2.1. The European Union against mass human-rights violations and atrocity crimes 53

2.1.1. Legal framework 53

2.1.2. EU capacity regarding prevention 55

2.2. Prevention in the activities of the Organisation for Security and Cooperation in Europe 57

2.2.1. The High Commissioner on National Minorities – the oldest European institution dedicated to prevention 59

2.2.2. The Office's for Democratic Institutions and Human Rights mandate 60

2.2.3. OSCE Missions – prevention in the field 61

2.3. The preventative role of the Council of Europe 64

III. The Problem of Preventing Mass Human-Rights Violations and Atrocity Crimes in Non-European Institutions 67

3.1. Human rights and the African Union security system 67

3.2. The evolution of the Economic Community of West African States in respect of the protection of the population 69

3.3. The International Conference on the Great Lakes Region on Genocide Prevention 72

3.4. The preventative capacity of other sub-regional groups in Africa 74

3.5. The role of the Organization of American States 76

3.6. The Responsibility to Prevent in South East Asian institutions 79

3.7. Middle Eastern organisations in the prevention of mass human-rights violations and atrocity crimes 81

IV. Prevention of Mass Human-Rights Violations and Atrocity Crimes in the Foreign Policy of States 85

4.1. Human rights, prevention and sovereignty of states 86

4.2. States towards preventing mass violations of human rights and atrocity crimes 90

4.3. International cooperation of countries interested in the prevention 95

V. The Role of Non-Governmental Organisations in the Prevention of Mass Human-Rights Violations and Atrocity Crimes 101

5.1. The potential of non-governmental organisations 101

5.2. Types of non-governmental organisations and their forms of engagement 104

VI. International Instruments for the Prevention of Human Rights Violations and Atrocity Crimes 111

6.1. Early warning 111

6.2. Diplomatic instruments 117

6.3. Economic instruments 120

6.4. Legal instruments 123

6.5. Military instruments 127

Part Two: Case Studies 133

VII. Chechnya: An Attempt at Self-Determination 135

7.1. Background: Chechen independence aspirations and the first Russian-Chechen war 135

7.2. Institutions involved and instruments applied 138

7.3. Results and evaluation 148

VIII. Rwanda – Prevention After Genocide 151

8.1. Background: causes and consequences of genocide in 1994 ... 151

8.2. Institutions involved and instruments applied 155

8.3. Results and evaluation 170

IX. Côte d'Ivoire's Elections of 2010 173

9.1. Background: the fight for power 173

9.2. Institutions involved and instruments applied 176

9.3. Results and evaluation 181

X. The Conflict in Libya and the Intervention of International Force 185

10.1. Background: the collapse of the dictatorship and the outbreak of the civil war 185

10.2. Institutions involved and instruments applied 187

10.3. Results and evaluation 193

Concluding Remarks: Factors Contributing to the Prevention 199

Bibliography 209

Books 209

Articles and chapters 215

Documents, reports, statements 221

Index of Names 237

Preliminary Remarks

The problem of preventing mass human-rights violations and atrocity crimes is one of the key issues in the international relations. It also has implications for other areas, such as conflict prevention, peace and security. Reflections on the prevention of mass violence appeared for the first time in Raphael Lemkin's writings. At the International Conference on the Unification of Criminal Law in Madrid in 1933, he prepared a proposal for an international agreement that would have provided for the prohibition of acts of barbarity and vandalism, and for the punishment of their perpetrators. By introducing the concept of genocide in the famous 1944 "Axis Rule in Occupied Europe" – in reference to crimes committed in the wider context of the Second World War – Lemkin did not limit his work to the genocide, also electing to recommended actions by which crimes might be avoided in the future. He once again advocated reviews of international and national law on the prohibition of genocide and on the practice as regards punishing criminals, as well as the establishment of institutions and mechanisms that would allow for effective control of practice during enemy occupations.[1]

The idea of the prevention of future wars, as included in the United Nations Charter of 1945, as well as the prevention of genocide taken into account in the Convention on the Prevention and Punishment of the Crime of Genocide from 1948, represented important steps in the fight against violence, but did not prevent great suffering of populations on a fairly regular basis, as in Cambodia, Iraq, Guatemala and Tibet in the Cold War era, or in the former Yugoslavia, Chechnya and Rwanda in the 1990s. However, the cases arising after 1989, when both countries and international institutions showed their ineffectiveness (e.g. in the former Yugoslavia) and/or their passivity and indifference (e.g. in Rwanda) constituted motivation for a change of thinking regarding the essence of human-rights protection and the role of both states and the international community in that regard. The disasters surrounding responses in Somalia and Srebrenica drew them to prevention, as UN Secretary General Kofi Annan stated explicitly,

1 Lemkin R. (1944), Axis Rule in Occupied Europe. Laws of Occupation – Analysis of Government – Proposals for Redress, Washington: Carnegie Endowment for International Peace, 79–95.

in a famous speech at the UN Human Rights Commission in 1998. For him, the upcoming new century had to be the age of prevention.[2]

The issue of prevention was also an important part of the concept of Responsibility to Protect set out in the 2001 Report of the UN's International Commission on Intervention and State Sovereignty, as well as the key element thereof accepted and adopted by the General Assembly in 2005. It was clear that progress in the approach to the prevention of mass human-rights violations and atrocity crimes would not be possible without prior discussion and work on conflict prevention. In the 2001 Report on the prevention of armed conflicts, Secretary-General Kofi Annan referred to a transition to a preventive culture, and also the need to look through a prevention lens as action in the name of development was taken.[3] Furthermore, the concept of the prevention of conflicts and mass human-rights abuses and atrocities has been taken on board by the United Nations, regional organisations, numerous non-governmental organisations and states in line with the basic fact that prevention seems certain to generate fewer costs – of both a human and material nature – than responding to crises. In practice, the international reaction has often come too late in the past, and thus been accompanied by civilian casualties and refugee flows.[4]

It is important to recognise as positive (in both practice and research terms) the shift from interest confined to the prevention of international conflicts to one in which the prevention of internal conflicts is also on the agenda. Similarly, there has been a move beyond the perspective and paradigm of security towards one of civil protection, the combating of inequalities, and the building of national preventative capacity.

All of this means that research into the prevention of mass human-rights violations and atrocity crimes requires an interdisciplinary approach of relevance to researchers in international relations.

2 Speech by the UN Secretary-General Kofi Annan at the opening of the 54th session of the Commission on Human Rights, March 18, 1998, SG/SM/6487HR/4355.

3 Report of the UN Secretary-General, *Prevention of Armed Conflict*, June 7, 2001, A/55/985–S/2001/574.

4 See Bieńczyk-Missala A. (2019): 'Kosovo: the First War for Human Rights' in: Madej M. (ed.), *Western Military Interventions After the Cold War*, London-New York: Routledge, 53–73.

Conceptualisation of the terms

For the purposes of this work, it is necessary that the categories of prevention and mass human-rights violations and atrocity crimes should be defined. Both are problematic, however. Researchers on the prevention of genocide and other crimes often refer to the definition of prevention presented in the Carnegie Commission's (1997) Final Report on Preventing Deadly Conflict.[5] The authors there distinguished the categories of "structural prevention" and "operational (direct) prevention", where the former concerns long-term action vis-à-vis the root causes of conflict, taken with a view to achieving security, wellbeing and justice for all. This is then a matter of solving structural and systemic problems, including helping a state to build democracy and socio-economic infrastructure. The Report also recognised peace-building activities as part of structural prevention, which thus demonstrates a broad and comprehensive approach adopted.

In turn, the aforesaid operational prevention encompasses actions taken in the face of a sudden crisis and immediate danger. It entails perpetrators being deterred, and their actions impeded. If that does not bring the desired results, it then becomes critical for violence to be stopped, and the escalation of conflict and numbers of subsequent victims averted. Operational prevention can thus be taken to include preventative diplomacy, investigations and peace-keeping activities.[6]

Mass violations of human rights and atrocity crimes, though potentially both causes and consequences of conflicts, are also committed in time of "peace" or in the context of internal riots. In defining prevention for the purposes of this study, the author assumes that prevention means taking action to avoid massive human-rights violations and atrocity crimes. However, unlike in conflict prevention, here greater attention is paid to the goal than to situations such as crises, which should not be prerequisites for the taking of action to prevent mass human-rights violations and atrocity crimes.

The aforementioned 2001 Responsibility to Protect Report dealt with civil protection and response to severe suffering, and thereby introduced a division of action potentially taken by the international community into the spheres of prevention, response and reconstruction. It is worth mentioning that the extent of prevention corresponds in part to the response to human suffering and to the

---

5 *Preventing Deadly Conflict: Final Report,* Carnegie Corporation of New York.

6 *Preventing Deadly Conflict: Final Report,* Carnegie Corporation of New York, XVIII–XX.

restoration of protection for human rights. For example, the use of economic sanctions can be regarded as a response and prevention tool at one and the same time. Likewise, post-conflict reconstruction is often aimed at preventing any recurrence of human-rights abuses. This all ensures that a precise definition or delimitation of the scope of preventative action will not prove fully possible.

Attempts to address mass human-rights violations not defined in international human rights law also raise doubts. Violations of human rights can concern individuals or have an individual character, or may be mass and systematic. The relevant literature also identifies gross or serious violations of human rights. The distinction between individual cases and mass human-rights violations is not easy, as the latter obviously comprise large(r) numbers of individual violations. It is difficult to establish a limit of how many individuals must be affected for violation to be considered to have assumed a mass-scale. The burden of infringements is an equally important issue. Violations of not all human rights will be considered gross, with attention tending to be confined to the most fundamental and important rights, especially the right to life, as well as freedom from torture, slavery or arbitrary deprivation of liberty.[7] The importance of the right to life should be emphasised. It is the number of victims and the fear of arbitrary deprivation of life, systematic, targeted attacks on the population and all actions aimed at eliminating population groups that have proved most outrageous and mobilising for both the public opinion and the international community.

Along with the concept of Responsibility to Protect, a category of atrocity crimes was arrived at. This was not set out in the 2001 Report itself, but did arise in the wake of the adoption of the 2005 General Assembly Final Document. Thus, the latter's scope was narrowed to genocide, crimes against humanity, ethnic cleansing and war crimes.[8] The definitions of these (except in the case of ethnic cleansing) are as provided for in the Statute of the International Criminal Court. Other similar categories include: mass crimes, mass atrocities, mass murder, muss killings and mass violence. However, none of these categories are fully satisfactory, and nor are they in fact crucial for preventive action to take place. For, at the stage of prevention, it is impossible to decide whether there will

7 See Conclusions of the Maastricht Seminar on the Right to Restitution, Compensation and Rehabilitation for Victims of Gross Violations of Human Rights and Fundamental Freedoms, which took place between 11 and 15 March 1992.

8 Crimes do not have to be mass crimes, but article 8 of the Statute of the ICC states that the Tribunal specifically deals with war crimes committed in the execution of a plan or policy, or when these crimes are committed on a large scale.

be genocide or crimes against humanity and, in relation to that, to differentiate actions taken and make choices of instruments in line with the situation. The effort made by the Special Advisor for the Prevention of Genocide relates to the early warning stage, with any attempt to qualify crimes in advance of their even being committed necessarily having a limited impact on ways in which institutions become further involved.

Attempts to address mass human-rights violations not defined in international human rights law also raise doubts. Violations of human rights can concern individuals or have an individual character, or may be mass and systematic. The relevant literature also identifies gross or serious violations of human rights. The distinction between individual cases and mass human-rights violations is not easy, as the latter obviously comprise large(r) numbers of individual violations. It is difficult to establish a limit of how many individuals must be affected for violation to be considered to have assumed a mass-scale. The burden of infringements is an equally important issue. Violations of not all human rights will be considered gross, with attention tending to be confined to the most fundamental and important rights, especially the right to life, as well as freedom from torture, slavery or arbitrary deprivation of liberty. The importance of the right to life should be emphasised. It is the number of victims and the fear of arbitrary deprivation of life, systematic, targeted attacks on the population and all actions aimed at eliminating population groups that have proved most outrageous and mobilising for both the public opinion and the international community.

Along with the concept of Responsibility to Protect, a category of atrocity crimes was arrived at. This was not set out in the 2001 Report itself, but did arise in the wake of the adoption of the 2005 General Assembly Final Document. Thus, the latter's scope was narrowed to genocide, crimes against humanity, ethnic cleansing and war crimes. The definitions of these (except in the case of ethnic cleansing) are as provided for in the Statute of the International Criminal Court. Other similar categories include: mass crimes, mass atrocities, mass murder, muss killings and mass violence. However, none of these categories are fully satisfactory, and nor are they in fact crucial for preventive action to take place. For, at the stage of prevention, it is impossible to decide whether there will be genocide or crimes against humanity and, in relation to that, to differentiate actions taken and make choices of instruments in line with the situation. The effort made by the Special Advisor for the Prevention of Genocide relates to the early warning stage, with any attempt to qualify crimes in advance of their even being committed necessarily having a limited impact on ways in which institutions become further involved.

This study adopted the category of mass human-rights violations and atrocity crimes, which refer to international human rights law and criminal law. The goal is to achieve the widest and most comprehensive consideration of the multi-annual achievements of the international system of human-rights protection. And, in the field of structural prevention, it is the activities of the international human-rights institutions that play an important role.

Assumptions and research hypotheses

Thus, the prevention of mass human-rights violations and atrocity crimes in the first place requires the involvement of states and national institutions. Protecting the population is primarily the task of governments, which in turn bear the primary responsibility-cum-liability should mass crimes arise. However, post-1989 there was a steady increase in states' interest in enriching their foreign policies with consideration of serious and mass human-rights violations. States declared that the violation of rights elsewhere falls within their own legitimate interests at the CSCE forum in Moscow in 1991 and in the context of the Vienna Declaration adopted at the end of the 1993 Vienna Human Rights Summit. The 1990s' discussion on the role of the international community, including a possible role intervening on humanitarian grounds, was a natural continuation of changed thinking as regards human rights and the vulnerability of populations. As it took shape, the key concept of Responsibility to Protect encompassed a new approach to state sovereignty, holding that a government's failure to ensure protection domestically gives rise to a responsibility of the same nature at the level of the international community.

The involvement of states and international institutions in the prevention of mass human-rights abuses and atrocity crimes, as well as the instruments applied and their significance, have all been the subject of this study.

Two time intervals turned out to be significant in the course of the research. First, the end of the Second World War and the establishment of the United Nations (UN) in 1945, accompanied by the idea of saving future generations from the suffering of war. It was also the beginning of the formation of an international system of human rights protection with a significant preventive "load." The second symbolic moment was the aforementioned announcement by the UN Secretary General in 1998 to increase the Organisation's efforts to prevent genocide and other crimes. On the one hand there was an increase of the interest in the problem of preventing mass human suffering, and on the other hand, in the potential and competences of international institutions, especially after the recognition of Responsibility to Protect in 2005 by the UN General Assembly.

The course of the research summarised here has seen many questions raised. Which international institutions are directly and indirectly involved in prevention, and how are their capacities and roles changing in this area? Which instruments at the disposal of countries and international institutions are used to prevent mass human-rights violations and atrocity crimes? Has the acceptance of Responsibility to Protect contributed quantitatively and qualitatively to the involvement of certain actors, and increased the adequacy of instruments used? How does the internal and international context affect the international community's involvement and effectiveness?

The purpose of the work detailed here has thus been to achieve a systematisation in regard to actors involved and tools available vis-à-vis the prevention or limitation of mass violations of human rights and atrocity crimes. There has also been detailed and comprehensive analysis and evaluation of the effectiveness of both actors and instruments. Factors contributing to the success or failure of prevention have then been identified, through analysis of their application in the context of security, political, ethnic and economic determinants. A relationship between such determinants and the results of preventative action has also been sought, while the adequacy of international instruments used in situations where atrocity crimes are most likely to occur has been assessed.

The main research hypotheses formulated were that:

1. International institutions increased their capacity to prevent mass violations of human rights and atrocity crimes under the influence of the experiences of mass crimes in the 1990s in Europe and Africa and by developing the concept of responsibility for protection. However, they did not create a coherent system of prevention.
2. It is not possible to consistently and effectively apply instruments to prevent mass violations of human rights and atrocity crimes due to the overly complex and rapidly changing nature of the context – internal and international conditions – in which the threat of mass violations is present.

This is also the basis for the following sub-hypotheses:

1. By virtue of its nature and its achievements in the fields of human rights and security, the UN has at its disposal the widest range of instruments which can be used to prevent mass violations of human rights and atrocity crimes.
2. Since 2005, there has been limited qualitative change in laws, institutions, and practice in recognition of R2P, but this has not been extensive enough in relation to the components of the UN system focusing on the protection of human rights.

3. Prevention of genocide and other atrocity crimes has been a stronger driver of change in intergovernmental organisations outside Europe than in the European institutions.
4. The foreign policies of individual states remain the most important driving mechanisms in international prevention efforts.
5. NGOs play an important role in early warning, but cannot lead in terms of operational prevention.
6. The capacity of international institutions to prevent mass human-rights violations in countries that are Permanent Members of the UN Security Council is extremely limited.
7. The presence of international staff on the ground promotes adequacy and effectiveness of international prevention efforts.
8. There are problems with the unequivocal assessment of armed intervention as an instrument for preventing or stopping mass atrocities.
9. The experience of genocide can be a powerful factor in mobilising the international community to support efforts to stabilise situations and prevent future crimes.

The above hypotheses are verified in the course of ten chapters. Six of these form a first part in which the capacity of international institutions to prevent mass human-rights violations and atrocity crimes is outlined. Considerations here begin with a characterisation of the United Nations, given its universal character, but also because it has been a precursor of reflection and action on conflict prevention, genocide and other crimes. In subsequent chapters, the competences of regional European and non-European organisations, states and non-governmental organisations are considered. There is then and attempt at the systematisation and analysis of the international instruments used to prevent mass human-rights violations, in particular with a breakdown into those relating to early warning, diplomacy, the economy and trade, the law and the military.

The second part of the study presents four cases in which international instruments for preventing mass human-rights violations have been used. These are the cases of Chechnya, Rwanda, Côte d'Ivoire and Libya. The choice thereof has been dictated by the contexts specific for each case. The first case of Chechnya is one of an ethnic group seeking independence and engaging a state enjoying the status of Permanent Member of the UN Security Council. The Rwandan case in turn refers to the instruments used in the wake of genocide, and in the presence of a real threat that further mass crimes would be committed. Côte d'Ivoire then exemplifies the action taken by the international community in the face of severe tensions and violence surrounding a change of power in a state and organised elections. Finally, Libya represents a situation in which internal conflicts were ongoing, and numerous institutions and instruments involved, up to and including international military intervention to protect the population.

This choice of cases allows for the analysis of what might be seen as "typical" situations in which mass human-rights violations arise in the context of national or ethnic group self-determination, ethnic divisions, power struggles and attempts to overthrow a dictatorship. To achieve further systematisation, analysis of the cases is based on a fixed analytical model. This begins with the internal and international context, with a view to the sources of threats of mass human-rights violations being defined, along with the state of involvement of international actors. International activities are then presented, in respect of the institutions and instruments deployed to prevent mass violence from breaking out. The final element of the analysis then entails presentation of the results of international engagement, as well as an evaluation thereof. Each time, the specificity of the situation and the changing conditions are taken into account. Such a cohesive approach to the analysed cases allows for comparison and the drawing of conclusions at the end of the work.

A serious limitation to the presentation of research results here lies with our basic inability to prove if preventative measures have been effective. In the case of repeated mass violations of human rights and atrocities, it is easy to say that instruments applied are ineffective at a specific place and time, but in the long term it is very difficult to formulate such conclusions. Still, the search for answers to the question why massive human-rights violations occur in a given situation, but not in others, and what determines the success of national and international prevention efforts, certainly represents one of the most important and interesting tasks facing the modern humanities. And naturally, this task goes far beyond the scope of this work alone, and indeed beyond the field of international relations alone.

Research methods and techniques

The research underpinning this study has drawn on several different research methods. The initial phase saw analysis of institutions and legal instruments, in order to achieve identification of the legal bases for the actions taken by states and international institutions as they seek to prevent mass human-rights violations and atrocity crimes. It was important to analyse both the legal instruments defining the obligation to prevent and the powers of international institutions in this area. It was equally important to identify the scope and nature of those relevant institutions (be these intergovernmental or non-governmental, expert or political), as such factors impact in a concrete way on the strength of their influence. The decision-making method was a complement that proved important in identifying decision centres, processes and implementation decisions. Its usefulness was manifested in particular in situations of the inadequacy of activities of organisations or states in the face of threats of mass human-rights violations and atrocity crimes; or when the implementation of decisions was seen to go beyond a given mandate.

The systems analysis was particularly helpful in respect of selected aspects of the international human-rights protection system and, to a lesser extent, the international security system. It allowed for exploration of the institutional and functional capacities of individual international organisations in the area of prevention to the extent necessary for the goals of the present work to be achieved. It also allowed for some encapsulation of the changes taking place in international organisations and in relations between states under the influence of complex cases of mass violence and unsuccessful international reactions or cases of apparent indifference to mass crimes. The study of the relationship between international organisations in the context of the threat of mass human-rights violations and atrocity crimes proved equally important, most especially where the United Nations and regional organisations were concerned. It was about the possibility of capturing manifestations of cooperation and competition in the face of the need to take action. It was equally important for the role of NGOs and their participation and impact on preventative action to be identified.

Particular elements made subject to systematic analysis were states in the world that have the capacity to engage directly and indirectly in solving problems in international relations, by way of their influence on processes taking place in international organisations. They are a particularly fascinating part of the analysis because of the dilemmas associated with the actions they take, which are influenced by various political, economic and security interests often seen to take precedence even when mass killings are in prospect. The systematic analysis has thus allowed for some grasp of the interrelationships between internal and international conditions, the involvement of institutions and the choice of instruments. It has also served to investigate whether the problem of preventing mass human-rights violations has affected the existing international human-rights system.

The elements of comparative methodology applied in the context of case studies allow conclusions to be drawn concerning institutions involved and international instruments used. Above all, they favoured identification of the relationship between internal and international conditions and the instruments used and their effectiveness. The adopted time interval also allowed for comparison before and after the adoption of Responsibility to Protect, in terms of the competences of international institutions, the identification of common features which could possibly foster cooperation and increased operational effectiveness.

The work leading to the present study has seen written sources analysed, and data collected in the course of visits to places affected by mass violations of human rights and atrocity crimes, as well as to the seats of international institutions. In the first case, literature used included monographs and articles, as well as legal acts, Reports and Resolutions. The latter were collected during archival searches at the United Nations Library in Geneva and the International Law Library at the Peace Palace in The Hague, among other places. Invaluable talks and interviews were held at the Permanent Representation of Poland to the United Nations Office in Geneva, the Office of the High Commissioner for Human Rights in Geneva, the Office of the United Nations Special Rapporteur for the Prevention of Genocide in New York, the Auschwitz Institute for Peace and Reconciliation, and the Budapest Centre for the Prevention of Mass Crimes. The study visit to Rwanda was also an important part of the work, allowing for exploration of the policy of national memory, and for interviews with government officials, NGOs and survivors. None of this would have been possible without the support of the National Science Centre of the Republic of Poland, to which the author extends her heartfelt thanks.

Part One: States, International Institutions and Instruments

I. The United Nations as a Universal Institution for The Prevention of Mass Human-Rights Violations and Atrocity Crimes

The United Nations (UN) is a universal organisation committed to the prevention of mass crimes. It was in fact obliged to be so from the moment the United Nations Charter of 26 June 1945 came into existence. After the traumatic experience of the Second World War, states obliged themselves to protect future generations from disasters of war, and to restore faith in basic human rights and human dignity.[1] However, notwithstanding the deaths of 40 million civilians during the Second World War, mass crimes were not considered a separate sphere of international relations requiring separate regulations and specialised institutions.

Indirectly, a collective security system based on the Security Council, together with its competence to maintain international peace and security, was intended to serve the above purpose also. However, it could not suffice in the event of mass crimes, since it did not cover the internal policies of countries that could also lead to massacres, as in the case of Cambodia. Nor was the period of the Cold War, dominated by the rivalry between the United States and the Soviet Union, the Eastern and Western blocs, conducive to the issues of human rights and the prevention of mass violations. Literally interpreted terms relating to the sovereignty of the state and non-interference in the internal affairs thereof, which in practice meant putting the interests of the state before the rights of individuals, constituted the conceptual impediment. During the Cold War, the Security Council almost did not deal with human rights.

In the 1990s, beginning with Security Council Resolution 688/1991 on the situation in northern Iraq,[2] which called on all members of the organisation to improve the humanitarian situation, the United Nations engaged in a more systematic addressing of the issues of human rights and crimes. Internal conflicts

---

1 Preamble to the Charter of the United Nations, https://www.un.org/en/about-us/un-charter/full-text.

2 UN Security Council Resolution, 688/1991, April 5, 1991.

and atrocity crimes were then perceived as a threat to international peace and security.

At that time, the UN was focused into conflict prevention and, where mass crimes were concerned, into reacting. Hence the decisions on humanitarian interventions in Somalia (Resolution 794/1992) and then in Bosnia-Herzegovina (Resolution 816/1993).[3] For its part, the humanitarian intervention in Kosovo undertaken by the North Atlantic Alliance without the original authorisation of the UN Security Council gained the latter's approval post-factum.

Equally, there were numerous situations in which the UN remained passive. It did not intervene in Rwanda, where within a period of just three months about 800,000 people lost their lives,[4] or in Sri Lanka, where – as a result of conflict between SLA and Tamil Tigers – some 90,000 people died.[5] Srebrenica was a great embarrassment for the organisation as well, given the massacre of some 8000 Bosnian Muslims, despite the Council's declaration of civilian security zones and the stationing of UN troops.[6]

The United Nations failures of the 1990s made it clear to states that the UN was incapable of responding adequately and effectively to atrocity crimes. Indeed, the very idea of response or reaction denotes a loss, since the crimes will already have taken place, leaving many thousands of victims. Given this reality, the United Nations shifted its work towards the prevention of atrocity crimes such as genocide, ethnic cleansing, crimes against humanity or war crimes, a symbolic beginning of which was UN Secretary-General Kofi Annan's statement of 18 March 1998, in which his determination that the next century must be the age of prevention was announced.[7] The ability of the UN to prevent atrocity crimes is

---

3 Lillich R.B. (1995) 'The Role of the UN Security Council in Protecting Human Rights in Crisis Situations. UN humanitarian intervention in the post-cold war world,' *Tulane Journal of International and Comparative Law*, Vol. 3, 5–11.

4 Report of the Independent Inquiry into the actions of the United Nations during the 1994 genocide in Rwanda, December 15, 1999, S/1999/1257.

5 Report of the Secretary-General's Panel of Experts on Accountability in Sri Lanka, March 31, 2011.

6 Report of the UN Secretary-General pursuant to General Assembly resolution No. 53/35, November 11, 1999, https://www.un.org/en/ga/search/view_doc.asp?symbol=A/54/549.

7 Statement by Secretary-General Kofi Annan at the opening of the fifty-fourth session of the Commission on Human Rights, March 18, 1998, Press Release SG/SM/6487 HR/4355.

now seen to derive from law adopted, institutions capable of taking preventative action established and appropriate mechanisms developed.[8]

1.1. The issue of prevention in universal human-rights instruments of the UN

Preventative motives were the basis for the creation of a universal system of human rights protection in response to the atrocities of the Second World War. This was to contribute to the principle set out in the preamble to the Charter of the United Nations entailing the protection of individuals against war, given that the latter usually involves serious human-rights violations and mass crimes. States were driven by revolutionary motives – a humanitarian, almost idealistic message, which addressed the fate and good of the individual,[9] as well as the prevention of traumatic events in the future.

Under Articles 1, 55 and 56 of the Charter of the United Nations, Member States commit themselves to addressing humanitarian concerns and to working together to promote universal respect for human rights and fundamental freedoms for all, regardless of race, sex, language or religion.[10] Importantly, no countries have raised objections to the above articles and other human-rights clauses.

The Convention on the Prevention and Punishment of the Crime of Genocide of 9 December 1948 was the first legal instrument in which states committed themselves to prevention. It acknowledges that genocide is a crime in international law and must be prevented. From the viewpoint of UN bodies, the most important provisions are contained in Article VIII, which provides that any State Party to the Convention[11] may request that the competent authorities of the United Nations adopt the measures provided for in the Charter that they deem appropriate to prevent or suppress acts of genocide or other acts referred

8 Bieńczyk-Missala A. (2016): 'Early Warning and the Prevention of Atrocity Crimes. The Role of the United Nations' in: Bachmann K., Heidrich D. (eds.), *The Legacy of Crimes and Crises. Transitional Justice, Domestic Change and the Role of the International Community*, Frankfurt am Main: Peter Lang Edition, 199–207.

9 Henkin L. (1978): *The Rights of Man Today*, Boulder: Westview Press, 95 et seq.

10 Charter of the United Nations, June 26, 1945, https://www.un.org/en/about-us/un-charter/full-text.

11 There were 147 States Parties to the Convention on the Prevention and Punishment of the Crime of Genocide. State as of September 23, 2016, according to the base of the International Committee of the Red Cross, https://ihl-databases.icrc.org/applic/ihl/ihl.nsf/INTRO/357?OpenDocument.

to in Article III, such as: the purpose of committing genocide, direct and public incitement to crime, complicity and others.

However, the said Convention fails to specify what the nature and scope of the obligation to prevent genocide are. Following Raphael Lemkin, the originator of the concept of genocide and drafter of the Convention, it was believed that a sufficient precautionary instrument would be to punish the crime of genocide.[12] States have therefore been obliged to adopt the appropriate law to convict the guilty of genocide irrespective of whether they are constitutionally responsible members of the government, public officials or private persons (Art. IV).[13]

The day after the adoption of the Convention on the Prevention and Punishment of the Crime of Genocide, the UN General Assembly adopted the ground-breaking Universal Declaration of Human Rights, which gave rise to a further development of standards regarding human rights, as well as to the adoption of control mechanisms that in fact served in a preventative role, among other things. In the Preamble to the Declaration, states acknowledge that lack of respect and contempt for human rights had led to acts of barbarism that had shocked the conscience of humanity, as well as recognising that the inherent dignity and equal and inalienable rights of all members of the human community are the foundation of freedom, justice and peace in the world.[14]

It is also recognised that what the Declaration enshrines, including the right to life, freedom and security of persons (Article 3) and to equality and non-discrimination (Articles 2 and 7), the prohibition of slavery (Article 4) and torture (Article 5), and the right to religious freedom (Article 18) represent a common standard of achievement. states are to strive for greater respect for these rights and freedoms, and to ensure their universal and effective recognition and respect, among both peoples of the states themselves and those residing in territories under those states' jurisdiction.

---

12 This corresponded to the intentions of Raphael Lemkin, who argued – in his *Axis Rule in Occupied Europe* – that punishing the perpetrators of the genocide of the Second World War would help avoid repetition of the crime in the future, Lemkin R. (1944): *Axis Rule in Occupied Europe: Laws of Occupation – Analysis of Government – Proposals for Redress*, Washington, D.C.: Carnegie Endowment for International Peace, 93–94.

13 Ben-Naftali O. (2009): 'The Obligations to Prevent and to Punish Genocide' in: Gaeta P., (ed.) *The UN Genocide Convention. A Commentary*, Oxford: Oxford University Press 2009, 36–44.

14 Universal Declaration of Human Rights, December 10, 1948, https://www.un.org/en/about-us/universal-declaration-of-human-rights.

Human rights instruments such as the International Covenant on Civil and Political Rights (ICCPR) and the International Covenant on Economic, Social and Cultural Rights (ICESCR) of 16 December 1966, call for the creation of such conditions as allow every individual to benefit from accepted human rights.[15] States undertake to respect and ensure that all persons within their territory and under their jurisdiction have rights in the Covenants recognised, regardless of any differences of race, colour, gender, language, religion or belief. A further undertaking entails steps necessary to implement rights, including adoption of appropriate legislation.

The Covenants made no direct reference to the prevention of human-rights violations, but set out standards that were significant in terms of prevention. The most important of these, apart from ones recognised previously in the Universal Declaration of Human Rights entailed the statutory prohibition of propaganda of war and the promotion of any national, racial or religious hatred inciting discrimination, hostility or rape (Article 20), as well as a prohibition on depriving persons belonging to ethnic, religious or linguistic minorities of rights to their own cultural life, to practice their own religion and to use their own language (Article 27).

A direct message regarding prevention was enshrined in the International Convention on the Elimination of All Forms of Racial Discrimination of 21 December 1965. In it, states concerned by cases thereof expressed a strong will to abolish racial discrimination, but also to prevent the emergence of doctrines and racist practices. To do this, they agreed, among others, to take on obligations to punish the dissemination of ideas based on superiority or racial hatred, all acts of violence or incitement to such acts against any race or group of people of different colour or other ethnic origin, and assistance in the conduct of racist activities, including the financing of such activities. They committed themselves to the prohibition of organisations seeking to promote racial discrimination or incitement thereto (Article 4).

In addition, Parties undertook to ensure effective protection against all acts of racial discrimination (Article 6) and to take urgent measures, especially in the fields of education, culture and information, to combat the prejudice which lead

15 International Covenant on Civil and Political Rights, preamble, G.A. res. 2200A (XXI), 21 U.N. GAOR Supp. (No. 16) at 52, U.N. Doc. A/6316 (1966), 999 U.N.T.S. 171; *International Covenant on* Economic, Social and Cultural Rights, preamble, G.A. res. 2200A (XXI), 21 U.N. GAOR Supp. (No. 16) at 49, U.N. Doc. A/6316 (1966), 993 U.N.T.S. 3.

to racial discrimination and to promote mutual understanding, tolerance and friendship among nations and racial or ethnic groups (Article 7).

In the latter regard, the Declaration on race and racial prejudice adopted by the United Nations General Conference on Education, Science and Culture, on 27 November 1978, played an important role. It emphasised that, for preventative purposes, states should take all possible steps, including in terms of legislation, especially in the sphere of education, culture and communication, and promote knowledge about the prevention of racial prejudice and attitudes. The states also identified the media and those who control it as well as organised groups within communities as responsible for promoting understanding, tolerance and friendship between racist individuals and groups (Article 5).

The above instruments corresponded to the Convention on the Prevention and Punishment of the Crime of Apartheid of 30 November 1973. This included an obligation for all necessary legal and other measures to be taken to both eradicate – and prevent the emergence of any support for – apartheid, as well as racial segregation policy in general (Article 4). Article 6 thereof in turn undertook to recognise and give effect to all decisions of the Security Council aimed at preventing, combating and punishing apartheid crimes, and supporting the decisions of other competent authorities in this regard.

The premise of prevention also accompanied the fight against torture. In Article 2 of the Convention on the Prohibition of Torture and Other Cruel, Inhuman or Degrading Treatment or Punishment of 10 December 1948, states undertook to take effective legislative, administrative, judicial and other measures to prevent torture throughout the territory under their jurisdiction. The Optional Protocol to the Convention of 18 December 2002 added some suggested national measures for education, and, for preventative purposes, and established a system of regular visits to places in which persons deprived of their liberty are located. These are carried out by national authorities under the so-called National Prevention Mechanism and International Subcommittee of the UN Committee Against Torture.

These instruments adopted at the UN appear crucial to the development of the concept of the prevention, but there have also been further measures concerning groups vulnerable to human-rights violations, which assume the need for violations of the law to be prevented. The Convention on the Elimination of All Forms of Discrimination against Women of 18 December 1979 provides guidance on the prevention of discrimination against women at work (Article 11.2). The International Convention for the Protection of the Rights of All Migrant Workers and Members of Their Families of 18 December 1990 in turn calls on states to cooperate for the prevention of trafficking of migrant workers

(Article 68). The Convention on the Rights of Persons with Disabilities involves states committing themselves to steps that prevent all forms of violence and exploitation of persons with disabilities, including through appropriate educational assistance and support for the avoidance, identification and reporting of violence and exploitation. A provision regarding the monitoring of activities and programmes for people with disabilities by independent and competent bodies also had preventative goals (Article 16). The Convention also refers to the prevention of the concealment, abandonment, negligence or segregation of children with disabilities (Article 19).

A prevention obligation is also imposed on states by the Optional Protocol to the Convention on the Rights of the Child on the Involvement of Children in Armed Conflict, adopted on 25 May 2000. This stipulates that armed groups or other armed forces of a given country should not under any circumstances recruit or engage in the armed forces persons under the age of 18; and that states are to take all possible measures to prevent such recruitment and exploitation, including by adopting remedies necessary if such practices are to be prohibited and punished (Article 4).

Similarly, the Optional Protocol on the Sale of Children, Child Prostitution and Child Pornography adopted on the same day provides for the prevention of the offences listed in its title. Article 9 therein deals with the strengthening, implementation and dissemination of law, administrative measures, social policies and programmes capable of preventing the relevant crimes. In addition, special attention is paid to activities increasing awareness in society, including among children themselves, through, among others, education and training. States also pledge to strengthen international cooperation over the prevention of the crimes referred to (Article 10).

As they ratify the various Conventions relating to human rights, states pledge to promote, respect and protect human rights. Beyond that, many of the instruments also lay down obligations to the effect that infringements of human rights need to be prevented. Records thus show efforts made to identify risk factors, as well as to seek practical measures by which violations are to be prevented.

1.2. Prevention as the foundation of Responsibility to Protect (R2P)

Looking for a way to increase the effectiveness of the United Nations in the event of atrocity crimes, the UN referred to the conclusions of the distinguished International Commission on Intervention and State Sovereignty (ICISS), which heralded a declaration on Responsibility to Protect in December 2001.[16] This dealt with possible actions to be taken by the international community in the face of the severe suffering of people caused by internal conflicts, uprisings or repression. The Commission proposed, among others:

- a new understanding of state sovereignty, also as a responsibility for citizens of a state to be protected,[17]
- transfer of the responsibility to protect to the international community, should a state fail,
- three dimensions to the responsibility of the international community, i.e. regarding prevention, reaction and reconstruction, where the latter is understood as a restoring of a situation in which human rights are respected,
- recognition of military intervention as the instrument of last resort, triggered by the following criteria: the occurrence or serious threat of occurrence of mass crimes, extremity, legitimate intent, proportionality and a chance to improve the situation.[18]

Over time, this new concept has become subject to both intergovernmental and expert debate at the UN. Secretary-General Kofi Annan set up the High-Level Panel on Threats, Challenges and Change, which recommended to the United Nations the adoption and implementation of the "Responsibility to Protect" concept.[19] This became possible thanks to the conclusions of the UN World Summit in September 2005. In paragraphs 138 and 139 of the Outcome Document, states recognise the legitimacy of the R2P concept, including the primary responsibility of states where civil protection is concerned, but also the complementary responsibility of the international community.[20]

---

16 Report of the International Commission on Intervention and State Sovereignty, The Responsibility to Protect, December 2001, https://undocs.org/pdf?symbol=en/a/57/303.

17 Axworthy L. (2011): 'RtoP and the Evolution of State Sovereignty' in: Genser J., Cotler I. (eds.) *The Responsibility to Protect. The Promise of Stopping Mass Atrocities in our Time*, Oxford University Press, 3–16.

18 Report of the International Commission on Intervention and State Sovereignty, The Responsibility to Protect, December 2001, https://undocs.org/pdf?symbol=en/a/57/303, 32–37.

19 United Nations (2004): Report of High-Level Panel on Threats, Challenges and Change, *A More Secure World: Our Shared Responsibility*, 1, 17, 65–66, 72–73.

20 UN General Assembly, 2005 World Summit Outcome, par. 138–140, http://www.un.org/en/preventgenocide/adviser/pdf/World%20Summit%20Outcome%20Document.pdf#page=30.

The UN has limited the situations to which R2P relates to: genocide, crimes against humanity, war crimes and ethnic cleansing. It also departed from the division of responsibility for prevention, response and reconstruction, with the greatest importance being assigned to prevention.[21] The document announced the provision of preventative support for civil protection, including the building of states' internal capabilities in this area. The need for the UN to develop early-warning capabilities was also acknowledged.[22]

The choice of instruments at the disposal of the international community with a view to its assisting in the protection of a population is limited to the possibilities set out in Chapters VI and VIII of the UN Charter. On the other hand, the authorisation of military intervention remains a matter for the Security Council, in accordance with Chapter VII. No attempt is thus made to resolve the dilemma of responsibility for a decision to intervene should the Security Council remain passive.

The above provisions were adopted by consensus among all Member States of the United Nations Organisation. Given the concerns raised previously, this represented an undoubted success. While smaller states had feared that the concept could become an instrument used for military intervention against them.[23] In turn, large states, primarily the United States, did not agree to take on an obligation denoting military intervention whenever a crime was committed. Article 139 merely recognises a readiness (not a duty) for collective armed action to be resorted to when those criteria are fulfilled.[24]

---

21 For the key importance of prevention, see also Nambiar S. (November 2011): 'The Emerging Principle of the Responsibility to Protect: An Asian Perspectives,' *Strategic Analysis*, Vol. 35, No. 6, 959.

22 UN World Summit Outcome Document, par. 138–139.

23 Grzebyk P. (2015): 'Miejsce interwencji zbrojnej w koncepcji "odpowiedzialność za ochronę"', *Stosunki Międzynarodowe*, No. 3, Vol. 51, 61–76.

24 Knight W.A., Egerton F. (2014): *The Routledge Handbook of the Responsibility to Protect*, New York: Routledge; Glanville L. (2012): 'The Responsibility to Protect Beyond Borders,' *Human Rights Law Review*, Vol. 12, 8–15.

1.3. Main UN bodies and institutions competent to prevent mass human-rights violations and atrocity crimes

1.3.1. The crucial role of the Security Council in the operational prevention

The Security Council can be considered the UN body with the most serious competencies to prevent atrocity crimes, especially since its decisions are legally binding. Its instruments derive from the role accorded the Council by virtue of the UN Charter, as regards the maintenance of international peace and security (Article 24.1),[25] due to the connection between mass crimes and disruptions in this sphere. Possible actions referred to in Chapters VI and VII of the Charter may be used for both crime prevention and response. This is true of preventative diplomacy, the call for negotiation, research, reconciliation or the search for a judicial decision, but also the possibility of force being used.

In its Article 8, the Convention for the Prevention and Punishment of the Crime of Genocide provides that any State Party thereto may request that the competent authorities of the United Nations take the measures provided for in the UN Charter that they deem appropriate to prevent or suppress acts of genocide or other acts referred to in Article 3, such as: the purpose of committing genocide, direct and public incitement to crime, complicity and others. While the Security Council did not in fact gain explicit designation as a competent authority of body, it has the most serious instruments by which atrocity crimes might be prevented or responded to.

During the Cold War, the Security Council confined interpretation of its mandate to the maintenance of international peace and security. Its Resolutions made no reference to the Genocide Convention, while only rarely referring to human-rights issues either.[26] In contrast, post-1989 the Council made increasing reference to mass offenses, as well as to internal conflicts as threats to international peace and security.[27]

---

25 Schabas W. (2007): 'Preventing the "Odious Scourge": The United Nations and the Prevention of Genocide,' *International Journal on Minority and Group Rights*, Vol. 14, 383.

26 Ben-Naftali O. (2009): 'The Obligations to Prevent and to Punish Genocide' in: Gaeta P. (ed.), *The UN Genocide Convention. A Commentary*, Oxford: Oxford University Press, 36–44.

27 Ramcharan B. (2002): *The Security Council and the Protection of Human Rights*, Hague: Martinus Nijhof Publishers, 15–34; Genser J., Ugarte B.S. (2014): *The United Nations Security Council in the Age of Human Rights*, New York: Cambridge University Press, 30–31.

Atrocity crimes in the Balkans in the 1990s and in Rwanda, often carried out in the absence of any reaction on the part of the Security Council, contributed to discussion of the idea of humanitarian interventions that might amount to military interventions, where the context was one of international crimes or the threat thereof. Military intervention was thus seen as an instrument of both response to and the prevention of human suffering. The NATO intervention in Kosovo in 1999 launched without the authorisation of the Security Council represented an important moment. States started to seek an answer as to whether the international community might intervene on humanitarian grounds, in the event of inactivity on the part of the Security Council, or whether it too was to remain idle in those circumstances.

The International Commission on Intervention and State Sovereignty, recognising the Council's responsibility for maintaining peace and security, saw it as the key institution in the field of R2P. At the same time, it considered that the international community should develop additional mechanisms by which military intervention might be resorted to in the event of the decision-making process in the Council being blocked by one of its Permanent Members. It pointed to the General Assembly, regional organisations or coalitions of states. Nevertheless, cy adopting the R2P concept in 2005, the General Assembly did not go beyond the UN Charter on Security Council competencies.

However, UN Secretary-General Kofi Annan proposed that a principle of unity be adopted in situations of systematic and massive human-rights violations.[28] This idea has met with particular favour among French politicians.[29] In 2015, France issued a political declaration on the suspension of the veto in mass-murder cases, as addressed to Permanent Members of the Security Council. In addition, on 23 October 2015, on the 70th anniversary of the UN, a Code of Conduct[30] was presented, having been elaborated by the 24 members of the ACT

---

28 See especially the speech of the UN Secretary-General Kofi Annan at the UN General Assembly in its 1999 session, UNIS / SG / 2381, September 21, 1999.

29 The idea of refraining from use of the veto in situations involving mass crimes was supported by French Foreign Minister Hubert Védrine in 2001 and President François Hollande, who announced it in a speech at the UN General Assembly in 2013. An article on this subject was published in the *New York Times* by Foreign Minister Laurent Fabius, October 4, 2013.

30 The Code of Conduct has been developed by 24 members of the ACT (Accountability, Coherence and Transparency) Group. i.e. Saudi Arabia, Austria, Chile, Denmark, Estonia, Finland, Gabon, Ghana, Ireland, Jordan, Costa Rica, Liechtenstein, Luxembourg,

(Accountability, Coherence and Transparency Group). The Code held that the prompt action of the Security Council might be necessary if crimes of genocide, crimes against humanity or war crimes were to be prevented or stopped, with all states that were or might become Members of the Security Council thus invited to not vote against credible draft Resolutions within the Security Council aimed at stopping or preventing such crimes (Article 2).[31] The Code has currently won the support of 112 countries.[32] China, Russia and the United States are the most sceptical here, as they exercise the right of veto most frequently.[33]

The interest of the Security Council in preventing atrocity crimes rose following the jubilee 2005 UN summit,[34] and this gained its reflection in Council decisions adopted by resolution. Most of them referred to R2P and conflict prevention at the same time. Adopted to mark the 20th anniversary of the acknowledgment of the crime of genocide, Resolution 2150 of 14 April 2014 on the prevention of genocide by UN Member States was particularly significant. The Security Council, referring to the provisions of the 2005 Outcome Document and R2P, called for the prevention and combating of genocide and other international crimes. It recommended that states develop educational programmes in this area and called upon the Secretary-General to develop coordination between various international early-warning mechanisms.[35] The Security Council provided support to the institutions of Special Advisers for the Prevention of Genocide and Responsibility to Protect.[36]

The Council also referred to prevention in Resolutions on the protection of civilians during armed conflicts. The first Resolution on this matter was adopted by the Council on 28 April 2006. For the first time, the Council referred therein

---

The Maldives, Norway, New Zealand, Papua New Guinea, Peru, Portugal, Slovenia, Switzerland, Sweden, Uruguay and Hungary.

31 Code of Conduct Regarding Security Council Action Against Genocide, Crimes Against Humanity or War Crimes, New York, October 23, 2015.

32 As of 29 March 2017, the Code of Conduct was supported by 112 states, see *UN Security Council Code of Conduct*, https://www.globalr2p.org/resources/code-of-conduct-regarding-security-council-action-against-genocide-crimes-against-humanity-or-war-crimes/.

33 Source: http://www.un.org/depts/dhl/resguide/scact_veto_table_en.htm.

34 The Resolution on Kosovo was an exception, as in it the Council called for the prevention of the humanitarian catastrophe in 1998. S/RES/1203 (1998).

35 Resolution of the UN Security Council S/RES/2150, April 16, 2014.

36 See examples of UN Security Council Resolutions: S/RES/2171 (2014), S/RES/2150 (2014), S/RES/2250 (2015).

to the results of the 2005 UN Summit on R2P, and reaffirmed its desire to prevent genocide, war crimes, ethnic cleansing and crimes against humanity. It recognised the role of education in preventing and combating civilian violence, combating armed conflict, and preventing sexual exploitation, trafficking in human beings and violation of international humanitarian law in the field of child recruitment. It decided to ensure that all peace-support operations would take all possible measures to prevent violence against civilians, especially women and children. The Security Council seemed to combine efforts to prevent conflicts with the prevention of mass crimes in this case.[37] In the following years, the Council likewise held open debates on the situation of civilians in armed conflict, reaffirming as it did so the main responsibilities of the state as regards R2P and prevention.

In Resolutions relating to national situations, the Security Council called, among others, for prevention of attacks on civilians (Sudan in 2006[38]), the use of heavy weapons against civilians (Côte d'Ivoire in 2011[39]), the return of violence (South Sudan in 2011 and 2013),[40] human-rights violations (Libya in 2012[41]), violations of international humanitarian law (Central African Republic in 2013[42]), violence between religious communities (Central African Republic in 2014[43]), violence against children (Mali in 2015[44]), the abuse of children in violation of international law (Sudan in 2015[45]), and clashes between communities (Sudan, 2016[46]). It also adopted more than 90 Resolutions reminding national authorities of their responsibilities when it came to civil protection,[47] including the prevention of genocide, crimes against humanity, ethnic cleansing and war crimes.

37 Resolution of the UN Security Council S/RES/1738, December 23, 2006.
38 Resolution of the UN Security Council S/RES/1706, August 31, 2006.
39 Resolution of the UN Security Council S/RES/1975, March 30, 2011.
40 Resolution of the UN Security Council S/RES/1996 (2011), July 8, 2011, resolution of the UN Security Council S/RES/2109, July 11, 2013.
41 Resolution of the UN Security Council S/RES/2040, March 12, 2012.
42 Resolution of the UN Security Council S/RES/2121, October 10, 2013.
43 Resolution of the UN Security Council S/RES/2134, January 28, 2014.
44 Resolution of the UN Security Council S/RES/2227, June 29, 2015.
45 Resolution of the UN Security Council, S/RES/2228, June 29, 2015.
46 Resolution of the UN Security Council, S/RES/2296, June 29, 2016.
47 See the list of Security Council Resolutions related to R2P at the site of Global Centre for the Responsibility to Protect, https://www.globalr2p.org/resources/un-security-council-resolutions-and-presidential-statements-referencing-r2p.

1.3.2. The General Assembly as a debate forum on the prevention

The General Assembly has expressed regular interest in the prevention of human-rights violations and atrocity crimes. This is the most representative forum, at which equality of states applies, and which has adopted the aforementioned legal instrument by virtue of which the concept of prevention has taken shape. The General Assembly has also sought institutional solutions in this area. On 20 December 1993, it conferred a role in the prevention of human-rights violations on the United Nations High Commissioner for Human Rights.[48] By the same token, in the case of the establishment of the Human Rights Council by virtue of a Resolution of 3 April 2006, the Assembly envisaged action to prevent infringements through dialogue and cooperation.[49]

The competence of the General Assembly regarding prevention arises primarily out of the Charter of the United Nations. The General Assembly can address the issue of prevention in its debates, as well as give recommendations in this area to the Security Council. In Article 139 of the UN Outcome Document of 2005, the need to continue discussions on Responsibility to Protect the population against genocide, war crimes, ethnic cleansing and crimes against humanity was documented.

The first such debate took place in July 2009, leading to the adoption of Resolution 63/308 on 14 September 2009,[50] in which the Assembly referred to the Report of Secretary-General Ban Ki-moon on "Implementing the Responsibility to Protect,"[51] and decided to continue the debate over that issue. At the same time, it emerged that prevention was an idea about which almost all countries were convinced, as Rwanda's representative noted. The only controversy was aroused by the issue of possible armed intervention in the name of R2P. Representatives of Nicaragua, Venezuela, Cuba, Iran, Sudan and North Korea were of the opinion that, if the R2P concept was about intervention and the use of armed force, it might easily become an instrument for strong states to use against weak ones.

Ultimately, the support for the further development of R2P by the African and Asian states was affected by two factors. First, a North-South divide was avoided in the case of this particular debate. Most developing countries agreed

---

48 Resolution of the UN General Assembly, 48/141, December 20, 1993.

49 Resolution of the UN General Assembly 60/251, April, 3 2006; Ramcharan B. (2010): *Preventive Human Rights Strategies*, New York: Routledge, 78–80.

50 Resolution of the UN General Assembly, 63/308, October 7, 2009.

51 Ki-moon B., *Implementing the Responsibility to Protect*, Report of the Secretary-General, A/63/677, January 12, 2009.

with the Secretary-General's message that Africa had contributed to the emergence of R2P by taking into account the right to intervene in the African Union Founding Act, with the idea of non-interference in this way yielding to that of non-indifference.[52] This idea was supported by Egypt and the entire Movement of Non-Aligned States. Second, the assumption concerning the prevention of atrocity crimes proved easy to accept, with the aforesaid Rwandan representative calling for African experience and commitment vis-à-vis the prevention of mass crimes to be made use of, and in this way helping to convince African and Asian states.[53] It was decided at that point that the essence of R2P would be the prevention of atrocity crimes, rather than armed intervention.

At that time, the General Assembly also accepted a proposal from the Secretary-General that the R2P concept be split into the aforesaid three dimensions, i.e. state responsibility for civil protection, international assistance to states in their duties and international response.[54] In its resolutions concerning Syria and Democratic People's Republic of Korea the General Assembly recalled the responsibility of states to protect their populations from atrocity crimes.

Each year, the Assembly also hosts a so-called informal interactive dialogue in which willing states examine the annual reports and recommendations of the UN Secretary-General regarding R2P. Most of these have been concerned with prevention, and have been based on Reports prepared by the Secretary-General himself. On 14 December 2011, it was early-warning mechanisms that gained discussion,[55] while on 12 July 2011 the role of regional and subregional organisations, on 5 September 2012 the issue of timely and decisive response, on 11 September 2013 the responsibility of states as regards prevention, on 8 September 2014 international support, including in the context of prevention, on 8 September 2015 the implementation of the responsibility to protect, on 6 September 2016 the mobilisation of collective action in this field and on 6 September 2017 the accountability for prevention. In 2018 and 2019 the General

52 Art. 4 of the African Union Constitution of 4 July 2000.

53 Official Records of the General Assembly, Sixty-Third Session, Plenary Meetings, 96th to 101st Meetings (A / 63 / PV.96-101), and: Luck E. (2010): 'Building a Norm: the Responsibility to Protect Experience' in: Rotberg R.I. (ed.) *Mass Atrocity Crimes. Preventing Future Outrages*, World Peace Foundation, 108–124.

54 Ki-moon B., *Implementing the Responsibility to Protect*, Report of the Secretary-General, A/63/677, January 12, 2009.

55 Ki-moon B., *Early Warning, Assessment, and the Responsibility to Protect*, Report of the Secretary-General, A/65/864, July 14, 2010.

Assembly debated on the Secretary-General reports on early action and lessons learned for prevention.

The message of prevention was also accompanied by the decision of the UN General Assembly to establish 9 December as the International Day of Remembrance and Dignity for the Victims of Genocide Crimes and the Prevention of Crime.[56] The Assembly encouraged all states, international and non-governmental organisations and individuals to celebrate this day in order to increase awareness of the need to prevent and combat crime.

1.3.3. The UN Secretary General – the *spiritus movens*

It was thanks to UN Secretary-General Kofi Annan that the topic of atrocity crimes gained momentum in intergovernmental discussion. He announced at the forum of United Nations Commission on Human Rights in 1998, that the next century would be the age of prevention.[57] The initial focus was on genocide. In 2004, on the tenth anniversary of the Rwandan crimes, the UN put forward a five-point plan of action to prevent similar events in the future, entailing:

1) prevention of armed conflicts that promote genocide, 2) protection of civilians during armed conflicts, 3) an end brought to impunity through better use of national and international judiciary systems, 4) information gathering and early warning through the UN Special Adviser for the Prevention of Genocide, 5) fast and effective involvement, including the possibility of armed action.[58]

It is difficult to overestimate the importance of the report *In Larger Freedom: Towards Development, Security and Human Rights for All*[59] of 2005, which recommended the strengthening human rights as one of the pillars of the UN. Kofi Annan gave his support to the concept of Responsibility to Protect, creating the High-Level Panel on Threats, Challenges and Change, which has recommended that the United Nations adopt and implement the concept.[60]

---

56 Resolution of the UN General Assembly, 69/323, September 11, 2015.

57 Speech by Secretary-General Kofi Annan at the opening of the 54th session of the Commission on Human Rights, March 18, 1998, SG/SM/6487HR/4355.

58 *Action Plan to Prevent Genocide*, speech by the UN Secretary-General in Geneva on 7 April 2004, http://www.preventgenocide.org/prevent/UNdocs/KofiAnnansAction-PlantoPreventGenocide7Apr2004.htm.

59 Annan K., *In Larger Freedom: towards development, security and human rights for all*, Report of the Secretary-General, A/59/2005, March 21, 2005.

60 United Nations (2004): *A More Secure World: Our Shared Responsibility*, Report of the High-Level Panel on Threats, Challenges and Change, 1, 17, 65–66, 72–73.

However, the degree of generality and lack of precision, as well as the political nature of the 2005 Outcome Document, necessitated the further discussion of details that the involvement of the Secretaries-General made possible. Due to misuse by the US of human-rights concepts and slogans to justify military action in Iraq after 2003; or by Russia during its war with Georgia in 2008, many countries remained sceptical about R2P in the first years following the Jubilee Summit.

In 2007, Ban Ki-moon set up two institutions to develop and implement the concept: the Special Adviser on the Prevention of Genocide and the Special Adviser on the Responsibility to Protect.[61] Through subsequent reports, he also made the greatest conceptual contribution to the development of R2P. In the report of January 2009, *Implementing the Responsibility to Protect,* the Secretary General acknowledged implementation of R2P as his priority. He was also the originator of the three dimensions to R2P, encompassing: state responsibility for civil protection, international assistance to states in discharging their duties, and international response.[62]

Another report, *Early Warning, Assessment, and the Responsibility to Protect,*[63] presented to the General Assembly on 14 July 2010, dealt directly with prevention, especially early warning. The Secretary-General identified the problems that should be resolved in order for prevention to be effective. First, he considered that transfer of information between UN institutions is limited. Second, the collection and analysis of information are often in isolation from the specificity and needs as regards liability for the prevention of mass crimes (Articles 138, 139 and 149). Third, in line with Articles 138 and 139 of the Outcome Document of the 2005 Summit, special emphasis should be placed on developing instruments for a careful, adequate and unbiased assessment of the situation and its development on the ground. Only then will it be possible to choose the best possible response.[64]

Effective early warning and prevention are possible only if there is close cooperation between states and international institutions, so the report on UN

---

61 The function was performed by Edward C. Luck in 2007–2012 and Jennifer Welsh from 2013.

62 Ki-moon B., *Implementing the Responsibility to Protect*, Report of the Secretary-General, A/63/677, January 12, 2009.

63 Ki-moon B., *Early Warning, Assessment, and the Responsibility to Protect*, Report of the Secretary-General, A/65/864, July 14, 2010.

64 Burke-White W.W. (2011): 'Adoption of the Responsibility to Protect,' *Public Law Research Paper*, University of Pennsylvania Law School, 33–34.

cooperation with regional and subregional institutions *The Role of Regional and Subregional Arrangements in Implementing the Responsibility to Protect* was a natural continuation. The Secretary-General defined the role that regional organisations can play in prevention by establishing regional control and support mechanisms.[65] He pointed to the mandate of the OSCE High Commissioner on National Minorities in the framework of early warning and prevention, to ambitious EU membership criteria that have contributed to the enhancement of human rights, and to the International Conference of the Great Lakes Region, which made efforts to create committees supporting states over their responsibility to respect human rights. The Secretary-General also pointed to the preventative role of regional human-rights tribunals operating within the Council of Europe, the Organization of American States and the African Union, as well as the International Criminal Court.

The introduction of a division into structural and operational prevention was a conceptual novelty of the report. The essence and purpose of structural prevention was to change the situation from one vulnerable to violence and mass crimes to one in which these would become less likely. Operational prevention is already a response to the immediate threat of crimes that include cases of violence.[66] On the occasion of the Report, the impossibility of precisely separating the sphere of preventative action from that of reaction (pillar III) made itself apparent.

These dilemmas were confirmed by Secretary General Ban Ki-moon in his report, *The responsibility to protect: timely and decisive response*,[67] presented on 5 August 2012. This was based on the third pillar – the potential for international action in high-risk situations or in the circumstances of mass crimes. In turn, in his *State Responsibility and Prevention* Report of 5 August 2013,[68] Ban Ki-moon focused on the responsibilities of states as regards prevention. He assumed a need for national law and institutions to be developed and for society to be shaped in such a way that risk factors relating to mass crimes might be responded to. Under

---

65 Ki-moon B., The Role of Regional and Subregional Arrangements in Implementing the Responsibility to Protect, Report of the Secretary-General, A/65/877-S/2011/393, July 12, 2011.

66 For an interesting position on this subject see: McLoughlin S. (2014), *The Structural Prevention of Mass Atrocities*, New York: Routledge.

67 Ki-moon B., *The Responsibility to Protect: Timely and Decisive Response*, Report of the Secretary-General, A/66/874–S/2012/578, July 25, 2012.

68 Ki-moon B., *State Responsibility and Prevention*, Report of the Secretary-General, A/67/929–S/2013/399, July 9, 2013.

this term he opted to include discrimination and violation of human rights in the past, hate speech, propaganda or exclusion ideology, increased activity of armed groups and militias, actions to facilitate crime such as changes in law or the control of armed groups, weakness of state structures and the occurrence of crimes. In addition, the Secretary-General presented instruments serving prevention that he deemed to be at the disposal of countries, such as the building of internal capacity, the promotion and protection of human rights and the adoption of crime-prevention instruments through, for example, the establishment of institutional mechanisms, dialogue with society, and education.

Prevention as the most important action was also recognised by the Secretary-General in his Second-Pillar (11 July 2014) Report on the responsibility of the international community, entitled *Fulfilling our collective responsibility: international assistance and the Responsibility to Protect*.[69] Ban Ki-moon there identified forms of international assistance to countries primarily of a typically preventative nature: counselling, and encouraging respect for human rights on the part of states and international organisations, supporting national institutions, assisting with the assessment of the risk of mass crimes being committed, and responding to factors such as ethnic tensions and hate speech. He also undertook to provide direct help, e.g. in mediation, assistance with the prosecution of criminals, refugee assistance, etc. In the course of the General Assembly's interactive dialogue over the report, the Secretary-General acknowledged that R2P is primarily a preventative doctrine.[70]

Similarly, in a Report published 10 years after the adoption of R2P by the UN General Assembly, entitled *A Vital and Enduring Commitment: Implementing the Responsibility to Protect*, the Secretary-General acknowledged the priority of prevention and urged states to recognise that status, making concrete efforts to prevent genocide, war crimes, ethnic cleansing and crimes against humanity. The Secretary-General recognised non-state armed groups and new technologies as new obstacles where prevention was concerned. He also pointed to six core R2P priorities for the next decade, i.e. (1) signalling political commitment at the national, regional and global levels to protect populations from atrocity crimes; (2)

69 Ki-moon B., Fulfilling our Collective Responsibility: International Assistance and the Responsibility to Protect, Report of the Secretary-General, A/68/947S/2014/449, July 11, 2014.

70 Summary of the Sixth Informal Interactive Dialogue of the UN General Assembly on the Responsibility to Protect, held on 8 September 2014, Global Centre for the Responsibility to Protect, September 2014.

elevating prevention as a core aspect of the responsibility to protect; (3) clarifying and expanding options for timely and decisive response; (4) addressing the risk of recurrence; (5) enhancing regional action to prevent and respond to atrocity crimes; and (6) strengthening international networks dedicated to genocide prevention and the responsibility to protect. The report *Mobilizing collective action: the next decade of the responsibility to protect* from 22 July 2016 represented a continuation of the recommendation.[71]

Next years the Secretary-General continued to be focused on the idea of prevention. He devoted his 2017 report to accountability for prevention,[72] 2018 report to early warning and early action[73] and 2019 report to lessons learned for prevention.[74] In 2020 he published the report on *Prioritizing prevention and strengthening response: women and the responsibility to protect*, which focuses on the gendered dimension of atrocity prevention and R2P.[75]

Through the annual dialogues organised by the General Assembly on the basis of the Reports of the Secretary-General, states have had the opportunity to exchange opinions on the concept of R2P and the prevention of mass crimes, and to align their positions.

The recognition of the link between the prevention of human-rights violations and the prevention of mass crimes is also recognised as a contribution of the UN Secretary-General. This perspective is expressed by the Human Rights Up Front Action Plan proposed by the SG in December 2013.[76] It addresses broad-based prevention and the various challenges facing the UN, including life-threatening situations. The programme assumes alignment of the entire UN system and UN work on the ground to, among others, prevent serious violations of human rights and international humanitarian law. The Secretary-General proposed three types

---

71 Ki-moon B., *A Vital and Enduring Commitment: Implementing the Responsibility to Protect*, Report of the Secretary-General, A/70/999–S/2016/620, July 22, 2016.

72 Guterres A., *Implementing the Responsibility to Protect: Accountability for Prevention*, Report of the Secretary-General, A/71/1016-S/2017/556, August 10, 2017.

73 Guterres A., *Responsibility to Protect: From Early Warning to Early Action*, Report of the Secretary-General (A/72/884-S/2018/525), June 1, 2018.

74 Guterres A., *Responsibility to Protect: Lessons Learned for Prevention*, Report of the Secretary-General (A/73/898-S/2019/463), June 10, 2019.

75 Guterres A., *Prioritizing Prevention and Strengthening Response: Women and the Responsibility to Protect*, Report of the Secretary-General, (A/74/964 – S/2020/501), July 23 2020.

76 United Nations (2014): *'Rights Up Front' Detailed Action Plan*, (updated) https://interagencystandingcommittee.org/system/files/detailed_hruf_plan_of_action.pdf.

of change: (1) a cultural change that is meant to increase awareness among UN staff and units of the mandate of the Organisation under the UN Charter, (2) an operational change involving the integration of UN pillars of peace and security, development and human rights and better cooperation over early warning and the reaction to problems, and (3) a change towards deeper involvement of the UN in problems identified at the level of the UN Member States.

The Violent Extremism Action Plan presented by the Secretary-General at the General Assembly on 15 January 2016 was an initiative to respond to the increasing role of non-state actors in mass crimes. The report primarily concerned terrorist organisations like Bokoharam or the so-called Islamic State of Iraq and the Levant. It contained 20 recommendations for prevention addressed to states, regional organisations and the UN itself.[77]

1.3.4. The Office on Genocide Prevention and the Responsibility to Protect: institutionalisation of prevention

The concept of preventing atrocity crimes from Kofi Annan as UN Secretary-General included the appointment of a Special Adviser for the Prevention of Genocide. This was motivated by Security Council Resolution 1366 of 2001, in which the Council called on the Secretary-General to present information and analysis of the UN system in regard to serious violations of international law, including human-rights and international humanitarian law, as well as potential emergencies arising from ethnic national or territorial causes.[78]

In a letter to the Chair of the Security Council dated 12 July 2004, the Secretary-General presented the mandate of the Special Adviser. He was to be engaged in (1) collecting information on mass and grave violations of human rights and international humanitarian law motivated racially or ethnically and capable of leading to genocide, (2) acting as an early-warning mechanism for the Secretary–General, and through him for the Security Council, (3) submitting recommendations to the Security Council for the Prevention of Genocide, (4) cooperating within the UN system to prevent genocide and strengthen the UN capacity in this area. The Secretary-General acknowledged that the Special

---

77 Ki-moon B., *Plan of Action to Prevent Extremism*, Report of the Secretary-General, A/70/674, January 2016.

78 Resolution of the UN Security Council, S/RES/1366 (2001), August 30, 2001.

Adviser would not deal with the qualification of crime, and that his methodology would consist of careful verification of facts, data analysis and consultations.[79]

In his work, the Secretary-General received support from the Advisory Committee on Genocide Prevention set up in May 2006, which included experienced people from a variety of areas relevant to the prevention of mass crimes. The Special Adviser for the Prevention of Genocide on a full-time basis at the level of Under-Secretary-General was finally appointed in May 2007. He was Francis Deng, who served in 2007–2012.[80] Then, in the light of the need to develop and operationalize the R2P concept, the Secretary-General sent a letter to the Security Council on the appointment of Edward Luck as the Special Adviser on the Responsibility to Protect (2008–2013).[81] The similar nature of the work of advisers and the growing belief that prevention was to be the main message of R2P led to the decision to create a Joint Office on Genocide Prevention and the Responsibility to Protect, which the General Assembly voted for n 2010, by its Resolution64/245.[82] Such a solution was supposed to foster closer cooperation between Special Advisers and, in the long term, contribute to the strengthening of prevention.

The Special Adviser for Prevention routinely collects data on cases of mass violations of international law that may lead to the most serious crimes. The Office is working with all UN institutions in the field. It collects information that is analysed using indicators developed under the co-called Framework Analysis for Atrocity Crimes, such as inter-ethnic relations, weakness of state structures, discrimination, arms transfers, intentions of group destruction and others,[83] and then assesses the risk of crime. If it determines that a risk of genocide exists, it issues warnings and recommendations that are passed to the Secretary-General and the Security Council. Information also reaches the relevant institutions of the UN system, regional organisations, states and non-governmental organisations.

Despite the inclusion in the name of the institution of the word genocide, the Office does not deal exclusively with the prevention of the crime of genocide.

---

79 Letter dated 12 July 2004 from the Secretary-General to the President of the Security Council, S/2004/567.

80 Advisers on the Prevention of Genocide: Adama Dieng (2012–2020), since 10 November 2020 Alice Wairimu Nderitu.

81 Letter dated 31 August 2007 from the Secretary-General to the President of the Security Council, S/2007/721.

82 UN General Assembly resolution 64/245, 24 December 2010.

83 *Framework Analysis for Atrocity Crimes. A Tool for Prevention*, United Nations Office on Genocide Prevention and the Responsibility to Protect, New York 2014.

That would be impossible as it would require identification of the crime prior to its perpetration. The Special Rapporteur is not involved in the identification of categories of crime at all, engaging in a broad interpretation of the mandate, examining cases of serious violations of international law. Extension of the scope of the crime was also a natural consequence of the establishment of a single Office for Advisers.

Thus far, the Adviser on the Prevention of Genocide has issued warnings in the cases of Burundi, Sudan, South Sudan, Syria and the Central African Republic. He personally presented the situation in the above countries to the Security Council, though it seems reasonable to suggest that the potential was not used by the Council.

The main task of the Special Adviser on the Responsibility to Protect has been to continue the conceptualisation of R2P and to build consensus among states as to instruments for its implementation. Due to countries' lack of consent to the adoption of criteria for military intervention that could lead to serious human suffering; and in line with the belief that prevention should be a key area of international engagement in R2P, the activities of the Special Adviser on the Responsibility to Protect correspond closely with the involvement of the Special Adviser on the Prevention of Genocide.

Apart from early warnings and mobilisation of the UN to take preventative action, the Office of Special Advisers also undertakes numerous training initiatives, and offers technical assistance as regards investigation of the sources and dynamics of atrocity crimes and possible preventative measures. It plays a significant role by raising awareness of the need for prevention among UN personnel and the whole system, but also at the level of national institutions. Both Advisers often participate in quiet diplomacy, in consultation with relevant UN agencies.[84] Undoubtedly, the prolonged war in Syria since 2011 has had the greatest impact on the perception of the Office's activities, and has shown its limitations in the face of a lack of cooperation with the Security Council.

---

84 Statement by Special Advisor on RtoP Jennifer Welsh at the Thematic Discussion in the UN General Assembly on "*Ten Years of the Responsibility to Protect: From Commitment to Implementation*," February 26, 2016; Akhavan P. (2006): 'Report on the Work of the Office of the Special Adviser of the United Nations Secretary-General on the Prevention of Genocide,' *Human Rights Quarterly*, No. 28 Vol. 4; Hehir A. (2011): 'The Special Adviser on the Prevention of Genocide: Adding Value to the UN's Mechanisms for Preventing Intra-State Crises?' *Journal of Genocide Research*, No. 13, Vol. 1; 'An Analysis of Perspectives on the Office of the Special Adviser on the Prevention of Genocide' (2010) 5(3) *Genocide Studies and Prevention*.

1.4. The role of UN human rights institutions in the prevention of mass human-rights violations and atrocity crimes

1.4.1. The UN Human Rights Council's contribution

The Human Rights Council, established under Resolution 60/251 of the General Assembly of 15 March 2006, as the successor to the Human Rights Commission, is the principal UN specialised human-rights body,[85] having the status of an auxiliary body of the General Assembly. The scope of responsibilities of the Council includes the tackling of serious and systematic human-rights violations, as well as contributing through dialogue and cooperation to processes whereby human-rights violations are prevented and threats responded to.

The systematic monitoring of the UN's situation as regards human rights, the universal reviewing of human rights as culminating in recommendations for states, and thematic resolutions referring to national situations are all certainly contributing to the prevention of human-rights violations and mass crimes, as are individual notifications by the Council in respect of severe and systematic human-rights violations, pursuant to Resolution 5/1.

Both the Council and the previous Commission made direct reference to the issue of prevention in their thematic resolutions. The first problem raised was the prevention of genocide, solely with respect to the Convention. In 2003, the Human Rights Commission called on states to ratify the Convention for the Prevention and Punishment of the Crime of Genocide, and to implement relevant national legislation.[86] Two years later, the Commission underlined in its Resolution the importance of international cooperation in meeting the objectives of the Convention, and expressed its support for the Five-Point Action Plan presented by the Secretary-General, as well as for the appointment of the aforesaid Special Adviser for the Prevention of Genocide. It called on states to cooperate with that Adviser, and on the Adviser to establish relations with the UN institutions, including the Commission on Human Rights. It urged international organisations, states and non-governmental organisations to disseminate the idea that the crime of genocide needs both preventing and punishing.[87]

---

85 Resolution of the General Assembly, A/RES/60/251, March 15, 2006.

86 Resolution of the Commission on Human Rights 66/2003, E/CN.4/RES/2003/66, April 25, 2003.

87 Resolution of the UN Commission on Human Rights, E/CN.4/RES/2005/62, April 20, 2005.

The Human Rights Council addressed the issue of the prevention of genocide explicitly in its Resolution of 28 March 2008 on "Prevention of genocide". It made a positive reference to responsibility to protect, confirming that states had to protect their populations against international crimes. It also urged states to cooperate over and strengthen the operating mechanisms essential if there is to be early identification and prevention of massive, serious and systematic human-rights violations capable of leading to genocide. The Council welcomed UN efforts to strengthen institutions, including the Secretary-General and Special Adviser on the Prevention of Genocide.

The Council underlined the role of the UN human-rights system as a whole in collecting and comparing information on serious violations of human rights, in this way helping people to understand the complexity of genocide situations. It went on to encourage the Special Adviser to work for the continuous strengthening of the systematic exchange of information with human-rights institutions, particularly as regards ethnic, national, religious and racial groups. In addition, the Council recognised, as factors in need of analysis: the law; the existence of vulnerable groups; massive, systematic and serious violations of human rights; discrimination and hate speech.[88]

In its Resolution on the Prevention of Genocide (as adopted on 22 March 2013, the Human Rights Council focused primarily on states and their need to build domestic capacity for prevention and to use human-rights education as an instrument serving prevention. To this end, it was further suggested that a day commemorating victim of genocide and crimes against humanity be designated.[89] The discussion on this, which attested to a consensus among states as regards the need for prevention, continued during the 28th session in 2015,[90] 37th session in 2018[91] and 43rd session in 2020.[92]

In the Resolution of 30 September 2016 on human rights and transitional justice, the Human Rights Council highlighted the problem of impunity, which may be an incentive for the recurrence of mass crimes. It called on states to set up comprehensive justice strategies for the transition period, including through

88 Resolution of the Human Rights Council, A/HRC/RES/7/25, March 28, 2008.

89 Resolution of the UN Human Rights Council, A/HRC/RES/22/L30, March 22, 2013.

90 Resolution of the UN Human Rights Council, A/HRC.RES/37/26, April 7, 2015.

91 Resolution of the UN Human Rights Council, A/HRC/RES/28/34, March 23, 2018.

92 Resolution of the UN Human Rights Council, A/HRC.RES/43/29, June 22, 2020.

the use of judicial and extrajudicial means to deal with past crimes and help prevent further ones.[93]

In addition to the thematic resolutions, the Human Rights Council addressed the question of the responsibility of states to protect in country resolutions. Calls for preventative action were included in Resolutions on Central African Republic, Libya, Syria, North Korea, Republic of Congo, and South Sudan.[94]

The Human Rights Council's mandate is also to convene Special Sessions on situations threatening serious human-rights violations and atrocity crimes. Since 2006, such sessions have concerned Burundi, the Central African Republic, Cote d'Ivoire, Darfur, the Democratic Republic of the Congo, Iraq, Lebanon, Libya, Myanmar, the Occupied Palestinian Territory, South Sudan, Sri Lanka and Syria. The Council also dealt with threats from non-state actors such as Boko Haram, and the so-called Islamic State of Iraq and the Levant. Severe and systematic violations of human rights were condemned repeatedly.

Investigative Commissions, which can deal with the risk of genocide, war crimes, ethnic cleansing and crimes against humanity, as well as responsibility for crimes committed, are among instruments at the disposal of the Council, which appointed Commissions of this kind in regard to Burundi, the Democratic People's Republic of Korea, Eritrea, Gaza, Lebanon, Libya, Sri Lanka and Syria.

The link between prevention of human-rights violations and prevention of atrocity crimes in the Human Rights Council activity is very often addressed. In Resolution 14/5 on the role of prevention in the promotion and protection of human rights, adopted on 17 June 2010, it considered that it would contribute to the prevention of human-rights emergencies. It also presented the initiative to the United Nations High Commissioner for Human Rights, requesting consultations, using a questionnaire, with states, national institutions, NGOs and other stakeholders, as regards the conceptual and practical dimensions to prevention. It further undertook to publish the results.[95] Indeed, results of the Commissioner's work were also discussed at a Seminar he attended, which allowed for the development of a catalogue of prevention instruments presented by the Council in its Resolution of 23 September 2013. The Council called on states to: consider ratification and implementation of international conventions on human

93 Resolution of the UN Human Rights Council, A/HRC/RES/33/19, September 30, 2016.

94 See the list of Resolutions on the site of the Global Centre for the Responsibility to Protect, https://www.globalr2p.org/resources/un-human-rights-council-resolutions-referencing-r2p/.

95 Resolution of the UN Human Rights Council, A/HRC/RES/14/5, June 17, 2010.

rights and alliances; govern and improve democratic standards and the rule of law; ensure the full enjoyment of all personal, political, economic, social and cultural rights; tackle discrimination, racial discrimination, inequality and poverty; promote civil society; promote human-rights education and fight against corruption. It recommended to the UN Commissioner for Human Rights that the concept in question be developed further, with the Council kept informed regularly of progress with, and the practical application of, actions to prevent human-rights violations.[96] This theme was pursued further during the 33rd Human Rights Council Session convened on 29 September 2016.[97]

1.4.2. Treaty bodies: expert work at the base

Due to the obligation to prevent human-rights violations, as set out in the UN's human-rights treaties, expert treaty bodies play an important role in preventing individual and mass human-rights violations. Currently there are nine such bodies. i.e. the Human Rights Committee, the Committee on Economic, Social and Cultural Rights, the Committee on the Elimination of Racial Discrimination, the Committee on the Elimination of Discrimination against Women, the Committee Against Torture, the Committee on the Rights of the Child, the Committee on Migrant Workers, the Committee on the Rights of Persons with Disabilities, the Committee on Enforced Disappearances and the Subcommittee on Prevention of Torture and other Cruel, Inhuman or Degrading Treatment or Punishment.

The Committees, through interpretation of relevant treaties, set the standards for the legislation adopted. In addition, they review reports and individual notices against states periodically, along with information provided by non-governmental organisations, with a view to knowledge being acquired and threats to civil protection identified. By working with the Human Rights Council, the Office on Genocide Prevention and the Responsibility to Protect is involved in the early-warning process.

In turn, through concluding observations made to states as regards improved implementation of the Treaties, the Committees may make a direct contribution to States' better exercise of their competences regarding civil protection. This applies in particular to conventions concerning issues such as the right to life, the prohibition

---

96 Resolution of the UN Human Rights Council, A/HRC/RES/24/16, September 27, 2013.

97 Resolution of the UN Human Rights Council, A/HRC/RES/33/6, September 29, 2016. See more in: Ramcharan B. (2011): *The UN Human Rights Council,* New York: Routledge, 80–86.

of propaganda, discrimination, racism and torture, and vulnerable groups such as women, children, the disabled and people belonging to national and ethnic minorities.

Sadly, the activities of such treaty bodies have their limitations. These include, but are not limited to, the facts that not all states remain parties to treaties, while others fail to report, in spite of having taken on commitments to do so. Moreover, Committee recommendations are not legally binding. States do not take advantage of the possibility they enjoy to tackle mass violations of human rights by means of the State notices provided for by the treaties. Committees also have structural constraints. They meet several times a year on a session, while the scope of their work, given the large number of reports to review, often fails to allow them to address all the issues systematically.

The Committee on the Elimination of Racial Discrimination expressed the greatest interest in contributing to the prevention of genocide by adopting a special declaration on 11 March 2005.[98] It expressed its support and willingness to cooperate with the Special Adviser on the Prevention of Genocide, who announced the development of genocide indicators, as well as early-warning and action procedures.

As early as in 1993, the Committee had adopted principles by which to prevent and respond to violations of the Convention.[99] Over time, it developed early-warning and early urgent action procedures, which became part of the Committee's ongoing work.[100] If a threat of the situation escalating is identified, the Committee requests that a State Party to the Convention on the Elimination of Racial Discrimination provides information. It may also make a visit to the said state to collect first-hand information, and to offer good offices or technical assistance. It then submits requests to UN institutions. It can adopt a decision or statement in a case.[101] Since 1993, the Committee has launched the above procedures with more than 20

98 Declaration on the Prevention of Genocide, *The Committee on the Elimination of Racial Discrimination*, CERD/C/66/1, March 11, 2005.

99 The UN Committee on the Elimination of Racial Discrimination (1993): *Prevention of Racial Discrimination, Including Early Warning and Urgent Procedures,* A/48/18, Annex III. http://www.ohchr.org/Documents/HRBodies/CERD/EarlyWarning/A_48_18_Annex_III_English.pdf.

100 Schabas W. (2006): *Preventing Genocide and Mass Killing: The Challenge for the United Nations*, Report, Minority Rights Group International, 20–21.

101 The UN Committee on the Elimination of Racial Discrimination (2007): *Guidelines for the Early Warning and Urgent Action Procedures*, Annual Report, A/62/18, Annexes, Chapter III.

countries. It has made two field visits and in six cases has provided information to the UN Secretary-General and other UN agencies. The Prevention Mechanism is fostered by the Subcommittee on the Prevention of Torture, which began work in February 2007 on the basis of the Optional Protocol[102] to the Convention against Torture and Other Cruel, Inhuman or Degrading Treatment or Punishment. This was in some way the natural consequence of the provisions of Art. 2 of the Convention, in which states have been called upon to take effective legislative, administrative, judicial and other measures to prevent torture.[103]

The Subcommittee on Torture pays visits to the States Parties to the Protocol, visiting closed places and offering technical assistance with the establishment of national preventative mechanisms.

1.4.3. The High Commissioner's for Human Rights activities towards prevention

The mandate of the High Commissioner for Human Rights is concerned primarily with the promotion and protection of human rights. It also includes tasks to prevent human-rights violations around the world, and to play an active role in "removing current obstacles and in meeting the challenges of full realisation of all human rights."[104]

A Report on the role of prevention in the promotion and protection of human rights, discussed at the 33rd Human Rights Council, was the conceptual contribution of the High Commissioner for Human Rights to the prevention of human-rights abuses (including those of a mass character). The Commissioner noted that the obligation to prevent arose out of international treaties to which states are parties, and that this was part of respecting and protecting human rights. He distinguished direct and indirect prevention, with the first taken to entail elimination of risk factors and the establishment of legal, administrative and political

102 The UN Optional Protocol to the Convention had 91 ratifications as of 21 July 2021, http://tbinternet.ohchr.org/_layouts/TreatyBodyExternal/Treaty.aspx?Treaty=CAT-OP&Lang=en.

103 The UN Convention against Torture and other Cruel, Inhuman or Degrading Treatment or Punishment (to be completed), 10 December 1984. The Committee Against Torture has, among others, tackled prevention issues in its general comment in 2008, in which it defined the scope of the obligation, Convention Against Torture and Other Cruel, Inhuman or Degrading Treatment or Punishment, General Comment No. 2. 2, Implementation of Article 2 by States Parties, CAT/C/GC/2, January 24, 2008.

104 Resolution of the UN General Assembly, A/RES/48/141, December 20, 1993.

structures for prevention; while the second was acknowledged as a reaction to human-rights abuses, for example involving investigation and punishment of perpetrators, and extension to victims of the right to know the truth and to file a complaint. In addition, the Commissioner defined the roles concerning the prevention of human-rights abuses to be played by national institutions for the protection of human rights, civil society, private institutions, human-rights education, and international institutions and mechanisms.[105]

In pursuing his/her mandate, the Commissioner is contributing to the prevention of mass human-rights violations. In principle, the focus is on cases involving the most serious violations, especially those involving the right to life. The Commissioner works with both governments and international institutions, for example providing direct support to the Office of the Special Adviser on the Prevention of Genocide and Responsibility to Protect in respect of early warning.

From this point of view, the presence of Field Offices is important, as it provides an opportunity for the human-rights situation to be monitored, and response tools preventing mass offences searched for. In relation to need, the Office of the High Commissioner uses offices and regional centres, but also opens national offices (e.g. in Angola, Togo, Uganda, Tunisia, Yemen, Cambodia, Bosnia and Herzegovina, Serbia, Bolivia, Honduras, Colombia, Guatemala and Mexico). Representatives of the Bureau also participate in many peacekeeping operations (e.g. in Afghanistan, Burundi, Chad, the Democratic Republic of the Congo, Ethiopia, Georgia, Guinea, Haiti, Iraq, Liberia, Libya, the Central African Republic and Côte d'Ivoire).

The Rapid Response Unit within the Commissioner's Office is of particular practical importance, as it has a list of people who can be deployed in the field rapidly should a crisis occur. At the request of the Human Rights Council and the Secretary General, the Unit also organises investigative and research missions. Such missions have, among others, taken place in the occupied Palestinian territories, the Democratic Republic of the Congo, North Korea and Syria.[106]

---

105 Report of the Office of the UN High Commissioner for Human Rights, *The Role of Prevention in the Promotion and Protection of Human Rights*, A/HRC/30/20, July 16, 2015.

106 Ramcharan B. (2002): *The United Nations High Commissioner for Human Rights. The Challenge of International Protection*, The Hague-London-New York: Martinus Nijhoff Publishers, particularly 29–196.

II. Competence of Regional European Institutions in the Prevention of Mass Human-Rights Violations and Atrocity Crimes

2.1. The European Union against mass human-rights violations and atrocity crimes

2.1.1. Legal framework

The European Union has not developed separate instruments to prevent mass violations of human rights. However, its contribution can be recognised through actions to protect human rights, as well as to achieve conflict prevention.[1] The Union has a solid legal basis for engaging in these areas within the framework of both its internal and external policies.[2]

Respect for human rights is one of the values of the European Union (Article 2 of the EU Treaty) and the fundamental rights guaranteed by the European Convention for the Protection of Human Rights and Fundamental Freedoms, as well as the constitutional traditions of states, form part of the law of the Union (Art. 6.3 TEU).[3] Respect for human rights is also a prerequisite for EU membership, while serious violations may be reason enough for proceedings under Article 7 of the Treaty on European Union (concerning the possibility of suspending certain rights of a Member State) to be initiated.

Through its external relations, the EU contributes to the protection of human rights (Article 3.5 TEU), and its actions aim to support the universality and indivisibility of human rights and fundamental freedoms, as well as respect for human dignity (Articles 21, 42, 43 TEU). In its so-called 2012 Strategic Framework and

---

1 *Gothenburg European Council Programme 2001*, comp., as well as: *Council of the European Union, Conclusions on Conflict Prevention*, June 20, 2011. Schmidt J. (2016): 'EU and UN Partnership in Light of the Responsibility to Protect' in: Chappel L., Mawdsley J., Petrov P. (eds.) *The EU, Strategy and Security Policy: Regional and Strategic Challenges*, London: Routlege. 139–144.

2 Fiott Cf. D., Vincent M. (2013) 'The European Union' in: Zyberi G. (ed.) *An Institutional Approach of the Responsibility to Protect*, Cambridge University Press, 199–202.

3 Consolidated version of the Treaty on European Union, Official Journal of the European Union, October 26, 2012.

Action Programme on Human Rights and Democracy, the European Council confirmed that the EU would promote human rights in all areas of external action, and would also act to prevent violations thereof. It at the same time agreed to include the human-rights situation among early conflict indicators within an emerging EU early-warning system.[4] On 20 July 2015, the Council adopted a new Action Programme for 2015–2019, which announced the continuation of the Strategic Framework.[5]

Institutions of the European Union have also extended repeated support to the concept of responsibility to protect, including the idea of preventing mass violence, and perceived the EU's role in this area. In the Consensus on Development adopted in 2005, the EU expressed support for the responsibility to protect and the need to prevent mass atrocities, recognising that it cannot be passive when genocide, war crimes, ethnic cleansing and serious violations of international humanitarian law and human rights are committed.[6] A 2008 report reviewing the European Security Strategy includes sovereign governments assuming responsibility for the protection of the population from genocide, war crimes, ethnic cleansing and crimes against humanity.

In the same year, the relationship between state sovereignty and responsibility for civil protection was recognised by the European Council, which committed the EU to act in favour of R2P in line with the UNGA Resolution.[7] This denoted that its vision of R2P was narrower than the original concept proposed by the Expert Committee in 2001. It was decided to focus on prevention and reconstruction. In similar vein, the European Parliament, which considered conflict prevention as an element of R2P in 2013, expressed its stance.[8] The Council of

---

4 EU Strategic Framework and Action Plan on Human Rights and Democracy, Luxembourg, June 25, 2012.

5 Action Plan on Human Rights and Democracy (2015–2019) – Keeping Human Rights at the Heart of the EU Agenda, JOIN(2015) 16 final, April 28, 2015.

6 European Consensus on Development – 2005 to be completed; Similar wording was included in the European Commission's proposal for a new European Consensus of November 2016: Communication from the Commission to the European Parliament, the Council, the European Economic and Social Committee and the Committee of The Regions. Proposal for a new European Consensus on Development Our World, our Dignity, our Future. Strasbourg, 22 November 2016, COM(2016) 740 final.

7 European Council Report on the implementation of the European Security Strategy: Providing Security in a Changing World, Brussels 11 December 2008, S407/08.

8 European Parliament, Report with a proposal for a European Parliament recommendation to the Council on the UN Principle of the "Responsibility to Protect", March 27, 2013.

the European Union also recognised the need to operationalise R2P, primarily regarding prevention. It spoke in favour of integrating action taken to prevent conflicts with civil-liability requirements.[9]

2.1.2. EU capacity regarding prevention

The capacity of the European Union to prevent mass human-rights violations and atrocity crimes entails competences of both intergovernmental institutions (the European Council and Council of the European Union) and European institutions (the European Commission, European Parliament and EEAS), as well as instruments developed. The most important human rights policies are: guidelines, strategies and action plans, structural human rights dialogue and demarches. Financial support for non-governmental organisations is provided by the European Instrument for Democracy and Human Rights. The European Neighbourhood Policy and the European Endowment for Democracy aim to promote stability, including human rights, democracy and the rule of law, in neighbouring countries.

The European Union also has quite strong economic instruments. It has the capacity to provide development assistance and impose sanctions. However, most of these are used in response to serious human-rights violations, rather than preventatively. Human rights clauses are deployed in trade agreements,[10] which thus provide for termination in the case of serious human-rights violations. In addition, the Generalised System of Preferences (GSP) is used to promote values consistent with the responsibility to protect, and has again gained actual application, in this case against Belarus, Sri Lanka and Myanmar. The Instrument for Stability (IFS) is an important EU contribution to prevention and response at times of crisis. In addition, special missions, and humanitarian and military operations may play a preventative role at the operational level.[11] It is also worth noting that the EU Common Position on Arms Exports from 2008 relates to R2P criteria.

---

9 Council of the EU, 10809/09, No. 3, June 9, 2009.

10 Sviatun O. (2014): 'The Role of Human Rights Clause in the EU Agreements with Third Countries' in: Jaskiernia J., *Uniwersalny i regionalny wymiar ochrony praw człowieka. Nowe wyzwania – nowe rozwiązania*, Vol. 1, Warsaw: Wydawnictwo Sejmowe, 643–653.

11 For EU external policy instruments, see Szmigielski A. (2016): 'Prawa człowieka i demokracja w centrum działań zewnętrznych Unii Europejskiej,' *Przegląd Zachodni*, No. 1, 12–15.

New opportunities emerged in 2011, with the founding of the European External Action Service (EEAS), as headed by the EU's High Representative for Foreign Affairs and Security Policy. The presence of EEAS Delegations in 139 countries has provided new opportunities for information-gathering, and for a practical impact on reality to be exerted. EU Special Representatives are being assisted in the promotion of EU policies in areas particularly vulnerable to destabilisation. At the time of writing, the EU has appointed Special Representatives for Afghanistan, Bosnia and Herzegovina, Central Asia, the Horn of Africa, Kosovo, the Sahel, the Middle East, Sudan and Georgia, among other countries and areas.

The only human-rights mandate *per se* has been that conferred upon the Special Rapporteur on Human Rights, who can contribute to the pursuit of EU human-rights objectives. However, he in fact concentrates more on the promotion of human rights and EU policy in this respect than on operational engagement. The European Union has established a R2P focal point, but it does not engage in operations to prevent mass atrocities. First and foremost, it is engaged in maintaining external contacts, mainly with the United Nations. In January 2019 the European External Action Service officially launched the 'Toolkit for Atrocity Prevention' to coordinate European responses to atrocities.

The European Union has not yet created an early warning system for atrocity crimes. Although it acquires information from various sources, including Member States, the COREU system, multilateral meetings of working groups of PSC ambassadors, INTCEN, the EU Intelligence and Situation Centre (IntCent), EUMS-INT and non-governmental organisations, and although it classifies states in terms of their fragility, it does not take threats of mass human-rights violations into account, or analyse the situation in the long term.[12] These deficiencies hamper the EU assessment of the situation, and especially its practical involvement.

However, the European Union case can serve as an example of success in the prevention of armed conflict and mass human-rights violations on its own territory. The principles accompanying integration, such as cooperation and solidarity, respect for human rights and democratic values, as well as economic development, certainly contributed. In external policy, the EU has not decided to set up a separate institution or instrument for the prevention of mass

12 *The EU and the Prevention of Mass Atrocities. An Assessment of Strengths and Weaknesses*, Budapest Centre for the International Prevention of Genocide and Mass Atrocities, Hungary 2013.

human-rights violations. It also has no early-warning system in this regard, which makes appropriate action in due time look difficult to achieve. The EU is, however, an institution with a significant prevention potential seen to lie in its broad political, diplomatic, economic, social and other instruments, as well as the Member States' general appreciation of the need for preventative action to be taken.

2.2. Prevention in the activities of the Organisation for Security and Cooperation in Europe

The Organisation for Security and Cooperation in Europe (OSCE) was created as a result of the transformation of the Conference on Security and Cooperation in Europe (CSCE) and is a regional organisation within the meaning of Chapter VIII of the Charter of the United Nations. It was one of the first institutions to address the topic of prevention. The very idea of the CSCE as a platform for dialogue between the Eastern and Western blocs during the Cold War contained the "element" of prevention – the intention to warm relations between competing blocs and facilitate cooperation to prevent war from breaking out. Established standards and mechanisms, such as review conferences, security and confidence-building measures, and disarmament initiatives were all largely preventative.[13]

Enhancing human rights was one element to the idea of prevention espoused by the CSCE/OSCE. At as early a stage as the 1975 Helsinki Conference, the relationship between human rights and security was recognised, with the then Declaration taking account of the principles governing mutual relations between states participating, in respect of both rules on security (e.g. refraining from the threat of the use of force or its use, or peaceful settlement of disputes) and human rights (respect for human rights and fundamental freedoms).[14] This union was

---

13 R. Kuźniar and others (2020): *Bezpieczeństwo międzynarodowe*, Warsaw: Wydawnictwo Naukowe Scholar, 283–292; Bielecka M. (2004): 'KBWE/OBWE jako forma instytucjonalizacji współpracy międzynarodowej w dziedzinie bezpieczeństwa' in: Parzymies S., Zięba R., *Instytucjonalizacja wielostronnej współpracy międzynarodowej w Europie*, Warsaw: Wydawnictwo Naukowe SCHOLAR, 286–307; Rotfeld A.D., *Polska w niepewnym świecie*, Warsaw: PISM, 210–226; Korey W. (1993): *The Promises We Keep. Human Rights, The Helsinki Process and American Foreign Policy*, New York: St. Martin's Press; Ghebali V.-I., Warner D. (eds.) (1999): 'The OSCE and Preventive Diplomacy,' *PSIO Occasional Paper*, No. 1.

14 CSCE Helsinki Final Act, August 1, 1975, https://www.osce.org/helsinki-final-act; Rotfeld A. D. (1990): *Europejski system bezpieczeństwa in statu nascendi*, Warsaw: PISM, 47–50.

also one of the foundations of the concept of cooperative security, in which one of the pillars was recognised as respect for human rights – the so-called human dimension. In line with the OSCE philosophy, all security efforts are activities preventing human-rights violations, with actions to respect these rights considered to promote security, including conflict prevention.

The Organisation did not develop separate instruments to prevent mass human-rights violations and atrocities. Rather, this problem forms part of conflict prevention, to which the OSCE attaches great importance. By the time of the Helsinki Summit in the summer of 1992, the states were designating the CSCE as an early-warning, prevention and crisis-management instrument;[15] while the Decision of the Ministerial Council of 7 December 2011 on elements of the state-conflict cycle decided to strengthen the OSCE's capabilities in respect of early warning and early action, facilitation of dialogue and mediation.[16] As a result of that Decision, Internal Early-Warning Guidelines were adopted in 2012,[17] and an open-ended list of early-warning indicators developed.

The decision-making powers of the OSCE in setting the direction of the Organisation's activities remain with the states, as represented on the Ministerial Council. Current decisions, including those concerning early response and early action, are taken by the Permanent Council, which meets weekly at the level of Permanent Representatives to the OSCE in Vienna, and is supported by the OSCE Secretariat and Presidency. In turn, a number of OSCE bodies and institutions acting in line with the human dimension and the OSCE play an important role in early warning and early action over security and human-rights situations. The most important bodies include the High Commissioner for National Minorities; the Office for Democratic Institutions and Human Rights; and OSCE field missions. The Conflict Prevention Centre,[18] the focal point for early warning in the Organisation, has a coordinating and support function vis-à-vis the main bodies and institutions of the OSCE. It collects information from various OSCE

15 CSCE Helsinki Document 1992: The Challenges of Change, Helsinki, July 10, 1992.

16 Decision No 3/11, Elements of the Conflict Cycle, Related to Enhancing the OSCE's Capabilities in Early Warning, Early Action, Dialogue Facilitation and Mediation Support, and Post-Conflict Rehabilitation, December 7, 2011 in: Organisation for Security and Co-operation in Europe, Eighteenth Meeting of the Ministerial Council, December 6–7, 2011, Vilnius, 11–16.

17 Internal OSCE Early Warning Guidelines, May 7, 2012,

18 The Conflict Prevention Centre was one of the first institutions established under the Charter of Paris for a New Europe, adopted 19–21 November 1990. Since January 1994 the Centre has been part of the CSCE / OSCE Secretariat.

sources, including missions and field operations, and then advises the Secretary-General and President on the potential for action.

2.2.1. The High Commissioner on National Minorities – the oldest European institution dedicated to prevention

The High Commissioner on National Minorities (HCNM) is the OSCE organ combining national minorities rights and conflict prevention. First appointment in 1992 was the result of the CSCE's search for means and methods of responding to conflict situations, including mass crimes, as happened at the time in the Balkans.

The mandate specifies that the Office of the High Commissioner is an "instrument of conflict prevention at the earliest possible stage". Its task is to identify and warn about problems of national minorities that could become conflicts. As an early warning, the Commissioner evaluates the situation of the parties involved, and the nature of the tensions, analysing the development of recent events and predicting their consequences for peace and stability in the OSCE region.[19]

To this end, the Commissioner visits given states, and contacts parties directly concerned, with the consequence that he/she has an opportunity to receive "first-hand" information. At the same time, the Commissioner works to promote dialogue, trust and cooperation between the parties. According to the HCNM mandate, in situations where the competences of the Commissioner are deemed to have been exceeded, a warning is to be issued to the Permanent Council.

As the involvement of the High Commissioner in a particular situation does not require the approval of any OSCE body or even the State concerned, we have a good indication of the fact that the Commissioner generally enjoys independence as he/she assesses whether or not a given situation requires action on his/her part. However, the operation of the Office is under the auspices of the OSCE President, and the High Commissioner is obliged to consult the President on planned departures and initiatives. On return, he/she submits a confidential report to the President, with data collected and information on the progress with actions in a particular case.

The High Commissioner cannot deal with violations of OSCE provisions against individuals belonging to national minorities, or with conflicts involving terrorist organisations. The mandate also fails to provide any practical

19 Helsinki decisions, Chapter II.

implementing measures for the Office of the High Commissioner.[20] In practice, the Commissioner uses "silent diplomacy," offers good offices, encourages dialogue and gives recommendations to the parties.

Thus far, the HCNM has, among others, been involved in the problems of the Russian-speaking population in Latvia and Estonia, the Hungarian minorities in Slovakia and in Romania, the Slovakian minority in Hungary, the Albanian minority in Macedonia and the Greek population in Albania. The issue of the Crimean Tatars in Ukraine has also been addressed, as have the problems of minorities in Georgia, Kazakhstan and Kyrgyzstan. The High Commissioner has also worked as a personal representative of the President-in-Office of Kosovo, and was involved in the Macedonian interstate situation, in which, following the dramatic increase in the number of Kosovo refugees, the "early warning" formula was issued for the first time to the Vienna Permanent Council, given the tense situation in the country (12 May 1999).[21] The High Commissioner also issued an early warning to the Permanent Council in regard to the situation in Kyrgyzstan in 2010.

2.2.2. The Office's for Democratic Institutions and Human Rights mandate

The Office for Democratic Institutions and Human Rights (ODIHR) is "the most important institution of the human OSCE dimension". Initially, it functioned as the Free Electoral Office, serving as a hub for the exchange of information and facilitating contacts between participating states regarding election choices. On the basis of the Helsinki Decisions (Chapters VI, 5–6, 15–22), the Budapest Decisions (Chapter VIII, sections 8–16, 23–25, 42–43) and the Decisions of the Ministerial Council taken in Prague and Rome, the Office has received a number of competences enabling it to develop a wide range of activities in the human dimension.

Efforts to promote democratic standards (including election monitoring); and practical support for the development of democratic institutions, civil society, the rule of law, respect for human rights and non-discrimination are of greatest importance in the context of preventing mass human-rights violations.[22]

---

20 Negotiating the mandate of the High Commissioner has been difficult. Many countries feared the escalation of demands from national minorities that could jeopardise their territorial integrity.

21 Report from the HCNM, *OSCE Newsletter*, May 1999.

22 *OSCE Handbook* (1999): Vienna, 105–111.

The ODIHR organises training and seminars, and sends experts to advise individual countries. It provides assistance to public authorities in their fight against hate crimes and other intolerance, among others, by organising training for law-enforcement officers and by strengthening the capacity of civil society to monitor and report incidents of hate crime.

By virtue of the Budapest Decisions, the ODIHR plays a special role as a Contact Point for the Roma people. It functions as an information-exchange centre and facilitates contacts between states, OSCE missions, international organisations (especially the Council of Europe), and representatives of the Roma community.

The ODIHR also organises OSCE Annual Review Conferences on Human Rights, which serve as systematic assessments of governments in their application of OSCE human-dimension standards. Similar seminars and implementation meetings are convened at expert level, and often devoted to selected issues in the field. Currently, their contribution to the early-warning function of the organisation is particularly underlined.

The Office exercises its functions under the general supervision of the Permanent Council, in respect of which it has consultative powers. It is also required to report on its activities. Through its educational, promotional, monitoring and advisory activities, it is an institution that contributes to the prevention of human-rights abuses, although it has no instruments to engage in atrocity crimes situations.

2.2.3. OSCE Missions – prevention in the field

Field missions and operations are perhaps the most important OSCE instrument for early warning and prevention. The missions, set up from the early nineties in an *ad hoc* manner on principles of trial and error depending on emerging needs and opportunities, are a manifestation of the flexible nature of the organisation based on political cooperation and the principle of consensus. They are a form by which political decisions are translated into practical implementation, and they demonstrate the ability of organisations to adapt to new conditions.[23]

The OSCE has the capacity to send short-term and long-term missions and other field operations. The former include expert, rapporteur, fact-finding and evaluating missions that may be ordered by the Permanent Council or the

23 See Höynck W. (1996): CSCE Missions in the Field as an Instrument of Preventive Diplomacy – their Origin and Development, Statements and Speeches, 1993–1996, Vienna, 116–131.

President of the OSCE, or else by the Office of Democratic Institutions and Human Rights. A mission to Albania in 1991 in view of the country's intention to join the CSCE was the first such expedition, seeking to evaluate whether the state accepted the standards developed during the Helsinki Process, was able to respect them, and expressed a readiness to recognise successive ones.[24] Gradually, explanatory missions came to be used as early-warning and conflict-prevention instruments in the OSCE area. They were tasked with identifying problems and sending first signals in an early-warning context, and sometimes also with the transmission of recommendations. Over time, the differences between explanatory and reporting missions became blurred, while similar functions also started to be performed by the assessment missions, whose task is assessment of situations in countries, regarding, for instance, the OSCE's human dimension.

In practice, the sending of explanatory and assessment missions is handled by most OSCE bodies and institutions. Missions dispatched by the ODIHR are of importance from the viewpoint of tasks related to the human dimension and the prevention of mass human-rights violations, serving in the assessment of a hosting country's needs concerning human rights, the rule of law and democracy. Information collected then forms the basis for the development of assistance projects, or the organisation of election-monitoring missions. Important tasks are also discharged by the missions initiated by the OSCE Presidency, which not only collect information but also perform ongoing tasks in conflict prevention and crisis management.

Nevertheless, it is the OSCE's long-term missions and so-called field operations that are of key importance. Long-term missions are founded by a decision of the OSCE body making political decisions. Since 1995 this has usually been the Permanent Council. The mandates of individual missions are negotiated by the OSCE Personal Representative. Initially they are valid for six months and then, depending on the situation in the region, the host country's will and the needs of the Organisation, they are extended by the Permanent Council. Missions cooperate with the host country based on a Memorandum of Understanding. The President is at the head of the mission, takes primary responsibility for it, and is required to inform the relevant OSCE bodies and Member States about it.

Operationally, a mission is supported by all the OSCE organs and institutions. The role of the Office for Democratic Institutions and Human Rights, the High Commissioner on National Minorities and the OSCE Representative on

---

24 Hałaciński A. (1995) 'Misje długoterminowe OBWE,' *Sprawy Międzynarodowe,* No. 2, 164.

Freedom of the Media is to support the mission in their respective fields. The Conflict Prevention Centre is responsible for the logistical and administrative servicing of a mission.

OSCE long-term missions represent the Organisation's greatest potential. Their mandates are diverse, tailored to the individual needs of each country. They perform tasks relevant to all phases of conflict and crisis situations, be this prevention, conflict management or stabilisation following completion. However, human rights and the whole human dimension remain at the "heart" of these tasks. They include, among other things, the collection of information, and assistance in the achievement of standards concerning human rights, the rule of law, democracy, the building of civil society and so on.[25]

The reports of a cyclical nature issued throughout the missions are extremely important for early warning. Thanks to their presence at the scene, representatives on a mission have an excellent opportunity to collect "first-hand" information, analyse and forecast and, if need be, to pursue on-the-spot initiatives capable of averting unfavourable developments. Periodic biweekly or monthly reports cover the whole situation in a given country and provide a solid basis for discussions within the Organisation, and then for appropriate action in line with the political will of the OSCE. Reporting is sometimes the most important task of staff, for example in OSCE Centres in Central Asian countries. Many of the reports are prepared specifically for the OSCE Chairman responsible for running the current policy. The reports go to all OSCE and participating countries, so the OSCE can be considered one of the best-informed organisations aware of the threats to the human dimension of the OSCE.

The OSCE has deployed a total of 34 long-term missions and field operations in the former Soviet Union and Balkan countries. Almost all of them had tasks within the human dimension of the OSCE, some of which were aimed at conflict prevention. Prevention was part of the OSCE mission in Estonia and Latvia in 1992, in Macedonia and in the initial phase of the mission in Ukraine (2014). Monitoring borders between Serbia and Montenegro (beginning of 1992), as well as of Kosovo (1998), Georgia and Chechnya (1999), Ingushetia (2001) and Dagestan (2003). Observation points in Donetsk and Gukowo (2014) were also founded, with a preventative function. Missions have also been involved in conflict resolution directly, with the effect several times being a so-called "freezing" of a conflict, and hence a

25 Bieńczyk-Missala A. (2005): '*Cele i funkcje misji Organizacji Bezpieczeństwa i Współpracy w Europie*,' *Stosunki Międzynarodowe. International Relations*, Vol. 32, No. 3–4, 53–74.

potential preventative effect. Such cases could be noted in Moldova, in respect of Transnistria (1993), and in Georgia with regard to South Ossetia (in this case, however, war broke out in 2008). One of the most spectacular failures was the mission of the OSCE Support Group in Chechnya established in 1995, which was unable to prevent mass human-rights violations during armed conflicts in Chechnya.[26]

In any case, the human rights situation is part of the mandate of each mission. Depending on the mandate, missions respond to human-rights violations by contacting host-country authorities, offering legal and institutional advice, initiating educational programs, supporting democratic institutions, and including free elections. All these activities are important in preventing mass human-rights violations. Indeed, they may provide a solid starting point for more advanced action on the part of the OSCE.[27]

The CSCE/OSCE exemplify failures and successes with conflict prevention and mass crimes. In addition to the unfortunate massacres that the Balkans experienced, mass crimes of the 1990s affected Georgia, Kyrgyzstan and Ukraine. The OSCE now has extensive experience in the prevention of conflict and of human-rights abuses. It has institutions at its disposal allowing threats to be rapidly responded to. At the same time, the fact that it is not barrier-free hinders the achievement of goals. Problems here include the political nature of commitments taken on,[28] the complex nature of the decision-making process, and the persistent consensus principle. The organisation has only soft-power means to deploy against states in violation of the OSCE human dimension. The Organisation may criticise or even condemn authorities for unlawful politics, but it does not impose sanctions. It uses cooperative methods of action which may not suffice, in the event of an outbreak of mass human-rights violations.

2.3. The preventative role of the Council of Europe

The Council of Europe has created the world's most effective system for the protection of human rights, working steadfastly towards unity between European states since 1949. Over that time, it has adopted more than 200 legal instruments

26 Zellner W., Evers F. and others (2014): *The Future of OSCE Field Operations (Options)*, OSCE Network of Think Tanks and Academic Institutions.

27 Bieńczyk A. (2000): *The Human Dimension in CSCE/OSCE Missions*, The Polish Quarterly of International Affairs, Vol. 9, No. 4.

28 Buchsbaum T. M. (1993): 'The Future of the Human Dimension of the OSCE,' *Helsinki Monitor*, Vol. 4, No.2; Bloed A. (1995): 'The Human Dimension of the OSCE: More Words than Deeds?,' *Helsinki Monitor*, Vol. 6, No. 4.

open for ratification, not only by Member States but also by third countries. The European Convention for Human Rights and Fundamental Freedoms of 4 November 1950,[29] together with the European Court of Human Rights, has been the CoE's jewel in the crown for years. Full respect for the Convention would in fact mean the absence of mass human-rights violations, to which the Court's case law contributes, setting standards that all Member States should strive for. Even if the Court deals with individual cases of human-rights abuses, and examines violations *ex post facto*, its decisions, and the compensation capable of being awarded may be important for the prevention of serious human-rights violations.[30] Rulings on the right to life and the prohibition of torture, especially in connection with ongoing military action against the Kurds in Turkey or the Chechens in Russia in the 1990s, provided important guidance for governments and judicial institutions alike.

The Council of Europe monitors the human-rights situation in the Member States systematically. This is supported by the reporting system, such as the Framework Convention for the Protection of National Minorities of 1 February 1995,[31] as well as by the competence of the High Commissioner for Human Rights. The Commissioner visits the states and motivates them to protect human rights through recommendations. The work of the European Committee for the Prevention of Torture and Inhuman or Degrading Treatment or Punishment (CPT)[32] is similar; it operates under the Convention for the Prevention of Torture and Inhuman or Degrading Treatment or Punishment, adopted on 26 November 1987. The idea of prevention was the basis for the adoption of the Convention and the appointment of the Committee, and is enhanced by regular visits to the states, as well as ad hoc visits and constant dialogue.

The expert activity of the European Commission against Racism and Intolerance, which deals with key issues in the prevention of mass crimes, deserves special attention. It monitors the problems of racism, xenophobia, anti-Semitism, intolerance and discrimination, on the basis of factors such as race, nationality,

---

29 The European Convention for Human Rights and Fundamental Freedoms, Strasbourg, November 4, 1950.

30 Smith R., Mallory C. (2013): 'The European System of Human Rights' in: Zyberi G. (ed.) *An Institutional Approach of the Responsibility to Protect,* Cambridge University Press, 439–456.

31 Framework Convention for the Protection of National Minorities, Strasbourg, February 1, 1995.

32 *European Convention for the Prevention of Torture and Inhuman or Degrading Treatment or Punishment,* Strasbourg, November 26, 1987.

ethnicity, colour, religion and language. In its reports, published every five years for each Member State, it draws attention to legal and institutional gaps and suggests changes in practice. The Council of Europe therefore pays special attention to groups that have been victims of atrocity crimes in the past, i.e. ethnic or ethnic and linguistic minorities, including Roma in particular.

According to experts, the Council of Europe has not addressed the issue of Responsibility to Protect sufficiently.[33] Through its position, it could make a greater contribution to the development of this principle and to its importance. Nevertheless, its contribution to the prevention and capacity which it holds in the sphere of structural prevention in particular are considered significant.[34]

33 Vlasic M.V. (2012): 'Europe and North America' in: Genser J., Cotler I., *The Responsibility to Protect. The Promise of Stopping Mass Atrocities in our* Time, New York: Oxford University Press, 181.

34 Michałowska G. (2007): *Ochrona praw człowieka w Radzie Europy i w Unii Europejskiej*, Warsaw: Wydawnictwa Akademickie i Profesjonalne, 91–175.

III. The Problem of Preventing Mass Human-Rights Violations and Atrocity Crimes in Non-European Institutions

3.1. Human rights and the African Union security system

The African Union (AU) and the African states themselves have made a significant contribution to the adoption and evolution of the concept of Responsibility to Protect, including the idea of prevention. The African Union Founding Act of 11 July 2000 alone can be regarded as one of the inspirations for the emergence of the concept. It states that the protection of human rights is the purpose of the AU (Article 2), and that the principles under which the AU functions formally include respect for democracy, human rights, the rule of law and good governance and the respect for the sanctity of human life (Article 4). The pioneering entry giving the Union the right to intervene in a Member State of the AU in the context of war crimes, genocide and crimes against humanity (Article 4) is considered the most radical expression of support for R2P,[1] in terms of both prevention and response.[2]

The African Union was quite radical about the possibility of intervening in atrocity crimes. In connection with the proposal from the UN High-Level Panel on R2P for the UN Security Council's 2005 Jubilee Session, according to which the intervention should be in conformity with the United Nations Charter, the AU stated in the "Common African Position on the reform of the United Nations" (The Ezulwini Consensus) of March 2005, that in the case of burdensome situations, regional organisations should act on their own, and be able to obtain the Security Council's approval even *post factum*. It was even recognised that a lack of action by the Security Council did not release the international community from its responsibility to protect.[3] However, this position does not denote

---

1 *Constitutive Act of the African Union*, Lomé, July 11, 2000, https://au.int/sites/default/files/pages/34873-file-constitutiveact_en.pdf.

2 On the sources and meaning of Art. 4 of the Founding Act, see Genser J., Cotler I. (2012): *Responsibility to Protect. The Promise of Stopping Mass Atrocities in our Time*, New York: Oxford University Press, 112–120.

3 Ezulwini Consensus, Executive Council 7th Extraordinary Session, March 7–8, 2005, Addis Abeba, Ext/EX.CL/2(VII).

a lack of criticism of African countries towards the understanding of R2P as armed intervention. In many cases, as in Darfur, where mass murders have taken place, the AU has not decided to carry out large-scale military operations.[4]

The AU's Peace and Security Council established by the Additional Protocol to the Founding Act of July 2002 plays the most important role where the implementation of the R2P by the African Union is concerned. This is the decision-making body for the prevention, control and resolution of conflicts, responsible for security, early warning and prevention, as well as reaction to conflicts and crises. It is supported by: the Commission, the Panel of the Wise and the Continental Early Warning Systems, the African Standby Force and the Special Fund. Included among the objectives of the Council laid down in Art. 3 are "promotion and support to democratic processes, good governance and the rule of law, protection of human rights and fundamental freedoms, respect for sanctity of life, international humanitarian law as part of efforts to prevent conflicts."[5] The Council's functions include early warning and preventative diplomacy (Article 6). The Council has broad powers to prevent mass crimes, including the anticipation and prevention of conflicts and policies that can lead to genocide and crimes against humanity. In addition, the Council may assemble and deploy peace-support missions, and recommend to the Assembly that there be intervention in respect of Article 4 of the AU Founding Act in serious circumstances such as those involving war crimes, genocide and crimes against humanity (Article 7). The ability to impose sanctions in cases of unconstitutional change of authority in a state is important as well, as such changes may often be accompanied by mass violations of human rights.

The Commission, like the UN Security Council, consists of 15 Members, but no state has a right of veto. In procedural matters, decisions are taken by a majority of votes, while in other cases a two-thirds majority is required. There is therefore no formal possibility of one state blocking a decision. In general, however, the Protocol assumes that decisions should be made through consensus (Article 8.12). The close cooperation of the African Union in regard to regional security mechanisms is also foreseen.

---

4 Williams P.D. (2007): 'From Non-Intervention to Non-Indifference: The Origins and Development of the African Union's Security Culture,' *African Affairs*, March 12, 2007, 278–279.

5 *Protocol Relating to the Establishment of the Peace and Security Council of the African Union*, Durban, July 9, 2002, http://www.peaceau.org/uploads/psc-protocol-en.pdf.

An important achievement in the field of prevention is the African Peer Review Mechanism (APRM) established in 2003 to ensure that all countries of the region follow the same values and principles of governance. APRM operates in line with the Declaration on Democracy, Political, Economic and Corporate Governance, which the states of the *New Partnership for* Africa's Development (NEPAD) adopted in July 2002 in the belief that human rights and democracy are central to the development and stability of the region.[6] APRM is a voluntary mechanism to which 33 African countries have so far acceded. It entails preparation – in cooperation with the given state – of a Report, along with recommendations regarding action. The assessment concerns several sectors, including human rights, democracy and good governance. An APRM Panel composed of heads of state and government has an impact on the Report's final shape.

Human-rights instruments, which the Union inherited from the Organisation of African Unity, could be considered an additional preventative capacity of the African Union. These are the African Charter on Human and People's Rights of 1981 and the African Court of Human and Peoples' Rights, the African Commission on Human and Peoples' Rights, the African Charter on the Rights and Welfare of the Child of 1990, the (2003) Protocol to the African Charter on Human and Peoples' Rights on the Rights of Women in Africa; and the (2007) African Charter on Democracy, Elections and Governance. However, poor performance would in fact seem to characterise the African system of human-rights protection, including the African Court. The possibility of complaints being filed with the Court should mass or serious violations of human rights arise would seem to limit the ability of the African institutions (including the Court itself) to take preventative action.

3.2. The evolution of the Economic Community of West African States in respect of the protection of the population

Hardly touched by mass crimes,[7] the states of the Economic Community of West African States (ECOWAS)[8] have incorporated into their system a protection

6 *Declaration On Democracy, Political, Economic And Corporate Governance*, July 8, 2002, http://www1.uneca.org/Portals/nepad/Documents/declaration-on-democracy-political-economic-corporate-governance.pdf.

7 In Liberia and Sierra Leone, Guinea Bissau, Côte d'Ivoire and Mali, among others.

8 Membership: Benin, Burkina Faso, Cape Verde, Cote d'Ivoire, Gambia, Ghana, Guinea, Guinea-Bissau, Liberia, Mali, Niger, Nigeria, Senegal, Sierra Leone, Togo.

of the population against regimes, war crimes and human-rights abuses. The Community has been focused on building a collective security system since the 1970s.[9] Among other things, it intervened in Liberia in 1990, with a view to mass human-rights abuses being prevented,[10] within the framework of an operation conducted without the authorisation of the Security Council.

Over time, ECOWAS has developed a normative basis for its commitments. The issue of the promotion of respect for human rights and the principles of democracy was first mentioned in the Declaration on Political Principles in 1991. In turn, in the 1993 Revised Treaty, ECOWAS reaffirmed the need for human rights to be recognised, promoted and protected, and for cooperation to be pursued with a view to internal and international conflicts being prevented (Article 58).[11]

These provisions formed the basis for the establishment of the Mechanism for Conflict Prevention, Management, Resolution, Peace-keeping and Security, and then for the initiation of R2P actions. The mechanism was established on the basis of a Protocol of 1999.[12] Established in order for tasks stemming from the Protocol to be implemented are: Heads of State and Government, an Executive Secretariat and a Council for Peace and Security. The design is not fully coherent, however. Although states have confirmed the human-rights obligations stemming from key UN and OAU instruments (Article 2), the prevention of mass crimes and human-rights violations has not been taken into account for the purpose of the mechanism, which relates primarily to security and conflict prevention (Article 3). Nonetheless, the states have assumed that one of the situations in which the mechanism may be launched relates to mass violations of human rights and the rule of law (Article 25). The ECOWAS liability section states that the Community will intervene to alleviate the suffering of a population, restoring normality in the wake of disasters and conflicts. The established mechanism has given ECOWAS an opportunity to resort to operational action in the case of Responsibility to Protect.

---

9 The basis was the *Non-Aggression Protocol* of April 1978 and *the Mutual Assistance Protocol* of May 1981.

10 *The ECOWAS Protocol on Non-Agression*, April 22, 1978; *The ECOWAS Protocol relating to mutual assistance on defence*, May 29, 1981, https://documentation.ecowas.int.

11 *The ECOWAS Revised Treaty*, July 25, 1993, http://www.ecowas.int/wp-content/uploads/2015/01/Revised-treaty.pdf.

12 *The ECOWAS Protocol Relating to the Mechanism for Conflict Prevention, Management, Resolution, Peace-keeping and Security*, December 10, 1999, http://www.zif-berlin.org/fileadmin/uploads/analyse/dokumente/ECOWAS_Protocol_ConflictPrevention.pdf.

The Complementary Protocol on Democracy and Good Governance adopted in 2001 lays down a number of principles shared by Member States. These include: the division of power into an executive, a legislature and a judiciary; change of government by way of free, fair and transparent elections; non-tolerance of changes of power achieved by unconstitutional means; participation in public life and the principle of the apolitical army. Implementation of these principles would represent an important contribution to the promotion of peace and to people's protection. The Protocol also provides for additional instruments for ECOWAS and a Mechanism for Conflict Prevention, Management, Resolution, Peacekeeping and Security. In the case of the suppression of democracy or mass human-rights violations, the possibility of sanctions being imposed on an ECOWAS Member State is envisaged, or even suspension of a member.

The development of ideas and instruments within ECOWAS led in 2008 to the next achievement – the adoption of the ECOWAS Conflict Prevention Framework.[13] It served to define the assignment of ECOWAS' mutual responsibilities and relationships with: its Member States, civil society, and external partners. There was also a strengthening of the system overall, as well as elaboration of a strategy for action. States have stated that their goal is a strengthening of human security, understood as the putting in place of conditions under which individual and collective rights, well-being, security and life are not threatened, while and human rights and democratic standards, as well as development, are supported (Article 6). It has been assumed that this may only be achieved through effective conflict prevention and support for peace-building in post-conflict situations.

The adopted Framework notes that ECOWAS has "supranational authority," and in that context the legal and moral justification to intervene on behalf of, if in agreement with, the Member States, the African Union and the UN – for the protection of human safety in the areas of responsibility to prevent, responsibility to react and responsibility to rebuild. Responsibility to prevent is defined as preventing the causes of armed conflicts (Article 41). This is to be done through activity in early warning, preventative diplomacy, democracy, human rights and the rule of law, media, natural resources management, cross-border initiatives, security management, disarmament efforts, women's initiatives, peace and security, youth empowerment, the ECOWAS Standby Force, humanitarian aid and peace education (Ch. VIII).

Adoption of the ECOWAS Conflict Prevention Framework represented the most comprehensive response to tasks arising out of the UNSC's R2P principle

---

13 *The ECOWAS Conflict Prevention Framework*, Regulation MSC/REG, January 1, 2008.

as set out in the 2005 Outcome Document. ECOWAS recognised the need for multilateral action, developing instruments to promote peace and stability in the security sphere, while also obliging Member States to respect human rights and democratic standards. While it is doubtful whether the Community has sufficient resources to implement ambitious goals, it does not escape the adoption of instruments. It suspended the membership rights of Guinea in 2008, for breach of standards; applied sanctions and threatened to use force against mass human-rights violations. Niger was also suspended in 2009, but ECOWAS was not able to put pressure on it to accept ECOWAS standards.[14] In addition, the Community has also intervened in Sierra Leone, while also setting up numerous operations, including in Côte d'Ivoire in 2003, Liberia in 2003, Guinea-Bissau in 2012, Mali in 2013 and Gambia in 2017.

3.3. The International Conference on the Great Lakes Region on Genocide Prevention

The African Union and the United Nations launched the International Conference on the Great Lakes Region (ICGLR)[15] in the 1990s, in the light of serious conflicts that had occurred in Burundi, Rwanda and Congo, the massacres accompanying them, and the massive destabilisation of the region as a result of flows of refugees.[16] This intergovernmental organisation operating under the Pact on Security, Stability and Development in the Great Lakes Region signed in December 2006 is eager to address the issue of preventing international crimes and human-rights violations.

As early as in the Declaration adopted at the First Summit held on 19–20 November 2004 in Dar-Es-Salaam, the states expressed regret over conflicts, massive human-rights violations, and the impunity that crimes of genocide, crimes against humanity and war crimes had been met with. They committed themselves to the development of a mechanism for conflict prevention (Article 17), to the fight against genocide in the Great Lakes region (Articles 18, 29), and to

14 See Aning K., Atuobi S. (2012): 'The Economic Community of West African States and the Responsibility to Protect' in: Knight W.A., Egerton F. (eds.), *The Routledge Handbook of the Responsibility to Protect*, London-New York: Routledge, 223–229.

15 Membership: Angola, Burundi, Democratic Republic of Congo, Kenia, Republic of Congo, Central African Republic, Rwanda, South Sudan, Sudan, Tanzania, Uganda, Zambia.

16 Resolutions of the UN Security Council No. 1291, Art. 18 and No. 1304 art. 18.

cooperation in the latter regard (Article 36).[17] It would be two years later, in the aforementioned Pact, that they formulated their vision concerning action, with a number of instruments introduced to serve the general objectives of security, stability and sustainable development (Article 2). Alongside the non-aggression and security provisions, the states put considerable emphasis on the promotion of human rights, democracy and good governance (Article 6 – Protocol on Democracy and Good Governance), recognising that the lack of a democratic processes and the rule of law had led to destabilisation and mass murder in the past.[18] It was also deemed important for crimes of genocide, war crimes and crimes against humanity, and all forms of discrimination to be prevented and punished.[19]

The most important implementing instrument of the Pact was the Regional Mechanism of Review, consisting of, among others, the Summit of Heads of State and Government, the Interinstitutional Steering Committee, the Secretariat and National Coordination and Cooperation Mechanisms (Articles 22–27). Financial support was to be provided by the Special Fund for Reconstruction and Development provided for in Article 21.

The Protocol for the Prevention and the Punishment of the Crime of Genocide, War Crimes and Crimes against Humanity and all forms of discrimination (Article 8) was part of the Pact. The states there committed themselves to abstention from, and to the prevention and punishment of, crimes, as well as condemning and seeking to eliminate all discriminatory practices. They also decided to ensure close monitoring of such practices by authorities and institutions, and to ban any propaganda and organisation whose the ideology is based on a conviction as to the superiority of a race or group of people of specified origin, or else any justification of discrimination caused by ethnic origin, race, religion or gender. They also promised to prevent sexual violence against women and children (Article 11), and to protect and help internal refugees (Article 12).

---

17 *Dar-Es-Salaam Declaration on Peace, Security, Democracy And Development In The Great Lakes Region*, International Conference on the Great Lakes Region, Dar-Es-Salaam, 2004.

18 See speech by the Secretary General of the ICGLR Amb. Liberaty Mulamuly during the II Regional Forum in Arusha, March 3–5, 2010, dedicated to the prevention of genocide.https://www.icglr.org/images/LastPDF/GENOCIDE_PREVENTION_Mulamulapaper_2.pdf.

19 *Pact on Security, Stability and Development in the Great Lake Region*, International Conference on the Great Lakes Region, Nairobi, December 15, 2006.

The states also decided to set up a Committee for the Prevention and Punishment of the Crime of Genocide, War Crimes and Crimes against Humanity and all forms of discrimination. This consists of one expert from each country distinguished by high moral standards, impartiality and competence. Article 38 indicates that the Committee's mission is to prevent crimes of genocide, war crimes and crimes against humanity in the Great Lakes region. The Committee's responsibilities include: regular review of the situation in each country in the context of genocide, war crimes and crimes against humanity and discrimination, the collection and analysis of information, informing summits in a timely fashion in order for them to take preventative action, the proposing of measures by which impunity might be combated effectively, with awareness also raised and education in the name of peace and reconciliation pursued through regional and national programmes, and policies and measures recommended with a view to victims of crime having their rights to truth, compensation and rehabilitation guaranteed. The gender perspective is also to be addressed, and national actions monitored in respect of disarmament, demobilisation, the rehabilitation and repatriation of child soldiers, and other tasks imposed by the Ministerial Committee. The Committee was granted the right to pursue any method of investigation, including the conducting of interviews (Article 41).[20] However, the Committee has not played a significant role thus far.

3.4. The preventative capacity of other sub-regional groups in Africa

The South African Development Community (SADC)[21] and the Intergovernmental Authority on Development[22] (IGAD) have not addressed the topic of mass crimes directly. However, in both cases, the states have agreed on peace and security, human rights, democracy and good governance.[23] They have

---

20 *Protocol for the Prevention and the Punishment of the Crime of Genocide, War Crimes and Crimes Against Humanity and all forms of Discrimination*, International Conference on the Great Lakes Region, Nairobi, November 21, 2006.

21 Membership: Angola, Botswana, Democratic Republic of Congo, Lesotho, Madagascar, Malawi, Mauritius, Mozambique, Namibia, South Africa, Seychelles, Swaziland, Tanzania, Zambia, Zimbabwe.

22 Membership: Djibouti, Eritrea, Ethiopia, Kenya, Somalia, Sudan, South Sudan, Uganda.

23 See Article 2: *Treaty of the Southern African Development Community*, Windhoek, August 17, 1992, http://www.sadc.int/files/9113/5292/9434/SADC_Treaty.pdf, as well as Article 7: *Agreement Establishing The Inter-Governmental Authority On Development* (IGAD), Nairobi, March 21, 1996, http://www.ifrc.org/docs/idrl/N527EN.pdf.

also developed mechanisms for conflict prevention, thanks to which they have instruments by which the prevention of mass human-rights violations may be engaged in.

The objective of the SADC's most important body – the Organ on Politics, Defence and Security, established in 1996 – is to work for peace and security, especially with a view to people being protected, and development in the region safeguarded against the destabilisation resulting from the breach of law and order and armed conflicts, with conflicts prevented, the development of democratic institutions promoted, and respect for universal human rights encouraged.[24] The Organ pursues specific tasks in this area on the basis of strategic plans adopted by SADC Member States. It can resolve any significant interstate conflict, and the word "significant" is, among others, taken to mean large-scale violence between social groups or between the population and the state, including by way of genocide, ethnic cleansing and human-rights abuses.[25] The SADC has also set up a regional early-warning system that precedes the use of diplomatic and legal instruments for preventative purposes. The SADC has had the opportunity to use its capabilities in the Democratic Republic of the Congo, Madagascar, Lesotho and Mozambique.[26]

The legal framework of the Intergovernmental Authority on Development has also enabled it to develop a Conflict Early Warning and Response Mechanism (CEWARN).[27] It is a large institutional structure empowered to collect data and recommend preventative actions, but the states have not addressed human rights or mass crimes by formulating a Mechanism. In its adopted cyclical strategies and action plans, IGAD focuses more on food security and humanitarian aid than on human-rights issues. It was involved in peace talks in Sudan, where it set up the operation Force for Security and Deterrence (PDF) in March 2014,

---

24 *Protocol on Politics, Defence and Security Co-operation,* Blantysa, August 14, 2001, http://www.sadc.int/files/3613/5292/8367/Protocol_on_Politics_Defence_and_Security20001.pdf.

25 *Revised Edition Strategic Indicative Plan for the Organ on Politics, Defence and Security Cooperation*, Southern African Development Community, Maputo, August 5, 2010, http://www.sadc.int/files/3213/7951/6823/03514_SADC_SIPO_English.pdf.

26 *African Regional Communities and the Prevention of Mass Atrocities,* African Task Force on the Prevention of Mass Atrocities, Budapest Centre for Mass Atrocities Prevention, Budapest 2016, 29.

27 *Protocol of the Establishment of a Conflict Early Warning and Response Mechanism for IGAD Member states,* 24.

and was considering intervening in Somalia;[28] but it did not prove determined enough (and was found to lack the resources) to undertake field missions.[29]

3.5. The role of the Organization of American States

In the area of the prevention of mass human-rights abuses, the most major asset of the Organization of American States (OAS) – the largest regional American organisation – is a system of human-rights protection. The key legal instrument is the American Convention on Human Rights of 22 November 1969; while the institutions that actually work to protect and prevent human-rights violations are: the Inter-American Commission on Human Rights and the Inter-American Court of Human Rights. In recent years the number of grievances raised by the Commission and Court has been rising steadily, and the OAS works constantly to improve the effectiveness of the system.[30] Countries that have not ratified the Convention (including the United States and Canada) are subject to the 1948 American Declaration on the Rights and Duties of Man.

The obligation to prevent human-rights violations was formulated in the Inter-American Convention to Prevent and Punish Torture of 9 December 1985, the Inter-American Convention on the Prevention, Punishment and Elimination of Violence against Women of 9 June 1994, the Inter-American Convention on Forced Disappearance of Persons of 9 June 1994, the Inter-American Convention against Racism, Racial Discrimination and Other Forms of Intolerance of 5 June 2013, the Inter-American Convention Against All Forms of Discrimination and Intolerance of 5 June 2013 and the Inter-American Convention for the Protection of the Human Rights of Older People of 15 June 2015. To monitor the implementation of the two conventions on combating discrimination and intolerance, the states envisaged the establishment of an expert Inter-American Committee for the Prevention and Elimination of Racism, Racial Discrimination and all Forms of Discrimination and Intolerance. The Committee is expected to work out its methods after the Convention enters into force, but that had not taken place as of 15 June 2017.

---

28 Bellamy A.J. (2009); 'Responsibility to Protect. Five Years On,' *Ethics and International Affairs*, Vol. 24, No. 2, 155–156; *The Responsibility to Protect (RtoP) and Genocide Prevention in Africa*, Report of the International Peace Institute, June 2009.

29 Kingah S., Seiwert E. (2017): 'The Contested Emerging International Norm and Practice of a Responsibility to Protect: Where are Regional Organizations?' *North Carolina Journal of International Law*, Vol. 42, March 2017, 140–141.

30 Insulza J.M. (2015): 'Democratic Governance,' *OAS 2005–2015*, OAS, 109–110.

In addition to protecting human rights, the OAS pays attention to the promotion and strengthening of democracy, which has been recognised as a valid system. Resolution No. 1080 of the General Assembly of the OAS of 1991 entitled "Representative Democracy" proved crucial, as it provided for a procedure whereby meetings of the Permanent Council of Foreign Ministers are held automatically in cases of the unlawful overthrow of democratically-elected governments.[31] One year later, the OAS Protocol to the Charter was adopted, providing for a state's suspension in a case of unconstitutional change of government.[32] An innovative tool, important for structural prevention, is the 2001 Inter-American Democratic Charter, which was widely accredited by the OAS in cases of serious violations of democratic standards. The Secretary-General was empowered to pursue diplomatic initiatives of any kind where an unconstitutional regime is deemed to have emerged. In turn, the right to run election monitoring missions that has been conferred upon the OAS serves to strengthen the democratic process (Articles 23–25).[33]

The 1959 Inter-American Commission on Human Rights is a key OAS institution contributing to protection, and the prevention of human-rights violations. Apart from dealing with complaints and referring cases to the Court, it has competences in respect of the monitoring of human-rights situations in Member States, carrying out on-the–spot visits, preparing reports and recommending preventative measures should serious human-rights violations arise. Since 1990, the work of the Commission has been supported by Rapporteurs with thematic mandates. The Commission mainly appoints such Rapporteurs where groups are considered particularly vulnerable to human-rights violations due to discrimination experienced previously. The first (1990) reporting was instigated in respect of indigenous peoples; as followed by women, migrants, people of African origin, LGBT groups and others. The main goal is to spread awareness and close co-operation among states, to identify problems and good practices, and to offer recommendations and technical support for their implementation.

---

31 OAS General Assembly Resolution No. 1080, OAS Doc. AG/RES. 1080 (XXI-0/91), June 5, 1991.

32 *Protocol of Amendments to the Charter of the Organization of American States*, Washington, December 14, 1992, http://www.oas.org/assembly2001/assembly/GAAssembly2000/Protocol%20of%20Washington.pdf.

33 *Inter-American Democratic Charter*, Lima, September 11, 2001, http://www.oas.org/charter/docs/resolution1_en_p4.htm. For activities undertaken by the OAS in the name of democracy, see also: 272–273.

The Commission also carries out early-warning tasks. On receipt of a notification regarding human-rights violations, it acquires knowledge about serious and systematic cases thereof, with the possibility to visit the state involved giving it the opportunity to investigate the situation and prepare a report. The Commission has in fact used these powers in the cases of Argentina, Peru, El Salvador, Guatemala and Nicaragua.[34] Measures taken by the Commission,[35] and interim measures managed by the Court on receipt of a proposal therefrom – in a situation of high risk regarding serious human-rights violations – can also be seen as of a preventative nature.[36]

While OAS documents have never made direct reference to the concept of Responsibility to Protect, the issue of atrocity crimes was taken up in 2001. Adopted in Quebec, the Action Program in this regard obliges states to fight genocide, crimes against humanity and war crimes under international law, while also calling for the ratification of the Statute of the International Criminal Court.[37]

In 2002, a debate on the concept of multidimensional security provided an opportunity for the General Assembly of the OAS to discuss the R2P concept, as presented a year earlier by the International Commission on Intervention and State Sovereignty. However, despite Canadian interest in this, the final Declaration does not address the problem as such.[38]

The 2009 Report of the Inter-American Commission on Human Rights concerning the Safety of Citizens and Human Rights addressed the issue more directly. There, the Commission outlined standards upon which people's security depends, and which strengthen the capacity of states to prevent and respond to

---

34 Hilaire Sobers O. (2013): 'The Inter-American System of Human Rights' in: Zyberi G. (ed.) *An Institutional Approach of the Responsibility to Protect,* Cambridge University Press, 471.

35 Rules of Procedure of the Inter-American Commission on Human Rights, Article 25, http:www.oas.org/en/iachr/mandate/Basics/rulesiachr.asp.

36 See Rules of Procedure of the Inter-AmericanCourt of Human Rights, Article 27, http:www.oas.org/en/iachr/mandate/Basics/rulesiachr.asp.

37 Plan of Action, Organization of American States, Quebec, April 22, 2001, Organization of American States, Plan of action, Quebec, April 22, 2001, https://www.state.gov/p/wha/rls/59664.htm.

38 Declaration of Bridgetown. The Multidimensional Approach To Hemispheric Security, Organization of American States, Bridgetown, June 4, 2002, http://www.oas.org/xxxiiga/english/docs_en/docs_items/agcgdoc15_02.htm; Paulo de Tarso L. Arantes (2013): 'Organisation of American States' in: Zyberi G. (ed.) *An Institutional Approach of the Responsibility to Protect,* Cambridge University Press, 271–277.

violence and crimes. However, due to the history of the region, the Commission confines its references to crimes against humanity, mainly in the context of the impunity of perpetrators being combated, along with the violence caused by criminal gangs.[39] Two years later, in the Declaration on the Safety of Citizens in the Americas it adopted, the OAS recalled its obligations to citizens, but did not go more deeply into the issue of prevention.

3.6. The Responsibility to Prevent in South East Asian institutions

The relatively modest level of discussion on the international protection of human rights in Southeast Asia, the strong attachment there to the principle of non-interference in domestic affairs, as well as the cultural avoidance of addressing disputes internationally have all ensured a relative lack of interest in regional institutions' developing instruments to prevent serious human-rights violations and atrocity crimes.[40]

The South Asian Association for Regional Cooperation[41] (SAARC), dealing primarily with socio-economic co-operation, avoids national debates, including on human rights. There is greater potential in this regard in the Association of Southeast Asian Nations (ASEAN),[42] a forum that has experienced a certain evolution towards the integration of human-rights issues into its work. All the provisions adopted by ASEAN have been accompanied by tumultuous discussion among its Member States, some of which (e.g. Singapore and Malaysia) expressed concerns that the issue of human rights would provide a pretext for

---

39 Report on Citizen Security and Human Rights, Inter-American Commission on Human Rights, OAS Doc. OEA/Ser.L/V/II. Doc. 57, December 31, 2009, at www.oas.org/en/iachr/docs/pdf/CitizenSec.pdf.

40 See Bellamy A.J., Beeson M. (2010): 'The Responsibility to Protect in Southeast Asia: Can ASEAN Reconcile Humanitarianism and Sovereignty?,' *Asian Security*, Vol. 6, No. 3, 262–279, Bellamy A.J., Drummond C. (2014): 'SouthEast Asia. Between Non-Interference and Sovereignty as Responsibility' in: Knight W.A., Egerton F., *The Routledge Handbook of the Responsibility to Protect*, New York: Routledge Handbook, 245–250.

41 Membership: Afghanistan, Bangladesh, Bhutan, India, Maldives, Nepal, Pakistan, Sri Lanka.

42 Membership: Brunei, Cambodia, Indonesia, Laos, Malaysia, Myanmar, Philippines, Singapore, Thailand, Vietnam.

interference in the internal affairs of states.[43] The ASEAN Charter adopted in 2008 recognises the need to respect and protect human rights, good governance, the rule of law and international humanitarian law,[44] but it has not affirmed any rejection of genocide, mass torture and other crimes, despite the recommendation of its Outstanding People Group, appointed to prepare the draft of the said Charter.[45]

The ASEAN Intergovernmental Commission on Human Rights, set up under Article 14 of the Charter, has not been empowered to monitor the human-rights situation in Member States, or to take any initiatives in this area. Its actions depend on the decisions of the Ministerial Conferences. It is therefore hard to expect that it will play a greater role even in structural prevention. Nevertheless, several projects have been completed, including the adoption of the ASEAN Declaration of Human Rights in 2012, which is broadly in line with universal standards.[46]

Furthermore, instruments adopted by ASEAN in the political and security spheres do afford opportunities for action regarding operational prevention to be taken. These have been elaborated within the ASEAN Political-Security Community (APSC), constituting the so-called first pillar of ASEAN. The Action Plan adopted in 2009 states that ASEAN is a people-oriented organisation, in which will participate, regardless of gender, race, religion, language, or social and cultural origin. It announced efforts to promote tolerance and diversity. In the political sphere, it assumed, among others, a strengthening of democracy and the rule of law, protection of vulnerable groups, promotion of education and awareness of human rights. In turn, in the security sphere expectations were that

---

43 Bellamy A.J., Drummond C. (2014): 'SouthEast Asia. Between Non-Interference and Sovereignty as Responsibility' in: Knight W.A., Egerton F., *The Routledge Handbook of the Responsibility to Protect*, New York: Routledge Handbook, 250–254.

44 The ASEAN Charter, November 20, 2007, http://asean.org/wp-content/uploads/images/archive/publications/ASEAN-Charter.pdf.

45 Report of the Eminent Persons Group on the ASEAN Charter, December 2006, http://www.asean.org/wp-content/uploads/images/archive/19247.pdf.

46 ASEAN Human Rights Declaration, November 18, 2012, http://www.asean.org/storage/images/ASEAN_RTK_2014/6_AHRD_Booklet.pdf; Clarke G. (2012): 'The Evolving ASEAN Human Rights System: The ASEAN Human Rights Declaration of 2012,' *Northwestern Journal of International Human Rights*, Vol. 11, No. 1, 1–28; Doyle N. (2014): 'The ASEAN Human Rights Declaration And The Implications of Recent Southeast Asian Initiatives In Human Rights Institution-Building And Standard-Setting,' *International and Comparative Law Quarterly*, Vol. 63, No. 1, 67–101.

cooperation over conflict prevention would develop, also in terms of creating an early-warning system and confidence-building measures, as well as resort to preventative diplomacy.[47]

The ASEAN Regional Forum (ARF),[48] created in 1994, also has a preventative measure at its disposal. It is the only form of cooperation in which ASEAN countries and powers like China, Japan, Russia and the United States are involved. The Forum's aim is to promote dialogue on regional political and security cooperation. The Forum addresses the issue of preventative diplomacy and the prevention of crisis and conflict situations. Non-governmental institutions, such as the Council for Security Cooperation in the Asia Pacific have in fact appealed for a greater role for the ARF in the promotion and implementation of Responsibility to Protect.[49] However, the facts that the ARF meets only occasionally (on average twice a year) and generates non–binding decisions hampers its practical involvement.

3.7. Middle Eastern organisations in the prevention of mass human-rights violations and atrocity crimes

It would scarcely be possible to point to organisations in the Middle East as particularly dynamic in developing the component of human-rights protection and the prevention of atrocity crimes. However, they accepted the UN 2005 Outcome Document and, in the discussion on the concept of Responsibility to Protect, confined expressions of concern to the aspect of armed intervention and the need for prevention. They also agreed that the international community should take action in worst-case scenarios.[50]

---

47 ASEAN Political-Security Community Blueprint, June 2009, http://asean.org/wp-content/uploads/archive/5187-18.pdf.

48 Membership as of 15 June 2017: Australia, Bangladesh, Brunei Darussalam, Cambodia, Canada, China, Democratic People's Republic of Korea, European Union, India, Indonesia, Japan, Lao PDR, Malaysia, Mongolia, Myanmar, New Zealand, Pakistan, Papua New Guinea, Philippines, Republic of Korea, Russia, Singapore, Sri Lanka, Thailand, Timor-Leste, United States, and Viet Nam.

49 Council for Security Cooperation in the Asia Pacific (CSCAP) Study Group on the Responsibility to Protect (RtoP), *Final Report*, 2011, http://www.cscap.org/uploads/docs/RtoP/CSCAP%20Study%20Group%20on%20RtoP%20-%20Final%20Report.pdf.

50 Helal M.S. (2012): 'Middle East' in: Genser J., Cotler I., *Responsibility to Protect. The Promise of Stopping Mass Atrocities in our Time*, New York: Oxford University Press, 212–220.

When it comes to the structural prevention of mass human-rights violations, a question would concern the capacity of the Cairo Declaration on Human Rights in Islam[51] adopted by the Organisation of the Islamic Conference on 5 August 1990 and the Arab Charter of Human Rights of the Arab League of 22 May 2004 to provide effective instruments. Both documents raise doubts from the perspective of universal human-rights standards.[52] In addition, the Declaration lacks implementation instruments, while the requirement to report to the Human Rights Committee on the basis of the Charter has not been transformed into an effective mechanism.

However, the League can take political and diplomatic action in situations of serious human-rights violations. It can exert pressure and suspend membership rights, as it did in respect of Libya and Syria in 2011; and can set up observation and military missions, as it did as a result of the 2007 Summit decision, for example in South Lebanon, Darfur, Somalia, Iraq and other places.

***

In his report on the role of regional and sub-regional arrangements implementing the Responsibility to Protect, the UN Secretary-General pointed to a need for synergies between UN, regional and sub-regional institutions seeking to prevent atrocity crimes.[53] He saw grounds for their engagement in Chapters VI and VIII of the Charter of the United Nations, as concerning the role of states in the peaceful settlement of disputes and the maintenance of international peace and security. It was this that also gained the endorsement of the UN General Assembly in the UN 2005 Outcome Document (Article 139), given its adoption of the R2P concept.

The legal framework in which organisations operate, institutional structure and instruments developed all reflect valuable historical experiences, often linked to mass crimes, lack of stability and security. This ensures that regional bodies mostly know the specifics of their region best, and are often more trusted than the UN among states still sensitive about their sovereignty. An important role is thus played in making states aware of their primary responsibility to

51 Cairo Declaration on Human Rights in Islam, Organisation of Islamic Conference, August 5, 1990, http://hrlibrary.umn.edu/instree/cairodeclaration.html.

52 Arab Charter on Human Rights, League of Arab States, May 22, 2004, http://hrlibrary.umn.edu/instree/arabhrcharter.html.

53 Ki-moon B., *The Role of Regional and Sub-regional Arrangements in Implementing the Responsibility to Protect*, Report of the Secretary General, A/65/877-S/2011/393, July 12, 2011.

prevent mass human-rights violations, as well as engage in structural and operational prevention. This is supported by both instruments adopted within the human-rights framework, and developing security systems.

IV. Prevention of Mass Human-Rights Violations and Atrocity Crimes in the Foreign Policy of States

With the development of international human rights protection after the Second World War, states have increasingly embraced human rights and prevention of genocide in foreign policy.[1] International law in this field, as well as membership of international organisations dealing with human rights have been effective in forcing states to act, both via multilateral fora and bilateral relations.

Human rights were first defined as a part of a foreign-policy programme by the administration of US President Jimmy Carter (1977–1981), which invoked them as an instrument in the struggle with the Eastern Bloc. Initially, this was treated with great detachment by the countries of Western Europe. Over time, however, the idea of human rights has become a permanent part of their foreign policy programmes.[2] This trend has been strengthened by a wave of democratisation, primarily in Central and Eastern Europe, as well as Latin America. New democracies have often sought advice as they seek to achieve lasting reform, and gain the image of countries respecting international standards.

The objectives of the discussion on humanitarian intervention, taking place in the 1990s; and then on the concept of Responsibility to Protect as such, were to settle the issue of how far a state, or the international community as a whole, might go in the face of situations entailing atrocity crimes. Much of that discussion referred to possible responses in the form of military interventions, and this naturally aroused controversy and fear among certain states. It was only after 2005 that states took up the issue of prevention under the R2P pillar proposed by the Secretary-General. This was a different matter, since – superficially at least – it did not arouse controversy. Indeed, in the declarative sphere, it is possible to note consensus regarding the need for genocide, crimes against humanity and war crimes to be prevented. In practice, the involvement of states in third countries combined with their desire to prevent mass killings may raise more questions than the need to respond to committed crimes. There are concerns about

---

1 Kuźniar R. (2000): *Prawa człowieka. Prawo, instytucje, stosunki międzynarodowe*, Warsaw: Wydawnictwo Naukowe SCHOLAR, 316–328.

2 Higgins R. (1987): 'Human Rights and Foreign Policy,' *Rivista di Studi Politici Internazionali*, 572–574.

true intentions, the desire to pursue business and even superpower ambitions. Prevention of atrocity crimes also requires much more involvement than just addressing human rights. For what is involved here is a multidimensional effort in the name of stability, security and development.

4.1. Human rights, prevention and sovereignty of states

The issue of sovereignty has always been accompanied by discussions on human rights in foreign policy. From the Treaty of Westphalia in 1648 onwards, the principle the sovereignty of states appeared in international relations. The principle was confirmed and reinforced by the provisions of Article 2 of the Charter of the United Nations. Nothing in the Charter authorises the United Nations to intervene in matters which, in essence, fall within the internal competence of any State (Article 2.7). All members refrain from threatening or using force against the territorial integrity or independence of any State (Article 2.4). However, with time, the situation evolved, in the sense that the number of states able to rely on these rules grew steadily, most especially in connection with decolonisation.

As long as human rights did not become an international issue, there was no need to decide on their place in foreign policy. During the Cold War, the relevant discussion arose out of the Cold War division into East and West. The dispute was primarily between the Soviet Union (USSR) and the United States. The USSR was of the opinion that human rights were among a state's internal affairs, to the extent that any addressing of these in the international-relations context represented a violation of (its) sovereignty and might even jeopardise the very peace that it saw as a precondition for progress in the field of human rights.

For their part, however, US administrations beginning with Jimmy Carter recognised that rights could be superior to governments' internal competence, and extended active support to the development of the international protection of human rights, and to the idea that states had a right to include human-rights protection internationally in their policies.[3] Thus, when President Carter opted to incorporate human rights into US foreign policy from the beginning of his term in 1977,[4] a key purpose was to furnish it with an instrument by which

3 Kuźniar R. (2000): *Prawa człowieka. Prawo, instytucje, stosunki międzynarodowe*, Warsaw: Wydawnictwo Naukowe SCHOLAR, 87–88.

4 The first impetus for American foreign policy to embrace human rights came from the Congress. In 1973, a debate on human rights took place at the Subcommittee on International Organisations, which led to the adoption by Congress of acts on foreign aid, international financial institutions and trade policy. They recognised that commitment

to strike at the Communist Bloc. The United States engaged in the serious and persistent criticism of the USSR and other Eastern Bloc countries from the viewpoint of human-rights abuses. While this had its moral side, it could never be ignored that the US also supported numerous anti-Communist regimes, even if they committed serious human-rights violations.[5]

The Conference on Security and Cooperation in Europe was one of the fora at which Soviet-American confrontation took place. The ground-breaking "Declaration on Principles Guiding Relations between Participating States" adopted by the two blocs on 1 August 1975 during the summit in Helsinki denoted respect for human rights and fundamental freedoms and the right of peoples to self-determination, thus sanctioning standards that Eastern Europeans might aspire to and justifying future consideration of the issue at subsequent CSCE meetings. In the years that followed, the United States and its allies in Western Europe raised human-rights concerns, thereby seeking to exert a liberal influence on communist systems in Europe. Responding to criticism, the communist countries referred to the principles of non-interference in internal affairs and respect for sovereignty, as well as those contained in the "Declaration on Principles."

The above confrontation continued until the end of the Cold War. The breakthrough on this issue was illustrated, among other things, by the documents signed at the end of the Vienna Review Conference of 1989, and after the meetings of the "Conference on the Human Dimension of the CSCE" (convened in Copenhagen and Paris in 1990 and Moscow in 1991). The Moscow document states that states "categorically and irrevocably declare that the commitments undertaken in the field of the human dimension of the OSCE are matters of direct and legitimate concern to all participating states and do not belong exclusively to the internal affairs of the State concerned."[6] A similar record was included in the

---

of US foreign aid should be conditional upon a given country's performance in the area of human rights, see especially: Forsythe D. P. (1988): *Human Rights and U.S. Foreign Policy: Congress Reconsidered*, Gainesville: University Press of Florida; Dobriansky P. J. (Spring 1989): 'Human Rights and U.S. Foreign Policy,' *The Washington Quarterly*, 153–156.

5 According to J. Donnelly, the foreign policy of the United States during the Cold War was marked by two elements: anti-Communism and a conviction as to its own uniqueness and superiority vis-à-vis other states, among others, as a reflection of internal human-rights regulations, see Donnelly J. (1998): *International Human Rights*, Colorado-Oxford: Avalon Publishing, 86–89.

6 Document of the Moscow Meeting of the Conference on the Human Dimension of the CSCE, October 3, 1991 in: *OSCE Human Dimension Commitments, A Reference Guide*, Warsaw: OSCE 2001, 241.

Vienna Declaration adopted by the World Conference on Human Rights in Vienna in 1993, which stated that "(...) the promotion and protection of all human rights is a legitimate concern of the international community (...)."[7]

The victory of such an interpretation was largely influenced by democratic processes after the end of the Cold War,[8] but also by many other factors like international human rights law,[9] and control mechanisms such as reports, inspections, investigative missions and monitoring. Huge contributions to this process have been made by international judicial institutions operating in the area of human rights and criminal law, as well as all intergovernmental organisations dealing with human rights. Membership of organisations forces even minimal engagement, given the need for a stand to be taken on various human rights issues, and given the opportunity provided for creative foreign policy relating to human rights to be developed.

The concept of Responsibility to Protect is the key one influencing today's perception of sovereignty. It is the result of dynamic discussion from the 1990s in regard to humanitarian intervention and the associated dilemma of violating the principle of sovereignty in the name of the prevention or cessation of international crimes. Its course was marked by the Rwandan genocide in 1994, as well as crimes committed during the Balkan wars. Proponents of humanitarian intervention pointed out that states simply could not stand idly by, looking on at government practices that deprived populations of fundamental rights, and/or entailed the committing of atrocities and engagement in persecution. While for example justifying NATO's intervention in Kosovo, they concur that violation of the Charter of the United Nations is possible. Some scholars have pointed more generally to contradictions in the UN Charter as to the use of force. Respect for human rights is enshrined in the Charter as a purpose of Members of the organisation; while Article 2.4 provides for a ban on the use of force "against the territorial integrity or independence of any State". Meanwhile, in principle at least, humanitarian interventions are not directed against these values, but are

---

7 See text of *Vienna Declaration*: Kuźniar R. (2000): *Prawa człowieka. Prawo, instytucje, stosunki międzynarodowe*, Warsaw: Wydawnictwo Naukowe SCHOLAR, 396–427.

8 Drzewicki K. (July-September, 1998): 'Prawa człowieka w Karcie NZ i w Powszechnej Deklaracji Praw Człowieka,' *Sprawy Międzynarodowe*, 9–16.

9 On the impact of international law on the policies of states see more especially: Henkin L. (1978): *The Rights of Man Today*, Boulder: Westview Press.

instruments by which the rights of a population can be protected and humanitarian aid provided.[10]

In existence in 2001, the International Commission on Intervention and State Sovereignty (which developed the concept of Responsibility to Protect) noted that even the greatest defenders of the sovereignty idea do not believe it gives states unlimited powers to do whatever they like with their citizens. While sovereignty in the external sense means respect for other states, sovereignty in the internal sense entails "respect for the dignity and fundamental rights of all people in the state", and indeed responsibility to protect the security and life of all people, and to promote their wellbeing.[11] This leaves a State responsible for what it does do, and also for what it fails to do. In its conclusions, the Commission also referred to the concept of human security, which focuses on the condition of individuals, rather than states.

The new dimension to sovereignty is also related to the abandonment of the language of confrontation. Responsibility to protect does not focus on states and their "right to intervene," but on accountability. Where human-rights issues are addressed in bilateral relations, and where development assistance advice on how to strengthen domestic institutions and conciliation initiatives are provided, this is to be viewed as action being taken to strengthen sovereignty, rather than undermine it, with the recipient state being assisted with the exercise of its own sovereign responsibility. This point of view was stressed in the UN 2005 Outcome Document.[12]

Obviously, it is easier to pursue activity of the above profile if authorities in the given state are keen on changing and strengthening their capacity for civil protection. If they are not interested in respecting human rights or are themselves responsible for minor or major violations of law, states and international

---

10 Lillich R. B. (ed.) (1992): *Humanitarian Intervention and the United Nations*, Charlottesville: University Press of Virginia; Kuźniar R. (2000): *Prawa człowieka. Prawo, instytucje, stosunki międzynarodowe*, Warsaw: Wydawnictwo Naukowe SCHOLAR, 290–293.

11 Report of the International Commission on Intervention and State Sovereignty, The Responsibility to Protect, December 2001, https://undocs.org/pdf?symbol=en/a/57/303, 8, 13–14.

12 Touko Piiparinen considers actions in the framework of Responsibility to Protect as sovereignty-building: Piiparinen T. (2012): 'Sovereignty-building: Three Images of Positive Sovereignty Projected Through Responsibility to Protect,' *Global Change, Peace&Security*, October 8, 2012, 405–424.

organisations have a difficult task, which continues to demonstrate the power of the argument of sovereignty and non-interference in internal affairs.

The greatest dilemmas regarding the prevention of mass human-rights violations and the respect for sovereignty of states concern the possibility of military intervention and change of power. While extensive expert and intergovernmental discussions, and the practice of the Security Council, point to the possibility of military intervention under certain conditions in situations of threat or atrocity crimes,[13] the possibility of bringing about regime change is highly unlikely. In the case of Kosovo or Iraq, the Security Council was in favour of democracy, but the overthrow of Muammar Gaddafi's government on the occasion of Libyan intervention in 2011 sparked strong protest from Russia and China, and halted discussions on international armed conflict.[14]

4.2. States towards preventing mass violations of human rights and atrocity crimes

There are two basic motives for engaging countries in the prevention of gross human-rights violations atrocity crimes: the humanitarian and the security-related. These largely reflect the relationship between poor situation of human rights and destabilisation – which often extends beyond the borders of a single state and thus leads to a further deterioration in the security situation. Atrocity crimes can be a consequence of armed conflict, or they can be a source of serious internal and international conflicts. States are eager to engage in their prevention, but mainly via international organisations that mostly have developed mechanisms for conflict prevention. States that consider respect for fundamental human rights as a prerequisite for peace and security in the world and

---

13 See for example Hehir A. (2012): *The Responsibility to Protect. Rhetoric, Reality and the Future of Humanitarian* Intervention, New York: Palgrave Macmillan; Badescu C. (2010): *Humanitarian Intervention and the Responsibility to Protect: Security and Human Rights*, New York: Routledge; Thakur R. (2006): *The United Nations, Peace and Security: From Collective Security to the Responsibility to Protect*, Cambridge: Cambridge University Press; Pattinson J. (2010):, *Humanitarian Intervention and the Responsibility to Protect: Who Should Intervene?*, Oxford University Press; Razali Kassim Y. (2014): *The Geopolitics of Intervention: Asia and the Responsibility to Protect*, New York: Springer.

14 Interview at the Office of the Special Adviser on Genocide Prevention and Responsibility to Protect, New York, February 2015.

the common interest of states also willingly engage in respect for human rights through their foreign policies.

After the Second World War, the development of the international human-rights protection system allowed a human-rights-based approach to develop. In addition, the need to prevent and respond to genocide and other crimes was also articulated by reference to the concept of human security, which has at its heart the interests and rights of individuals. The past involvement of states in solving humanitarian problems using foreign policy can be considered limited, with few international institutions playing a role in this respect.

However, to be included among the above cases is the International Committee of the Red Cross. Through the development of international humanitarian law, this organisation was able to address the matter of the protection of civilians during international and non-international conflicts. In the 1970s, refugee action was launched by the High Commissioner for Refugees and later by NGOs such as Doctors Without Borders.[15] An appreciation of the need for humanitarianism has also been propagated by the activities of the major UN bodies – the General Assembly and the Security Council, which in their Resolutions on Sudan in 1989 or Iraq in 1991 talked about people's right to humanitarian aid,[16] also with increased emphasis on the role of states (as opposed to international organisations) in the provision thereof.

States' interest in the situations populations face during humanitarian crises has also been increased through active media coverage. The growing availability of information on the situation of refugees, and on crimes and the existence of mass graves has done much to influence public opinion, with greater commitment from governments often being demanded. This is of course true of democratic states in particular, given much-vaunted commitments to the protection of human rights and democratic values. The whole process has been further facilitated by factors such as the establishment of universal suffrage, social control over government policy, constitutional protection of human rights in the state, free media, civil-society freedoms and much more. Overall, there would now seem to be broad public expectation that democracies should work for the

---

15 Cohen R. (2014): 'From Sovereign Responsibility To R2P' in: Knight W.A., Egerton F., *The Routledge Handbook of the Responsibility to Protect*, New York: Routledge, 11–12.

16 See UN General Assembly Resolution: A/RES/46/182, December 19, 1991; UN General Assembly Resolution: S/RES/688, April 5, 1991.

improvement of the human-rights situation in other countries, and provide humanitarian assistance.[17]

Moreover, the policy of democratic states gains particularly rigorous analysis in ethical terms. Governments pursuing foreign policy must take account of views existing in their societies, which often influence their actions towards a country in violation of human rights. Typically, when the public and the media do not speak, authorities tend to remain silent. Often, involvement in this area is also part of building an image for a state as responding to the needs of a suffering population and involving itself actively in human-rights issues. In the power-structures in democratic countries responsible for foreign policy, there are now separate cells tasked with the elaboration and implementation of human-rights policy, as well as separate departments dealing with humanitarian and development aid. These units can work constructively to prevent mass human-rights violations. In addition, the issue is routinely taken account of in the programme documents and speeches, as well as the action plans, of the relevant authorities. Since the adoption of the Responsibility to Protect concept, many countries have also appointed special R2P focal points to promote the obligations concerning R2P, and to participate in international cooperation.

Although states have similar political, diplomatic, social, economic or military instruments to prevent human-rights violations and atrocity crimes, they pursue their policies in a different way. Differences in approach are visible, among others, between the United States and European countries, with this for example reflecting differing potential, international standing, traditions and historical experiences. The American policy was long determined by Cold War conditioning, and was relatively willing to use military instruments. On the other hand, Europe's democracies are more likely to provide development aid to a state, albeit linking it directly with human-rights issues. Sometimes European states, such as The Netherlands or Norway, have taken a different stance from the United States, thus emphasising the independence of their policies and the credibility of human rights.[18]

---

17 Beetham D. (1998): 'Democracy and Human Rights: Civil, Political, Economic, Social and Cultural' in: Symonides J. (ed.), *Human Rights: New Dimensions and Challenges*, 71 et seq.

18 For example, just after the Pinochet coup, Sweden halted aid to Chile. In 1980, Canada, The Netherlands and the Scandinavian countries increased aid to Nicaragua. The Netherlands suspended all assistance to Suriname, its former colony, after a military coup in 1980, and sought to exert international pressure within the United Nations

In contrast, non-democratic states that commit themselves to human-rights violations are not normally interested in pursuing active foreign policy in this area. Indeed, they sometimes work to undermine the international system of the protection of human rights, or deploy their own conception thereof in pursuit of other interests. For example, the Russian Federation referred to the concept of Responsibility to Protect as it seized Crimea in 2014. In fact, that situation did not meet R2P criteria, leaving Russia to implement a plan for annexation of territory in the old-fashioned way.[19]

In addition, even countries that are guided by humanitarian motives in foreign policy are unlikely to be consistent, and will tend to be characterised by double standards in policy.[20] They direct selective criticism at those weaker than they are, while those that are stronger remain "under protection". This may be illustrated by states attitudes to mass human-rights abuses in Chechnya or Tibet in the 1990s, as well as frequent cases of support for dictatorships by states such as the United States and France in Africa and Latin America. Equally, the variously-motivated overthrow of dictatorships does not necessarily denote an improvement of the situation (including the human-rights situation) of a civilian population, as was clearly demonstrated by the cases of Iraq after the fall of Saddam Hussein in 2003 and Libya after the overthrow of Muammar Gaddafi in 2011.

Inconsistency may thus reflect various interests of states emerging as of greater importance to them than difficult involvement in the prevention of mass human-rights abuses, or the complexity of a situation in which there is no certainty of policy producing the desired results, and not in fact worsening an already-bad situation. There are also cases of concern for human rights serving as a means to achieve certain state interests. The instrumentalisation of human rights complicates the study of states' foreign policies in the area of human rights. Difficulties lie, among other things, in determining the actual intentions of states as they act. In certain situations declared interest in action with a view to human rights being promoted has to be accompanied by disbelief regarding actual intentions. Such cases include

---

to permanently raise the issue of the country's human-rights situation. In contrast, the United States tolerated even worse situations in countries like Guatemala or El Salvador.

19 Grzebyk P. (2014): 'Classification of the Conflict Between Ukraine and Russia in International Law (Ius ad Bellum and Ius in Bello),' *Polish Yearbook of International Law* 2014, Vol. 34, 39–60.

20 Neier A. (Winter 1996–1997): 'The New Double Standards,' *Foreign Policy*, No. 105.

controversy over NATO's involvement in Yugoslavia in 1999, and also surrounding the Libyan interventions of 2011.

With a view to such doubts concerning states' intentions being avoided, principles of foreign policy seeking to prevent violations were formulated by Secretary General Ban Ki-moon in his Report on the involvement of countries in prevention dated 11 July 2014. He pointed out that preventative measures taken in third countries should be inclusive – involving national authorities, both central and local. International assistance may then be more effective. In addition, help should not hurt and aggravate the situation or introduce additional divisions. Spontaneity should be avoided by a series of actions, including situational assessment, action planning and monitoring. Simultaneously, flexibility is indicated – i.e. a readiness to respond to changing needs.[21]

It is worth adding that a lack of consistency characterising the foreign policy of states concerning human rights and the prevention of atrocity crimes often result from a changing internal situation, as well as depending on who is in charge. President Barack Obama launched several initiatives to redirect policy from responding to prevention. In 2011, he appointed an Atrocities Prevention Board (APB), which was to alert the US Presidential Administration to risks of atrocity crimes arising in third countries, and to propose possible responses.[22] In practice, the APB issued, among others, recommendations concerning the situation in the Central African Republic, Burundi and Nigeria. It nevertheless received criticism for the lack of an effective response to the crises in Syria and Iraq. It also faced strong organisational constraints, not least as no separate budget was provided for it.[23]

President Donald Trump, who initially sought to place less emphasis on global issues and multilateral cooperation, did not continue to work with the Council. Likewise, there has also been a curtailing of the development of US

---

21 Ki-moon B., *Fulfilling our Collective Responsibility: International Assistance and the Responsibility to Protect*, Report of the Secretary-General, July 11, 2014. (A/68/947S/2014/449), 5–6.

22 Norris J., Malknecht A. (2013): *Atrocities Prevention Board Background, Performance, and Options*, Center for American Progress.

23 Finkel J. (2014): 'Atrocity Prevention at the Crossroads: Assessing the President's Atrocity Prevention Board After Two Years,' *Series of Occasional Papers*, Center for the Prevention of Genocide, No. 2.

Armed Forces' doctrine aiming to respond to and prevent atrocities, within the framework of the so-called Mass Atrocity Response Operations.[24]

Canada has also been involved in the development of Responsibility to Protect. It contributed greatly to the establishment and support of the aforementioned International Commission on Intervention and State Sovereignty (ICISS) of 2001, which came out with its "Responsibility to Protect" Report that same year. In addition, it has contributed to the success of the Ottawa Process, and the inclusion of human-security issues in the international debate. However, under the Conservative Party administration ruling Canada in the years 2006–2009, the state failed to show further interest in the concept of R2P, also declaring restraint in the years 2011–2015.[25]

The above examples show that, even in such a key area as the prevention of the worst crimes, states prove unable to achieve consistency of approach. Internal conditions, interests and a willingness to maintain good relations with states, even when their populations are subjected to repression, all work to hold governments back from engagement. For this reason, states are more likely to take up the matter of the mass violation of human rights atrocity crimes in the framework of multilateral, as opposed to bilateral relations.[26] They benefit from the established cooperation mechanisms, can appeal to accepted standards and are less likely than in the case of bilateral conditions to be accused of taking action purely in line with state self-interest.

4.3. International cooperation of countries interested in the prevention

Countries that care particularly about the prevention of genocide and other crimes organise various coalitions within which they can cooperate. In 2012, at

---

24 Sewall S., Raymond D., Chin S. (2010): *Mass Atrocity Response Operations: A Military Planning Handbook*, Army War College Carlisle Barracks Pa Peacekeeping and Stability Operations Institute.

25 Beck Ch. (5 October 2015): *From Founding Father to Backslider: Canada and R2P*, https://us.boell.org/2015/10/05/founding-father-backslider-canada-and-r2p.

26 This is particularly true of small states with little chance of achieving a goal by unilateral action. On differences in the foreign policy of small and large states vis-à-vis human rights see. Donnelly J. (1998): *International Human Rights*, Colorado-Oxford: Avalon Publishing, 110–114.

the initiative of Argentina and Brazil, 18 countries[27] established the Latin American Network for Genocide and Mass Destruction. The main objective here is to support regional and local initiatives by which Latin American states may build up their capacities to prevent mass crimes. The first meeting identified two main goals of the coalition: development and implementation of a curriculum for the prevention of atrocity crimes, and its integrating into mandatory curricula for national institutions; and regional cooperation and the development of national initiatives to prevent genocide. Within the curricula, seminars were organised in Auschwitz.

In a Declaration of 29 December 2015, states involved reaffirmed their will to transform the Latin American network into a regional prevention tool, and also endorsed the focal points for prevention,[28] which formed a sort of internal coalition structure. Over time, these have evolved towards national mechanisms for the prevention of genocide, bringing in the representation of various national Ministries. In this way, internal policies of states regarding the prevention of genocide might be shaped.[29]

The Latin American network for the prevention of genocide and mass atrocities is a good example of cooperation between states and non-governmental organisations. Close cooperation was established with the Auschwitz Institute for Peace and Reconciliation (the institute serves as a technical secretariat), the International School of Public Policy on Human Rights (IPPDH) and the Stanley Foundation. These organisations have provided significant organisational and educational support to countries organising, among others, meetings with national preventative institutions and Raphael Lemkin seminars for the education of representatives of governmental administration.

Latin American cooperation has resulted in a number of training initiatives in participating countries, for example in Panama a seminar on instruments for

27 Argentina, Bolivia, Brazil, Chile, Colombia, Costa Rica, Dominican Republic, Ecuador, El Salvador, Guatemala, Honduras, Mexico, Nicaragua, Panama, Paraguay, Peru, Uruguay and Venezuela.

28 Declaration of the Latin American Network for Genocide and Mass Atrocity Prevention, Santiago, March 29, 2015, http://www.auschwitzinstitute.org/wp-content/uploads/2015/08/Network-Declaration-EN.pdf.

29 See case study on the national mechanism for the prevention of genocide in Argentina: Riera R. (2016): 'The Argentinean National Mechanism for the Prevention of Genocide: A Case Study in Contemporary Preventive Institution-Building' in: Rosenberg S.P., Galis T., Zucker A., *Reconstructing Atrocity Prevention*, Cambridge University Press, 477–493.

the prevention of genocide and mass atrocities (24–25 March 2015), in Mexico a seminar on instruments for education of the armed forces and security forces in prevention (27 April 2016), and in Ecuador a seminar on the importance of memory in the process of intangible reparations (19–21 September 2016).[30]

Global Action Against Mass Atrocity Crimes (GAAMAC) is an example of a similar initiative. It was created in 2004 through cooperation between Argentina, Australia, Denmark, Costa Rica, Switzerland and Tanzania, as well as with the involvement of the UN and regional and non-governmental organisations, among others the Auschwitz Institute for Peace and Reconciliation, Global Centre for R2P, International Coalition for RtoP, FXB Centre for Health and Human Rights at Harvard University, School of Diplomacy and International Relations at Seton Hall University and the Stanley Foundation. GAAMAC's goal is to support states in the development of national structures for the prevention of mass crimes. It is an open, global forum for facilitating cooperation, networking, exchange of experience, support, information and advice to interested states and organisations.[31]

GAAMAC organises cyclical meetings every two years, as well as *ad hoc* meetings at the request of the Steering Group, which makes decisions by consensus. It is headed by the President. GAAMAC creates working groups and support groups to develop topics related to prevention.

So far, two Plenary Meetings have taken place: in San Jose in March 2014[32] and in Manila in February 2016.[33] More than 50 countries and representatives of international organisations participated in each of the meetings. In both cases,

30 See more in: *Annual Report 2015,* The Latin American Network for Genocide and Mass Atrocity Prevention, https://www.stanleyfoundation.org/publications/other/LAN-ANNUALRPT2015ENGLISH.pdf; *Annual Report 2016,* The Latin American Network for Genocide and Mass Atrocity Prevention, https://www.stanleyfoundation.org/publications/other/LAN-ANNUALRPT2016ENGLISH.pdf.

31 Founding Document, The Global Action Against Mass Atrocity Crimes, San Jose, March 4–6, 2014, http://static.gaamac.org/media/uploads/PDFs/gaamac_founding_document.pdf.

32 Chair Statement, First International Meeting of "Global Action Against Mass Atrocity Crimes" (GAAMAC), March 4–6, 2014 San José, Costa Rica.
http://static.gaamac.org/media/uploads/PDFs/gaamac_final_chair_statement_08.05.2014.pdf.

33 GAAMAC II Outcome Document, February 4, 2016, Manila,
http://static.gaamac.org/media/uploads/PDFs/gaamac_ii_outcome_document_final.pdf

the discussion focused on the internal competences of states where the prevention of mass crimes is concerned, as well as the role that a coalition might play. GAAMAC contributed to awareness-raising as regards the need for building capacity for prevention. There is no vision of how GAAMAC could become operational in prevention.

A similar organisation, the Group of Friends on R2P, which was set up in 2015 on the occasion of the tenth anniversary of the adoption of UN Responsibility to Protect, functions within the UN General Assembly. It brings together more than 50 countries expressing an interest in strengthening the principle of R2P in the UN system.[34] It participates regularly in informal dialogues organised by the GA and the Secretary General. In 2015, it voted in favour of an anniversary Resolution confirming that the international community should not be subjected to indifference and idle policies. The Kingdom of The Netherlands and Rwanda serve as Co-Presidents of the Group. However, the Group rarely adopts any position regarding the risk of mass infringements. However, it draws up Common Positions, including the one concerning developments in Libya dated 25 February 2010.

In addition, there are regular meetings of the countries that have established R2P focal points as part of the Global Network of R2P Focal Points. Although their role is to promote responsibility to protect within a country, most of them do not implement a national mandate, instead focusing on international cooperation. Most Contact Persons are appointed within a country's Ministry of Foreign Affairs and serve to demonstrate support for R2P. The Global Network of R2P Focal Points was established in August 2010 on the initiative of Denmark and Ghana, in collaboration with the Global Centre for the Responsibility to Protect. Among the countries most involved in the group's activities are Australia

34 Botswana, Netherlands, Rwanda, Ghana, Liberia, Mali, Morocco, Mozambique, Nigeria, Senegal, Sierra Leone, South Sudan, Sudan, Tanzania, Bangladesh, Japan, Qatar, Republic of South Korea, Singapore, Argentina, Chile, Costa Rica, Mexico, Panama, Uruguay, Belgium, Bosnia and Herzegovina, Czech Republic, Denmark, European Union, Finland, France, Germany, Hungary, Italy, Côte d'Ivoire, Liechtenstein, Luxembourg, Norway, Romania, Slovakia, Slovenia, Spain, Sweden, Switzerland, United Kingdom, Australia, New Zealand, Canada, United States; See Statement by the Group of Friends of the Responsibility to Protect in Geneva at the Informal Interactive Dialogue with Under-Secretary-General Mr. Adama Dieng, Special Adviser to Secretary General on the Prevention of Genocide, March 3, 2016, https://www.globalr2p.org/resources/statement-delivered-on-behalf-of-the-group-of-friends-of-r2p-at-the-31st-session-of-the-human-rights-council-1.

and Costa Rica, though in total there are 59 participating countries that have set up R2P specialists.[35]

The most important task of this coalition of states is to act in support of states as they build capacity to prevent mass crimes. The greatest achievement to date has in turn entailed the development of recommendations for countries that appoint R2P Contact Persons. The assumption has been for prevention of atrocity crimes to be integrated with internal policies – something that is only possible through interdepartmental cooperation, involving all competent national institutions. The daily work of specialists should also involve monitoring of situations and early warning.[36]

Thanks to these forms of cooperation, states which wish to pursue active foreign policy in the field of the prevention of atrocity crimes and responsibility to protect, have the opportunity to present their views, and to put forward ideas as regards observation and prevention. In the current, initial phase of concept development, constructive discussion is important. However, if this cooperation does not acquire an operational dimension, it is impossible to preclude states losing interest in its development and preferring to concentrate on the possibilities international organisations offer.

35 Albania, Angola, Argentina, Australia, Austria, Belgium, Bosnia and Herzegovina, Botswana, Bulgaria, Cambodia, Canada, Chile, Costa Rica, Côte d'Ivoire, Croatia, Czech Republic, Democratic Republic of the Congo, Denmark, Finland, France, Georgia, Germanz, Ghana, Greece, Guatemala, Hungary, Ireland, Italy, Japan, Jordan, Kenya, Liberia, Liechtenstein, Lithuania, Luxembourg, Montenegro, Mozambique, New Zealand, Nigeria, Paraguay, Peru, Poland, Qatar, Republic of South Korea, Romania, Rwanda, Sierra Leone, Slovenia, South Africa, Spain, Sweden, Switzerland, Tanzania, Timor-Leste, Uruguay, United Kingdom, the United States and the European Union.

36 'National R2P Focal Points Recommendations,' *Policy Briefs*, Global Centre for the Responsibility to Protect, July 26, 2012, https://www.globalr2p.org/publications/national-r2p-focal-points-recommendations.

V. The Role of Non-Governmental Organisations in the Prevention of Mass Human-Rights Violations and Atrocity Crimes

5.1. The potential of non-governmental organisations

International non-governmental organisations (NGOs) play a significant role in the prevention of mass violations of human rights and atrocity crimes. The growth in number and competences in recent decades has largely linked up with the development of international law, which has become an important reference point for the NGOs as they assess policy on human rights. At the same time, involvement has arisen in the face of states' deception in either allowing mass crimes to occur or remaining passive in the face thereof. NGOs determined to engage in humanitarian crises, having experienced their consequences, have been natural advocates of the idea of that human-rights abuses must be prevented.

Indeed, NGOs have been a driving force behind and initiator of many activities for decades now. Their specificity of actions reflecting independence from the government, observance of the principle of neutrality, presence on the ground and close relationships developed with local NGOs have all served to make them spokespersons for populations exposed to violations of human rights, on the one hand, and important partners for states and international organisations when it comes to preventing and resolving numerous problems, on the other.[1] The role of NGOs in this field is also foreseen in the 2001 ICISS Report on Responsibility to Protect, which acknowledges in particular the potential roles in early warning and in popularisation of the need for preventative measures in domestic and foreign public opinion.[2]

---

1 On the role of non-governmental organisations in the protection of human rights, see: Weissbrodt D. (2013): 'Roles and Responsibilities of Non-State Actors' in: Shelton D. (ed.) *The Oxford Handbook of International Human Rights Law*, Oxford University Press; Baehr P. (2009): *Non-Governmental Human Rights Organizations* in International *Relations*, New York: Palgrave Macmillan, 721–725; Kuźniar R. (2000), *Prawa człowieka. Prawo, instytucje, stosunki międzynarodowe*, Warsaw: Wydawnictwo Naukowe SCHOLAR, 243–261.

2 Report of the International Commission on Intervention and State Sovereignty, The Responsibility to Protect, December 2001, https://undocs.org/pdf?symbol=en/a/57/

NGOs play a role in several areas relating to prevention, i.e. the promotion of human rights, capacity-building in states and institutions where prevention is concerned, the implementation of development aid, early warning and conflict prevention. Preventative action also entails the provision of humanitarian aid, especially to people at risk of starvation. The very presence of international staff in the field is often a factor stopping violence.[3]

Contributing to the increase in human-rights awareness through education and the promotion of the issue, NGOs likewise serve structural prevention. The educational and training programmes they offer a wide variety of participants are also significant. Routinely involved in the education of children, adolescents and adults, they raise awareness in societies as regards human rights and vulnerability. They also provide knowledge on how a crisis can be responded to. The training of government officials who have decision-making powers and can take concrete action in the event of a threat of gross human-rights violations is obviously of at least equal importance.[4]

Importantly, non-governmental organisations often focus on groups particularly vulnerable to violations of human rights for racial, ethnic or religious reasons. They provide support, but also try to build a positive image of such groups in society. In post-conflict situations, they pursue projects aimed at reconciling conflicting groups and achieving cooperation with a view to violence being avoided in future.

In the context of mass human-rights violations and atrocity crimes, the role of NGOs in identifying risks and in early warning looks invaluable. Large international organisations have their representatives, field offices or local partners in most countries in the world. They thus collect information at first hand. They are active in both peacetime and during armed conflicts. They often send special investigative missions to carry out research, count victims and identify perpetrators of violations of international law. In many cases, they are the

---

303, 20. On non-governmental organisations in the context of Responsibility to Protect see: Steenberghe R. van (2013): 'Non-State Actors' in: Zyberi G. (ed.) *An Institutional Approach of the Responsibility to Protect*, Cambridge University Press, 33–57.

3 Violence is more commonly used against local NGO workers than foreigners, see Bieńczyk-Missala A., Grzebyk P. (2015): 'Safety and Protection of Humanitarian Workers' in: Gibbons P., Heintze H.-J., *The Humanitarian Challenge. 20 Years European Network on Humanitarian Action (NOHA)*, Switzerland: Springer.

4 Lord J.E., Flowers N. (2006): 'Human Rights Education and Grassroots Peacebuilding' in: Mertus J.A., Helsing J.W. (ed.), *Human Rights&Conflict. Exploring the Links between Rights, Law, and Peacebuilding*, Washington: United States Institute of Peace, 431–454.

only institutions collecting such data, as was the case during the Afghanistan conflict pre-2007, when the United Nations Assistance Mission in Afghanistan (UNAMA) was launched.[5]

NGOs are often the first to raise the alarm in regard to hazards, and to spread the word about serious violations of human rights, and crimes committed. They reach out to societies, the media, governments and international organisations, both through regular and current reports and news, and social media and personal meetings. Thanks to their presence on the spot they are well aware of the complexity of situations, and so can not only inform but also lobby and advise, as regards which states and institutions should act, how and by what means. They help imbue a political will to take action, as one of the key factors in helping prevention.[6] Non-governmental organisations reach decision-makers directly, but also influence public opinion, the media and institutions. They may also engage in prevention negotiations, more often locally than nationally.

It is problematic to define the role of non-governmental organisations in the area of operational prevention. In principle, they are not obliged to engage and their help is voluntary. They also bear no responsibility for preventative action. In practice, they do strive to prepare populations for the outbreak of humanitarian crises, or for an immediate threat of mass human-rights violations. This is only possible if they have a good grasp of the situation and the confidence of the local population.[7] Support includes monitoring the development of a situation and coming up with a warning system, preparing groups for evacuation, negotiating with potential perpetrators about escape routes, building temporary shelters or just respecting civil rights.

This kind of involvement, as well as the regular role in collecting evidence as regards crimes helping international organisations in reaching out to witnesses, ensures that NGO staff are regularly threatened seriously,[8] by their status

---

5 Madej M. (2019): 'Afghanistan: The Longest War, the Greatest Fiasco?' in: Madej M. (ed.), *Western Military Interventions After the Cold War*, London-New York: Routledge, 134–136.

6 Aall P.R. (February 1996): *NGOs and Conflict Management. Responses to International Conflict Highlights From The Managing Chaos Conference*, United States Institute of Peace, 8.

7 On the need for organisations to cooperate with local people and on possible field activities for the civilian population, see: Barrs C.A. (2009): *Preparedness Support: Helping Brace Beneficiaries, Local Staff and Partners for Violence*, The Cuny Centre.

8 *NGOs and the Prevention of Mass Atrocities Crimes: A Practical Workshop for NGOs to Develop and Share Strategies to Implement the Responsibility to Protect in the Asia-Pacific*

as inconvenient witnesses. There are examples of killings of people who took the risk to warn potential victims (e.g. Toni Locatelli's case in Rwanda). On the other hand, if non-governmental organisations refrain from providing information in the name of the principles of neutrality and impartiality, they can be perceived by victims of infringements as unreliable institutions contributing to impunity. Nevertheless, states and intergovernmental organisations should take a cautious approach to cooperation with NGOs, given that they should not rely on such organisations proving useful, without assuming any responsibility for their safety. Noting the potential of NGOs in a situation in which mass human-rights violations and atrocity crimes threaten, the financial support of credible, disciplined NGOs lies in the interest of states, as does enhancement of their competence and professionalism (e.g. in communication and negotiation).[9]

5.2. Types of non-governmental organisations and their forms of engagement

Depending on the interests represented and actions taken, there are several types of NGOs involved in the prevention of human-rights violations. First, there are the classic human-rights organisations like Amnesty International and Human Rights Watch that focus on monitoring government policies and raising the alarm regarding serious human-rights violations. Such organisations have large financial resources and staff at their disposal, allowing them to observe the situation in practically all countries. They document crimes, collect evidence against perpetrators and work to fight impunity.

They also engage in the systematic publication of current news and cyclical reports, providing the reliable source of data that makes assessment of the threat of mass violence in a given region possible. Some organisations focus on one aspect, such as democracy (Freedom House), corruption (Transparency International) or freedom of speech (Reporters Without Borders). Declining personal freedom, increasing censorship or corruption do not have to be, but can be, one

Region, November 23–24, 2009, *Outcome document*, Oxfam Australia, March 16, 2010, 11.

9 On the weaknesses of NGOs, coordination problems and enhancement of competencies, see P.R. Aall, (February 1996): *NGOs and Conflict Management. Responses to International Conflict Highlights from the Managing Chaos Conference*, United States Institute of Peace, 11–12.

of the signs that mass human-rights violations are taking place. They also attest to the need for structural measures to be resorted to in countering negative trends.

Second, there are organisations that try to focus directly on the issue of preventing atrocity crimes. Genocide Watch is active and well-respected in the field of early warning. Its work hinges upon the famous ten-stage genocide model of Gregory Stanton, which is the basis for the organisation's analysis of the risk of a crime being committed.[10] The organisation seeks to educate the public, but primarily to influence policymakers. It prepares concrete recommendations for institutions that should be involved in regard to a threat of genocide, and presents the desired instruments.

Genocide Watch publishes three types of alert. The first is the "Genocide Watch" whereby the organisation may state that a given state is now featuring a process typical of the initial stages of the Stanton genocide model; and continues to monitor the situation (e.g. in Uzbekistan, India, Sri Lanka, Angola, Burundi, Iran, Mali and South Africa). The second type of alert is the "Genocide Warning," issued when mass killings or genocide are deemed inevitable and single massacres are already occurring (e.g. in Nigeria, Chad, Equatorial Guinea, Yemen, Kenya and the Central African Republic). The third alert is the "Genocide Emergency," attesting to genocide *per se* taking place (e.g. in Syria, Sudan, the Democratic Republic of the Congo, Ethiopia and Burma).[11]

Genocide Watch also proposes concrete institutional solutions. At the outset, the organisation ran a campaign to have countries ratify the Rome Statute of the International Criminal Court – up to the time of its entry into force on 1 July 2002. In 2000, it proposed the appointment of the UN Special Rapporteur on the Prevention of Genocide.[12] It currently lobbies for the establishment of the Early Genocide Warning Centre within the United Nations Secretariat and the United Nations Rapid Response Team.

Genocide Watch also coordinates the Alliance to End Genocide (AEG).[13] This is an international coalition of organisations committed to spreading awareness

---

10 Stanton G.H., *The Ten Stages of Genocide* 2013. http://www.genocidewatch.org/genocide/tenstagesofgenocide.html.

11 See current alerts: https://www.genocidewatch.com/copy-of-current-genocide-watch-aler.

12 See intervention of G.H. Stanton on the occasion of the opening of the Budapest Centre for the Prevention of Genocide, October 2010, https://d0dbb2cb-698c-4513-aa47-eba3a335e06f.filesusr.com/ugd/e5b74f_cd65c6b605534d80b0ff6a6eca3011ba.pdf.

13 Earlier name: *International Campaign to End Genocide.*

and knowledge of the dangers of genocide and other mass crimes, as well as their progress and consequences. Organisations join forces to educate the public, provide early warning and fight the fight against impunity among mass criminals. Its purpose is to eliminate genocide from the practice of states completely. Members include organisations like the International Crisis Group, the Aegis-Trust, the Genocide Prevention Initiative, the Centre for Holocaust and Genocide Studies, Combat Genocide, International Alert, the Montreal Institute for Genocide and Human Rights Studies, TRIAL, and others.

Further significant institutions dealing with genocide warnings include the Simon Skjod Centre for Genocide Prevention at the Holocaust Memorial Museum in Washington. Its work is related to the activities of the Committee on Conscience established in 1995, the mission of which is to "move consciences, influence policymakers and stimulate international efforts"[14] with a view to a stop being put to genocide and crimes against humanity. The Centre takes various actions. Its recommendations are primarily addressed to the United States, then to intergovernmental organisations and to the international community. In 2008, it published recommendations for US foreign policy on prevention and response in relation to crimes of genocide and other mass crimes.[15] In August 2016, it was reported that the prevention of atrocity crimes should be at the centre of the agenda of the newly-elected UN Secretary General,[16] and in 2017 a report on transatlantic cooperation over the prevention and suppression of mass killings was published.[17]

Within the framework of a joint project with Dartmouth College, Early Warning has developed a methodology for monitoring and analysing situations that could lead to mass crimes. The historical experience of states, the tendency to commit crimes, political and economic instability, ideology, authoritarianism and state isolationism are just some of the factors that are taken account of as the

14 On the Committee on Conscience, see https://www.ushmm.org/genocide-prevention/simon-skjodt-center/committee-on-conscience.

15 *Preventing Genocide. A Blueprint for U.S. Policymakers*, Washington 2008, https://www.ushmm.org/m/pdfs/20081124-genocide-prevention-report.pdf.

16 Gowan R., Woocher L., Solomon D., *Preventing Mass Atrocities: An Essential Agenda for the Next UN Secretary-General*, September 2016, https://www.ushmm.org/m/pdfs/Preventing-mass-atrocities.pdf.

17 Feinstein L., Lindberg T., *Report: Allies Against Atrocities: The Imperative for Transatlantic Cooperation to Prevent and Stop Mass Killings*, Washington, March 2017, https://www.ushmm.org/m/pdfs/20170301-Allies-Against-Atrocities-March-2017-Report.pdf.

statistical risk of something negative happening is calculated. The second pillar of the analysis referred to involves the opinions of experts on the region and its problems, who answer questions concerning the dynamics characterising events.

A positive aspect of this type of institution reflects the public nature of the work carried out. Unlike many reports of intergovernmental organisations or national services, the knowledge or concrete assessment of a situation in the possession of Genocide Watch or the Centre for the Prevention of Genocide at the Washington Museum are publicly available,[18] thus ensuring a greater opportunity for countries, organisations and individuals to be pressured and motivated into taking preventative action.

Third, some organisations are typically of the think–tank type. The International Crisis Group, Carnegie Endowment for International Peace or US Institute for Peace conduct research in the areas of peace, conflict prevention and responsibility for protection, including prevention of crimes. The International Crisis Group publishes a monthly newsletter, "Crisis Watch", which serves as an early warning in the context of conflict prevention. It affects about 70 countries particularly vulnerable to crises or conflict. It also identifies positive trends. The strength of the Group lies in its field research, thanks to a network of collaborators located near potential conflict zones. The group has 110 experts from 38 countries around the world.[19] It pays homage to the principle of impartiality, maintaining contacts with all parties to a conflict, as well as local and international institutions. The expertise and reports of the International Crisis Group are examples of reliable research, which are used by entities dealing with conflict prevention, human-rights abuses and atrocity crimes, e.g. the Alliance to End Genocide.

The Budapest Centre for Mass Atrocity Prevention was set up in 2011 to motivate the European Union to take up international efforts in the name of prevention. The Centre defines its mission as filling the gap between early warning and early action. It advocates for an integrated early warning system and early-stage system. It also voices the need for the issue of preventing conflicts to be separated from that of preventing atrocity crimes.

The Centre's priorities include its Prevention Policy Planning Program, which aims to monitor the risk of mass crimes systematically in selected regions, including the Balkans and Central Asia, and to develop recommendations and response strategies for states and institutions. The Centre is in the phase

18 http://www.earlywarningproject.com.

19 On the methodology of work see: https://www.crisisgroup.org/how-we-work.

of developing its risk-assessment team. Through collaboration with numerous experts, academics and policy-makers, the Centre has developed several relevant reports on the capacity of the European Union,[20] regional organisations in Africa[21] and Visegrad Group countries[22] when it comes to preventing mass crimes and extremism.

The fourth type consists of organisations specialising in education and training. The leading body in this area is the New York-based Auschwitz Institute for Peace and Reconciliation (AIPR), which works closely with the United States authorities and the United Nations Office on the Prevention of Genocide and Responsibility to Protect. It organises specialised training for government employees, the police, armed forces and the staff of international organisations. The Raphael Lemkin seminar programme is the flagship educational project of the Institute. Seminars are held partially in Poland, in cooperation with the Auschwitz-Birkenau State Museum. So far, representatives of 60 countries have participated in them.[23]

The activities of AIPR also involve meetings of practitioners, experts, and dormitarians designed to ensure that each group may learn from the others, and benefit from their experience. Since 2012, the Institute has been successful in creating a Latin American network for the prevention of genocide and mass crimes, and then proceeded to put a similar form of cooperation in place in Africa. The activities aim, not merely at international cooperation, but also at the encouragement of states when it comes to their installing the aforementioned national preventative mechanisms, and developing their own preventative capacity.[24]

Some non-governmental organisations specialise in the concept of Responsibility to Protect, focusing on all of the prevention, response and reconstruction aspects. The Asia Pacific Centre for the Responsibility to Protect operates at the

---

20 *The EU and the Prevention of Mass Atrocities. An Assessment of Strengths and Weaknesses*, Budapest Centre for the International Prevention of Genocide and Mass Atrocities, February 2013, http://www.massatrocitiestaskforce.eu/Home.html.

21 *African Regional Communities and the Prevention of Mass Atrocities*, African Task Force on the Prevention of Mass Atrocities, Budapest Centre for Mass Atrocities Prevention, Budapest 2016.

22 *Capabilities of the Visegrad Group in Preventing Extremism*, Budapest Centre for Mass Atrocities Prevention 2017, https://www.genocideprevention.eu/files/Report_V4_2017_A4_web_copy1.pdf.

23 See more: https://aipr.wordpress.com/about/.

24 See the annual Auschwitz Institute for Peace and Reconciliation reports for 2009–2015, http://www.auschwitzinstitute.org/publications/#aipr.

University of Queensland. The Centre's work is primarily research-oriented, so its employees are the authors of major publications. It also develops cooperation in the Asia-Pacific region intensively, serving as the Secretariat for the Asia Pacific Partnership for Atrocity Prevention, which brings together 14 institutions involved in this area.

The Global Centre for the Responsibility to Protect is an example of non-governmental cooperation with the government. The goal of the Centre is to build support for the development of R2P, and the conversion of R2P from theory into practice. This is done through bilateral meetings with representatives of states held in Geneva and New York, motivating participating in annual discussions on R2P at the General Assembly, and co-organising ministerial meetings on R2P and meetings of R2P focal points. The Centre lobbies for approval of the Code of Conduct of the Security Council in the context of atrocity crimes, as well as the Kigali Principles on the Protection of Civilians.

Since 2012, the Centre has published the bi-monthly *R2P Monitor*, which presents the situation of populations exposed to atrocity crimes in the context of historical experiences, potential perpetrators and factors that promote violence. The Global Centre also monitors the actions taken by the UN, regional organisations and the International Criminal Court, suggesting concrete efforts to prevent or stop violations of the law.[25] Both institutions are members of the International Coalition for the Responsibility to Protect, which brings together non-governmental organisations and independent bodies dealing with R2P.

Due to the large number of organisations and institutions whose actions may prove important in prevention, it is impossible to present all those whose daily work contributes to raising awareness of the atrocity crimes problem, motivates state and intergovernmental organisations, and provides specific assistance to populations experiencing violence.

In the context of the prevention of atrocity crimes, the above primarily play a role in the sphere of structural prevention. In turn, it is more difficult to identify international non-governmental organisations directly involved in operational prevention in the field, in the face of the threat of mass violence. Certainly at this stage, local formations should be involved, given that they have the best discernment in the prevailing conditions; and only then third countries and intergovernmental organisations. On the other hand, it is important to connect with local or international NGOs, the work of which has a humanitarian or developmental

25 All bimonthly editions of "R2P Monitor" are available online: https://www.globalr2p.org/publications/.

dimension. They should also be able to take advantage of training on possible action to be taken in the event of a threat of mass violence emerging.

VI. International Instruments for the Prevention of Human Rights Violations and Atrocity Crimes

6.1. Early warning

Mass human-rights violations and atrocity crimes are rarely unpredictable and spontaneous acts. Most often, they result from long-lasting processes whose final outcome is predictable. This leaves the taking of preventative action critically dependent on reliable information regarding development of a given situation. For a long time, states conducted their own monitoring in countries where they have political or economic interests, or with which they have close links, most often as neighbours. For that purpose, use was made of embassies, special services, commercial contacts and non-governmental organisations. Information was also obtained from domestic and foreign media. Knowledge of the situation in neighbouring countries was generally in given states' possession, but that did not denote a readiness or ability to use instruments of prevention. Both the United Nations and regional organisations therefore recognised as worthwhile the creation of an early-warning system to increase the probability of involvement on the part of international institutions and the countries concerned.[1]

The reports that followed the genocides in Rwanda and Srebrenica in the 1990s were the impetus for work to start on an early-warning system. They highlighted the weakness of the information-management and alert systems at the UN. In the case of Rwanda, it was concluded that there was no institution within the United Nations capable of meeting the objectives of early warning and risk analysis.[2] There was also no adequate information flow, especially to the Security Council.[3]

---

1 Miskel J.F., Norton R.J. (1998): 'Humanitarian Early-Warning Systems,' *Global Governance*, Vol. IV, 325.

2 See *Report of the Independent Inquiry into the Actions of the United Nations During the 1994 Genocide in Rwanda*, December 15, 1999, S/1999/1257; Report of the Secretary-General Pursuant to General Assembly Resolution 53/35: The Fall of Srebrenica, A/54/549, November 15, 1999, https://digitallibrary.un.org/record/372298.

3 These conclusions do not imply that there were no warnings regarding the possibility of an outbreak of violence. The growing tensions and deteriorating situation in Rwanda were reported in the reports: Gen. Romei Dallaire, Head of the United Nations Assistance Mission for Rwanda (UNAMIR), Bacre Ndiay – Special Rapporteur

Early warning aims to ensure the provision, at the earliest opportunity, of reliable information for decision makers regarding possible outbreaks of mass human-rights violations and atrocity crimes. Early warning does not mean that quick and effective action will be taken, but it does increase the chance of a more adequate and decisive response.[4]

The Office of the UN Special Adviser on the Prevention of Genocide defines early warning as the collection, analysis and communication of sufficient information about the escalation of a situation that could potentially lead to genocide, crimes against humanity or mass and grave crimes, so that competent UN bodies can take effective preventive measures in a timely fashion.[5]

In the case of each early-warning system, the first step is the collection of the data on which the final effect will depend. The credibility of sources and ability to separate real information from false, manipulative messages play a huge role. An on-site presence is an important component of early-warning systems, in particular the UN and the OSCE through their offices and field missions. Monitoring is subject to trends such as government policy, the economic situation and social relations. To that end, it is crucial to monitor official and unofficial statements by national and community leaders, by reference to traditional and social media, and the reports and news published by think tanks and non-governmental organisations active in human rights and security. Interviews with representatives of government and non-governmental organisations and members of vulnerable groups are equally important.

---

on extrajudicial executions of the UN Commission on Human Rights in February 1994 and UNDP field mission, see Davis R., Majekodunmi B., Smith-Hohn J. (June 2008): 'Prevention of Genocide and Mass Atrocities and the Responsibility to Protect: Challenges for The UN and International Community in the 21st Century,' *Responsibility to Protect. Occasional Papers*, 9; Hehir A. (2010): 'An Analysis of Perspectives on the Office of the Special Adviser on the Prevention of Genocide,' *Genocide Studies and Prevention: An International Journal*, No. 5, 261–262, and in the case of Srebrenica, Colonel Thomas Karremans, a commander of the Dutch United Nations Protection Force (UNPROFOR), in charge of the UN Security Council's security zone for civilians, called for international support. See also: Hamburg D. A. (2003), *No More Killing Fields: Preventing Deadly Conflict*, Rowman & Littlefield Publishers.

4 See *Report of the Secretary-General pursuant to General Assembly Resolution 53/35. The Fall of Srebrenica*, November 15, 1999, A/54/549, par. 474.

5 Woocher L., *Developing a Strategy, Methods and Tools for Genocide Early Warning*, for: Office of the Special Adviser to the UN Secretary-General on the Prevention of Genocide, Center for International Conflict Resolution, New York: Columbia University, 26 September 2006.

Besides monitoring trends, it is important that current events and the daily behaviour of the population be observed, in order that any intensification of refugee flows can be noted. In this case, it is also helpful to use satellite imagery, GPS and drones.[6]

The Office of the Special Adviser on the Prevention of Genocide (OSAPG) uses data from numerous United Nations offices, peacekeeping operations, UNHCHR reports, United Nations organisations such as the World Health Organization (WHO), the United Nations International Children's Emergency Fund (UNICEF), the *United Nations Development Program* (UNDP), the World Food Program (WFP) and other UN entities such as the Department of Political Affairs or the Office for the Coordination of Humanitarian Aid (OCHA). They monitor the situation on the ground for their own needs, identify problems and report cyclically. Collaboration with UN entities provides a guarantee of data quality. The Office is also supported by the information states, the media and NGOs provide. However, UN agencies and institutions are not always willing to cooperate with the OSAPG, either because of the confidentiality of the data, or because of a certain competition between them.[7]

The next stage of the early-warning system consists of the analysis of collected data, with a view to the risk of outbreaks of atrocity crimes being assessed. The Office of the Special Adviser has developed the Framework of Analysis for Atrocity Crimes for this purpose.[8] It is an analytical tool by which to investigate the dangers of genocide, crimes against humanity and war crimes on the basis of 17 risk factors and indicators attributed to individual factors.

---

6 On data collection and early warning methods for humanitarian aid, see Leaning J. (2016): 'Early Warning for Mass Atrocities: Tracking Escalation Parameters at the Population Level' in: Rosenberg S.P., Galis T., Zucker A. (eds.), *Reconstructing Atrocity Prevention*, Cambridge University Press, 352–378; *Community Early Warning Systems: Guiding Principles*" International Federation of Red Cross and Red Crescent Societies, Geneva, 2013, 7, http://www.ifrc.org/PageFiles/103323/1227800-IFRC-CEWS-Guiding-Principles-EN.pdf; Pradhan B., Buchroithner M. (eds.) (2012): *Terrigenous Mass Movements: Detection, Modelling, Early Warning and Mitigation Using Geoinformation Technology*, Berlin-Heidelberg: Springer-Verlag.

7 See A. Hehir, (2010), 'An Analysis of Perspectives on the Office of the Special Adviser on the Prevention of Genocide,' *Genocide Studies and Prevention: an International Journal*, No. 5, 266.

8 *Framework Analysis for Atrocity Crimes. A Tool for Prevention*, United Nations Office on Genocide Prevention and the Responsibility to Protect, New York 2014.

The identification of risk factors denotes the emergence of conditions that make mass crimes more likely. Some may point to structural problems, such as the weakness of a state or discrimination against a particular group in the population. Others may be of an *ad hoc* and dynamic nature, for example relating to incitement to crime or an increased concentration of armed forces. Indicators are manifestations of risk factors – circumstances. The more indicators prove to be identifiable, the easier it is for the probability of a crime to be determined.

Amongst the 17 risk factors, the eight characteristic for all of the types of crime under consideration are a situation of armed conflict or other forms of destabilisation, serious violations of human rights and humanitarian law, the weakness of state structures, motives or incentives for crime, a capacity to commit crimes, an absence of mitigating factors, and the presence of favourable circumstances or preparatory actions and triggering factors. In addition, factors specific to each type of crime have been identified. In the case of genocide, the list includes tensions between groups or discrimination targeted at protected (ethnic, national, racial and religious) groups listed by the Convention on Genocide, and signs of an intent to destroy the said protected group in whole or in part. Signs of broad or systematic attacks against civilians, or a plan or policy of attacks have been identified as specific in the case of crimes against humanity. Where war crimes are concerned, the specific risk factors include serious threats to persons protected under international humanitarian law and serious threats to humanitarian and peaceful operations.

Risk factors and their indicators have a universal dimension ensuring their potential use in analysing the threat of atrocity crimes in all different parts of the world. They also discipline the data collection phase to a great extent in that, if a first risk factor (the occurrence of a situation of armed conflict or other forms of destabilisation) is identified, the Office recommends gathering information from various reliable sources on individual indicators, and then assessing whether a conflict is international or internal, whether there is a humanitarian crisis or a state of emergency, whether there is a unique, political, economic and social destabilisation, including a change in power, a rise of nationalism and extremism, extraordinary military movements, political repression, poverty, unemployment, mass protests, etc.

In turn, in the case of the risk factors characteristic of genocide, it is recommended that there be verification for the presence of such indicators as historical and current discriminatory, segregation and exclusionary practices against national, ethnic, racial or religious groups; the denial of the existence of protected groups, impunity among perpetrators of crimes committed in the past, tensions or conflicts between protected groups or relations with the state with respect to, for example, access to raw materials, socio-economic inequalities, official documents that indicate intent to destroy groups, dehumanisation, physical elimination of group members, attacks on cultural and religious symbols, and so on.

The methodology included in the Framework of Analysis is used by staff of the Office of the Special Adviser for the Prevention of Genocide, but is also recommended to all other centres that deal with threat detection and early warning. It is also worth noting that it is ancillary, encouraging systematic monitoring of the situation on the basis of the same criteria. However, even the presence of risk factors or indicators thereof does not prove that crimes will certainly take place.[9] However, it does certainly point to the need for national or international preventive measures to be launched.

Lists of factors or determinants are also found in the methodology of other early-warning systems, which are usually elements to the prevention of conflicts, but also humanitarian or economic crises. In the case of Conflict Prevention by the OSCE, they include the political system, military and security structures, socio-economic development, the environment, the occurrence of ethnic and religious minorities, the courts and tribunals and human rights, and the geopolitical situation.[10] In turn, for the European Union, the focus is on the kind of political system, lack of democracy, weak government, a bad human-rights situation, repression, social inequalities, ethnic composition, transnational relationships, killings, a history of conflicts and latest trends, the situation in neighbouring countries and access to raw materials.[11]

The factors analysed under the early-warning systems for conflict prevention are much more general in nature than the methodology developed by OSAPG; and the outbreak of a conflict does not have to prove crimes. At the same time, atrocity crimes are also committed in the absence of armed conflict. According to Alex Bellamy's statistics on 103 post-1945 episodes of mass killings investigated (and accounting for the lives of at least 5000 people), 69 of these (or 67%)

---

9 See more: Mucha W. (2014): 'The Next Spring is Certain to Come – and Certain to be Missed: Deficits in Conflict Prevention Research,' *Global Responsibility to Protect*, Vol. 6, No. 4, 2014, 382-406; Jacob C., McLoughlin S. (2015): 'Strengthening State Resilience for the Prevention of Mass Atrocity Crimes,' *R2P Ideas in Brief*, Vol. 5, No. 5, 2–4.

10 Conflict Prevention and Early Warning: The OSCE's Toolbox – presentation at the seminar "V4 prevention" organized by the Budapest Center for Mass Atrocities Prevention, 5–7 October 2015, Warsaw.

11 On indicators and various early warning systems see also: Davies J.L., Gurr T.R. (eds.) (1998): *Preventive Measures: Building Risk Assessment and Crisis Early Warning Systems*, Oxford: Rowman&Littlefield Publishers.

occurred during conflict, while 34 (33%) occurred beyond the scope thereof.[12] It can therefore be concluded that early-warning systems in the prevention of atrocity crimes and conflicts are mutually supportive, and that regional systems play a particularly important role because of their "proximity" to countries in which there is a potential for violence to arise.

The last stage of early warning entails issuance. The addressees are primarily states and UN and regional organisations, and in particular their decision-making bodies. The Special Adviser for the Prevention of Genocide may appeal to the Secretary-General of the United Nations and, through him, to the Security Council. This means there is no possibility of direct influence on the most important UN body being exerted, and this is an undoubted weakness of the system.[13] Success for early warning can be considered achieved where the international community is mobilised to act.[14] Alerts of non-governmental organisations addressed, not only to states but also to the public, are a great help. Public opinion then has a chance to put pressure on governments, and to contribute to the latter's prevention activities.

Issued warnings concern short-term prospects and require operational prevention. The implementation of structural prevention is supported by data obtained by international human-rights monitoring mechanisms involving the Human Rights Council and Special Rapporteurs, Treaty bodies and other universal and regional procedures.[15] In addition, attention needs to be given to indicators of the economic situation. Low GDP per capita and poverty, inequality, discrimination and large populations dependent on humanitarian aid all

12 Bellamy A.J. (2011): 'Mass Atrocities and Armed Conflict: Links, Distinctions and Implications for the Responsibility to Prevent,' *Policy Analysis Brief*, The Stanley Foundation, 2.

13 See A. Hehir, (2010), 'An Analysis of Perspectives on the Office of the Special Adviser on the Prevention of Genocide,' *Genocide Studies and Prevention: An International Journal*, No. 5, 265–266.

14 Chalk F., Matthews K., Barqueiro C. (2010): *Mobilizing the Will to Intervene: Leadership to Prevent Mass Atrocities*, The Montreal Institute for Genocide and Human Rights Studies at Concordia University.

15 In the context of minority rights, see *Preventing and addressing violence and atrocity crimes targeted against minorities*, Contribution of the United Nations Network on Racial Discrimination and Protection of Minorities to the Seventh Session of the Forum on Minority Issues, 25–26 November 2014, http://www.ohchr.org/Documents/Issues/Minorities/Contribution7thsession.pdf.

indicate the need for economic, developmental or humanitarian aid, which are also of preventative importance.[16]

6.2. Diplomatic instruments

Diplomatic instruments concern the sphere of states' official relations with the rest of the world. These can be applied at bilateral or multilateral level – within international organisations. States and international institutions may engage in confidential or so-called "silent diplomacy" – urge the government to change policy by way of unofficial talks, or draw attention to the human-rights situation in a given country by means of public speeches, express concern as to the imminent humanitarian crisis, call for a change of civil protection policy and also engage in condemnation of law-breaking and resort to inhumane practices. Substantial measures entail the cancellation or postponement of official state visits, and the lowering of the status of diplomatic representation or reductions in staffing. The withdrawal of an international mission from an area or the closure of an organisation's office, which is most likely to occur as a result of the escalation of a security situation, may have a similar effect. Such activities may have a symbolic dimension, signalling disapproval of the internal politics of a state; or be a prelude to the use of more major international instruments. For example, the withdrawal of the Kosovo Verification Mission from Kosovo in March 1999 was a prelude to the NATO decision to intervene.[17]

Furthermore, states may isolate the regime or even break off diplomatic relations, while international organisations have the option of suspending membership in Member States or – in extreme cases – of depriving a state of member status in the event of a drastic breach of international law. For example, Libya's membership of the UN Human Rights Council was suspended on 1 March 2011. However, it remains debatable how far the exclusion of the state or its isolation

16 *Integrating Conflict Prevention In Development Policy And Aid Agendas*, Policy Messages from the Wilton Park Conference: Conflict Prevention and Development Co-operation in Africa, a Policy Workshop, 8–11 November 2007, https://www.jica.go.jp/jica-ri/IFIC_and_JBICI-Studies/english/publications/reports/study/topical/prevention/pdf/001.pdf; Mosso D. (2009): 'Early Warning And Quick Response: Accounting in the Twenty-First Century,' *Studies in the Development of Accounting Thought*, Vol. 12. Bingley: Emerald Group, JAI Press.

17 Bellamy A.J., Griffin S. (2002): 'OSCE Peacekeeping: Lessons from the Kosovo Verification Mission' *European Security*, Vol. 11; Maisonneuve M. (summer 2000), 'The OSCE Kosovo Verification Mission,' *Canadian Military Journal*, 52–53.

has a preventive dimension and affects the situation of its population positively, or else may rather be regarded as a warning to other states.

The effects of such imposed isolation can be counterproductive. By acting in this way, the international community limits possibility to influence the given state, while hampering the situation of local organisations and groups particularly vulnerable to discrimination, exclusion and the violation of their rights, including by way of violence. The maintenance of contacts with all national, ethnic, religious, racial and political groups protected under international humanitarian conventions and all exposed to mass repression is important to the international community, in the context of both structural and operational prevention.[18]

Should atrocity crimes, an escalation of tensions or armed conflict threaten, international organisations and states are eager to use preventive diplomacy. This can be defined as diplomatic action taken as soon as possible to prevent escalation of a situation, and especially the outbreak of conflict or mass violence.[19] Such measures are initiated and deployed by both states and international organisations.

At the UN, the possibility of preventative diplomacy being initiated falls within the competences of the General Assembly, the Security Council and the Secretary-General. At the request of the Council, diplomats and officials like special envoys may engage in confidential or so-called "silent" diplomacy, urging a government to change policy by means of unofficial talks,[20] or drawing attention

---

18 Examples entail activities undertaken by CSCE/OSCE missions towards the opposition in such countries as Belarus and Bosnia-Herzegovina, see Bieńczyk A. (2000): '*The Human Dimension in CSCE/OSCE Missions*,' *The Polish Quarterly of International Affairs*, Vol. 9, No. 4.

19 For more information on UN institutional frameworks, see: *Preventive Diplomacy: Delivering Results*, Report of the Secretary-General, https://www.un.org/undpa/sites/www.un.org.undpa/files/SG%20Report%20on%20Preventive%20Diplomacy.pdf.

20 "Silent diplomacy" is one of the most effective preventative measures, using the basic task of diplomacy that is communication between states. See Vincent R. J. (1982): 'Human Rights and Foreign Policy,' *Australian Outlook*, Vol. 36, No. 3, 2–4, as well as the article by Max van der Stoel, High Commissioner for National Minorities of the OSCE, portraying, among others, the need for confidentiality if the mandate of the Commissioner is to be fulfilled: Van der Stoel M. (1998): 'Zapobieganie konfliktom w sytuacjach związanych z kwestiami mniejszości narodowych,' *Sprawy Międzynarodowe*, No. 3, 59–74. Other researchers believe that only the emergence of threats can bring results: Kohlschutter A.V. i Baechler G. (1998): 'A Pilot Study for an Early Warning System for the Swiss Foreign Ministry' in: Davies J.L., Gurr T.R. (eds.) *Preventive Measures: Building Risk Assessment and Crisis Early Warning Systems*, Oxford: Rowman&Littlefield Publishers, 183.

to the human-rights situation and factors favouring mass crimes in a given country in public speeches. The Secretary-General often undertakes diplomatic missions in person.[21] The greater the support forthcoming from states, UN institutions and regional arrangements, the greater an initiative's chance of success. Similarly, regional organisations, such as the European Union, OSCE, Organisation of African States and African Union, are eager to use this instrument. The mandates of the latter also include the provision of mediation and good offices.

International organisations make an effort to prepare their negotiators properly. At the UN, there is a Mediation Support Unit within the Department of Political Affairs, which advises and supports envoys and established missions. However, there are unfortunately no separate procedures for using preventative diplomacy in the face of a threat that mass crimes may be committed. Furthermore, as most initiatives focus on preventing armed conflicts or ending fighting, the problem of mass violations of human rights may find itself put to one side. Efforts to address serious human-rights violations and atrocity crimes may also cause difficulties in dealings with local authorities, only serving to stiffen their negotiating positions, especially if they fear criminal consequences. In principle, timely addressing of the issue of human rights should form part of the effort present in preventative diplomacy. However, as current mechanisms do not assume this directly, their inclusion often depends on individuals' awareness and commitment.[22] The Secretary-General, in his 2012 report on enhancing the role of mediation in peaceful dispute resolution and conflict prevention and resolution, highlighted the need for an awareness of human rights and international humanitarian law among mission officers involved in preventative diplomacy.[23]

The use of diplomatic and political instruments is extremely difficult if states are not interested in peace and do not demonstrate a political will to cooperate, especially with "outside" envoys, often seen as biased, or representative of

21 Ramcharan B. (2008): *Preventive Diplomacy at the UN*, Bloomington-Indianapolis: Indiana University Press, especially chapter 9, devoted to the prevention of genocide, 175–193.

22 On the subject of unused opportunities for preventive diplomacy in Libya, see Rashid S. (2013): 'Preventive Diplomacy, Mediation and the Responsibility to Protect in Libya: a Missed Opportunity for Canada?' *Canadian Foreign Policy Journal*, Vol. 19, No. 1, 39–52.

23 *Strengthening the role of mediation in the peaceful settlement of disputes, conflict prevention and resolution* Report of the UN Secretary-General, June 25, 2012, A/66/811. See also *Enhancing mediation and its support activities*, Report of the UN Secretary-General, April 8, 2009, S/2009/189.

external interests. It is therefore important to convince parties of the independence and disinterested position of negotiators, and of the humanitarian objectives of their mission. Other instruments to be used in this situation may involve sticks or carrots motivating efforts to ensure protection of the population.[24]

6.3. Economic instruments

As they engage in the promotion of human rights or resort to means of preventing mass trafficking, states and international organisations often use economic, financial means, which include the provision of economic and development aid, the imposition of restrictions and sanctions on trade and investment and efforts to ensure that loans and credits are made conditional upon respect for human rights, the rule of law and democracy. States use economic instruments directly in bilateral relations or by donating funds to multilateral institutions that work on specific projects supporting states in need; though this does not mean they are guided in their efforts by the will to prevent mass crimes.

Mass abuses of human rights and atrocities are more common in areas where there is poverty, underdevelopment, economic inequality between groups and high unemployment, and where states are not linked by a network of dependencies that largely force their leaders to adhere to international rules.[25] Thoughtful support for states' development, maintenance of trade relations and improvement in the quality of life of the population is indirectly preventative. In turn, in the face of the risk of withdrawal of direct financial support or necessary loans, violence and its consequences can become "unprofitable."

Funds transferred by states and international organisations reach various national institutions such as Ministries with portfolios relating to the economy,

---

24 On the preventive diplomacy, see: Steiner B.H. (2004): *Collective Preventive Diplomacy. A Study in International Conflict Management*, State University of New York Press, and on the role of mediation: Babbitt E.F. (2014): 'Mediation and the Prevention of Mass Atrocities' in: Serrano M., Weiss T.G. (eds.), *The International Politics of Human* Rights, London: Routledge, 30–44.

25 Harff B., Gurr T. R. (1988): 'Toward Empirical Theory of Genocides and Politicides: Identification and Measurement of Cases since 1945,' *International Studies Quarterly*, Vol. 37, No. 3, 359–371. See more in: Goldstone J.A., Bates R.H., Gurr T.R., Lustik M., Marshall M.G., Ulfelder J., Woodward M. (2005): *A Global Forecasting Model of Political Instability*, Conference paper, Washington, 1–4 September; authors of the project *Human Security Report* reached similar conclusions in 2009/2010, 2011, 2014. https://css.ethz.ch/en/services/organizations/organization.html/13296.

development, finance, and so on. This makes it difficult to monitor the flow of funds and to test the effectiveness of instruments used.[26] It remains unclear how the regime uses the funds received, in particular whether it is for military use and ultimately against the public.

Greater transparency applies to financial assistance targeted at specific, narrow projects, supported by non-governmental organisations. These aim to support pro-democracy projects, develop entrepreneurship or provide humanitarian aid. Settlements involve the submission by local NGOs of detailed project implementation reports. In some cases, however, work with non-governmental organisations is obstructed by restrictive internal laws regarding the financing of NGOs from outside, or by difficulties with reaching reliable partners.

Cases of human-rights violations or of the opacity of local government policy are often reasons for aid to be suspended, as was the case with Rwanda. After the 1994 genocide, high levels of international assistance began to arrive in that country. However, one of the effects of the accusations regarding this violation of standards was the new limiting of aid from 2012 onwards.[27] Decisions in this regard are each time controversial. Abstaining from or reducing aid to the government-perpetrator may be the cause of a stiffening of policy.

There are many funds, programmes and agencies operating within the United Nations that discharge tasks in support of the development of states. It was to increase their effectiveness that, at the initiative of the Secretary General, the United Nations Development Group was formed in 1997. This currently comprises 32 funds, programmes, agencies and other development bodies. The most important include: the United Nations Development Program, the United Nations Children's Fund, the World Food Program, the World Health Organisation and others. The United Nations signs Individual Development Assistance Plans with individual countries, which provide guidance to the institution about support. Their assumptions are in harmony with the Millennium Declaration and the Millennium Development Goals. The European Union and the Organisation

---

26 See case of development aid to Nepal: Skar H.O., Cederroth S. (2005): *Development Aid to Nepal. Issues and Options in Energy, Health, Education, Democracy and Human Rights*, Nordic Institute of Asian Studies, Report Series, No. 34, 69–73; On development aid in Africa see Resnick D., van de Walle N. (2013): *Democratic Trajectories in Africa Unravelling the Impact of Foreign Aid*, Oxford: Oxford University Press, as well as: Wilks A. (ed.) (2010): *Aid and Development Effectiveness: Towards Human Rights, Social Justice and Democracy*, Quezon: IBON Books.

27 International Development Statistics (IDS) online databases, http://www.oecd.org/dac/stats/idsonline.htm.

for Economic Co-operation and Development (OECD) are significant donors of development aid. These organisations endeavour to combine the assistance provided with the promotion of human rights.

Economic instruments can also be used as punishment where rights of the population are violated. At the same time they represent a form of pressure by which to change the policy of a state. The Security Council, pursuant to Art. VIII of the Charter of the United Nations, has the power to impose economic sanctions on undemocratic regimes whose policies threaten to use or use violence. Among other things, it has already used this instrument – against the regimes in Southern Rhodesia (in 1965–1979), South Africa (in 1986–1994) and Iraq (in 1990–2003). The effectiveness of the sanctions applied was assessed as ambiguous.[28] On the one hand, sanctions mobilised local entrepreneurs wishing to develop business activities to exert pressure on violent authorities. On the other hand, sanctions had an adverse effect on the condition of local populations, most often also in neighbouring countries. Reports on Iraq proved this.[29] Nor did sanctions lead to the expected regime change. The whole spectrum of sanctions was applied to Yugoslavia during the war in the Balkans in 1990s. Bans were imposed on arms deliveries and access to credit, followed by a freezing of Serbian assets abroad and a ban on investing in that country. This did not curb or stop the committing of crimes. However, in the long run, it motivated the Parties to conclude a peaceful agreement on 21 November 1995.[30]

In the light of doubts about the effectiveness of sanctions, and about the severity of their impact on a state's population, recent years have brought the application of targeted sanctions to specific individuals, notably the politicians and officials responsible for making decisions. These mainly involve bans on travel and the freezing of bank accounts. However, George A. Lopez maintains that sanctions should be extended to entire elites operating in support of decision-makers, including those related to an oppressive government.[31] Such sanctions

---

28 See Baehr P. (1996): *The Role of Human Rights in Foreign Policy*, London: Palgrave Macmillan; Higgins R. (1987): 'Human Rights and Foreign Policy,' *Rivista di Studi Politici Internazionali*, 578–580.

29 UNICEF – Results of the 1999 Iraq Child and Maternal Mortality Surveys, 2003 IRQ: Iraq Watching Briefs – Overview Report, July 2003.

30 Comras V.D (2012): *Pressuring Milosevic: Financial Pressure Against Serbia and Montenegro, 1992–1995,* November 6, 2012, ISN-ITH, *article originally* published by the Center for a New American Security.

31 Lopez G.A. (2016): 'Mobilizing Economic Sanctions for Preventing Mass Atrocities: From Targeting Dictators to Enablers' in: Rosenberg S.P., Galis T., Zucker A.

might also apply to specific raw materials and technologies. These instruments are more likely to be effective when used simultaneously by states and international organisations.[32] However, a dilemma continues to surround the issue of when sanctions might be triggered in order to have a preventative effect, rather than merely serving as a reaction to atrocity crimes. To this end, introduction should obviously take place following receipt of early warnings, with these also corresponding with diplomatic efforts.

6.4. Legal instruments

International legal instruments include accepted legal documents and the resulting procedures. To prevent mass human-rights violations and atrocity crimes one can use instruments deriving from the international human rights law and the international criminal law.

International treaties provide the basis for the examination of states' reports concerning implementation of treaties, with regular visits to states established, investigative missions and work to handle individual and state complaints. All of these procedures give international organisations the opportunity to recommend to states actions that should improve their human, political, social and economic situation.[33] Expert and judicial institutions have the capacity to indicate to states the direction of action which, if chosen, leaves no room for mass violations of human rights. The results of these procedures are an impulse and justification for action for states and international organisations, which is used by the international community, including the United Nations, the European Union, the Council of Europe, the Organization of American States and the African Union. Non-governmental organisations also refer to international

---

(eds.), *Reconstructing Atrocity Prevention*, Cambridge University Press, 379–386; see also: Stefanopoulos A., Lopez G.A. (2014): 'From Coercive to Protective Tools. The Evolution of Targeted Sanctions' in: Serrano M., Weiss T.G. (eds.), *The International Politics of Human* Rights, London: Routledge, 48–65.

32 On the effectiveness of the sanctions, see Biersteker T.J., Eckert S.E., Tourinho M. (eds.) (2016): *Targeted Sanctions – The Impacts and Effectiveness of United Nations Action*, Cambridge University Press; Neuenkirch M., Neumeier F. (2014): 'The Impact of UN and US Economic Sanctions on GDP Growth,' *Joint Discussion Paper Series in Economics*, No. 24.

33 Rodley N.S. (2013): 'The Role and Impact of Treaty Bodies' in: Shelton D. (ed.), *The Oxford Handbook of International Human Rights Law*, Oxford: Oxford University Press, 621–648.

procedures evaluating the practice of states. Each member state of the United Nations is a party to the selected treaties, hence all are subject to at least part of the procedures at both the universal and regional level. The smallest numbers of human-rights treaties have been ratified by: Bhutan, Democratic Republic of Korea, Myanmar and Southern Sudan.[34]

The limitations of these procedures lie in the voluntary nature of the participation of countries expressed through the ratification of treaties and additional protocols.[35] Non-democratic states in particular avoid their international obligations. While they are willing to ratify general international treaties such as the Convention on the Rights of the Child or the Convention on the Elimination of All Forms of Discrimination against Women, they are reluctant to ratify instruments involving the initiation of scrutiny procedures, notices and individual complaints.

In addition, many such states do not comply with recommendations that are not legally binding, representing soft-law[36] or treaty reservations,[37] and this does much to limit the impact of these instruments. Nevertheless, the above limitations do not render treaties entirely irrelevant. Even if they have not been ratified, they represent a good excuse for the international community to apply pressure in the name of their ratification. The European Union likewise uses the existence of international human-rights law to initiate and implement a structured human-rights dialogue. The UN Secretary-General, Treaty bodies and other institutions also call for the ratification of legal instruments.

Since 2007, a Universal Periodic Review (UPR) has application for all UN Member States. Every four-and-a-half years, thanks to information provided by states, international institutions and non-governmental organisations, the Human Rights Council has the opportunity to review the human-rights situation

---

34 *Human Rights Indicators. A Guide to Measurement and Implementation*, United Nation Human Rights Office of the High Commissioner, New York-Geneva 2012, 114.

35 Flood P.J. (1998): *The Effectiveness of UN Human Rights Institutions*, London: Praeger Publishers, 160–129.

36 Alebeek R. van, Nollkaemper A. (2012): 'The Legal Status of Decisions by Human Rights Treaty Bodies in National Law' in: Keller H., Ulfstein G., *UN Human Rights Treaty Bodies. Law and Legitimacy*, Cambridge University Press, 356–413.

37 On objections to the UN Human Rights Convention see Bieńczyk-Missala A. (2017): 'Cultural Determinants of the Development and Observance of Universal Human Rights' in: Michałowska G., Schreiber H., *Culture(s) in International Relations*, Peter Lang Edition, 253–272.

in each state and issue appropriate recommendations. There is no need for consent or involvement on the part of the said states.

Likewise, Council decisions to appoint a Special Rapporteur with a national mandate or a Committee of Inquiry do not require state consent, although absence of the latter usually denotes difficulties for established procedures.[38] The Human Rights Council also has an instrument for processing notices received from individuals, groups of individuals and non-governmental organisations, in the case of consistent patterns of gross and reliably attested violations of all human rights and all fundamental freedoms. The procedure is based on the Resolution of the Human Rights Council dated 18 June 2007, and does not require state consent, although its success depends on its will to cooperate.[39]

Improving the effectiveness of legal instruments in the field of human rights is necessary, and has a bearing on the prevention of mass offences. International law in the field of human rights is still being developed – especially when it comes to the development of new scrutiny mechanisms and opportunities. New possibilities are also being sought by which international institutions and procedures might be reformed. An example is the replacement of the Human Rights Commission with the Human Rights Council in 2006, the changes that have been made to the functioning of the UN treaty bodies,[40] or the reform of the European Court of Human Rights.[41]

Huge hopes were lodged with the preventative effect of international criminal-law instruments. These were expressed in the Convention on the Prevention and

38 *Institution-Building of the United Nations Human Rights Council*, Human Rights Council Resolution A/HRC/RES/5/1, June 18, 2007.

39 Kothari M. (2013): 'From Commission to the Council: Evolution of UN Charter Bodies' in: Shelton D. (ed.), *The Oxford Handbook of International Human Rights Law*, Oxford: Oxford University Press, 587–620; Alfredsson G., Grimheden J., Ramcharan B., Zayas A. de (2009): *International Human Rights Monitoring Mechanisms. Essays in Honour of Jakob Th. Möller*, Leiden-Boston: Martinus Nijhoff Publishers; Ramcharan B. (2009): *The Protection Roles of UN Human Rights Special Procedures*, Leiden-Boston: Nijhoff Law Specials.

40 On the reform, see: Ghanea N. (2006): 'From UN Commission on Human Rights to UN Human Rights Council: One Step Forwards or Two Steps Sideways? *International&Comparative Law Quarterly*, Vol. 55, No. 3, 695–705; Hampson F.J. (2007): 'An Overview of the Reform of the UN Human Rights Machinery,' *Human Rights Law Review*, Vol. 7, No. 1, 7–27.

41 Caflish L. (2006): 'The Reform of the European Court of Human Rights: Protocol No. 14 and Beyond,' *Human Rights Law Review*, Vol. 6, No. 2, 403–415.

Punishment of the Crime of Genocide of 9 December 1945. A similar objective accompanied the appointment of the International Criminal Tribunal for the former Yugoslavia (ICTY) and International Criminal Court (ICC) in the 1990s. In the Resolution establishing the ICTY, the Security Council expressed its hope that its operation would contribute to the restoration and maintenance of peace.[42] In turn, the States Parties to the Statute of the International Criminal Court have stated in the preamble that they are committed to putting an end to the impunity of the perpetrators of these crimes, and thus contributing to their prevention.[43] In both cases, it was expected that possibility of perpetrators facing justice would discourage or even deter them from committing the most serious crimes.[44]

In its rulings, the ICTY[45] has repeatedly pointed to deterrence as the purpose of its decisions, as has the International Criminal Tribunal for Rwanda (ICRR),[46] notwithstanding it having been established in response to the 1994 genocide.

Examining the preventative importance of international criminal law creates great difficulties. It is easy to say when a failure to perform the function occurred, as for example in relation to the genocide in Srebrenica, committed after the ICC commenced with its activities in July 1995.[47] By the same token, it is impossible to state that there was no crime at all under the influence of a Tribunal.[48] It is always difficult to assess the extent to which the punishment of criminals affects the thinking and behaviour of potential offenders, especially given operation in a complex, changing context.

---

42 UN Security Council Resolution, S/RES/827, May 25, 1993.

43 Statute of the International Criminal Court, Rome, July 17 1998, OJ, No. 78, item 708 from 9 May 2003

44 Ku J., Nzelibe J. (2006): 'Do International Criminal Tribunals Deter or Exacerbate Humanitarian Atrocities?' *Washington University Law Review*, Vol. 84, 777–833.

45 See e.g. *Aleksovski* Appeal Judgement, para. 185; *Čelebići* Appeal Judgement, para. 806; *Furundžija* Trial Judgement, para. 288; *Tadić* Sentencing Judgement, paras 7–9; *Kupreškić* Trial Judgement, para. 848.

46 *Kambanda* Trial Judgement, para. 28; *Rutaganda* Trial Judgement, para. 456.

47 Wieruszewski R. (2017): 'Wnioski z konfliktów w byłej Jugosławii' in: Bieńczyk-Missala A., *Civilians in Contemporary Armed Conflicts: Rafał Lemkin's Heritage*, Warsaw: Wydawnictwo Uniwersytetu Warszawskiego, 98.

48 See excellent text on the possibility of using theoretical models for the prevention of the function of international criminal law: Rosenberg S.P. (2016): 'Audacity of Hope: International Criminal Law, Mass Atrocity Crimes, and Prevention' in: Rosenberg S.P., Galis T., Zucker A. (eds.), *Reconstructing Atrocity Prevention*, Cambridge University Press, 151–174.

However, it can be assumed that not only court rulings but also warnings, accusations, and arrest warrants may prevent specific individuals from committing crimes, as well as exerting pressure on the UN Security Council to refer cases to the ICC. Obstacles to any combating of the "culture of impunity" by the International Criminal Court can be thought to reside in the principle of complementarity, which provides states with the illusion of independent criminal prosecution and no solution of the issue of delivering defendants to the Court. The most blatant example is the case of Sudan's President Omar al-Bashir, accused of genocide, crimes against humanity and war crimes in Darfur, for which the ICC issued an arrest warrant on 4 March 2009, to date going unenforced.

In addition, the ICC has no chance to judge perpetrators from countries that have not ratified the Rome Statute or retain the support of one or more Permanent Members of the Security Council (given that the latter has the capacity to refer cases to the Tribunal on the basis of Art. 53 of the Statute). In these cases, the Court's preventative influence is very limited.

6.5. Military instruments

The application of international military instruments is justified within the framework of both structural and operational prevention. Depending on the situation, the international community may provide assistance through the delivery of arms, the organisation of military training, the deployment of military operations, or the use of negative instruments (the latter including the breaking-off of military cooperation, imposition of an arms embargo or military intervention).

Negative instruments related to the imposition of military sanctions or the involvement of armed forces can be triggered both before the outbreak of mass human-rights abuses (and thus be purely preventative), or may represent a response to crimes that have already begun to be committed, though at the same time serving to prevent further crimes from arising. They also cause the greatest controversy.

Embargos on weapons are intended to limit resort to violence. The sudden interest of a government or armed groups in the purchase of more weapons and ammunition may be probable proof of planned crime. Rwanda is the most commonly cited example – in 1993 it brought 581 tonnes of machetes from China for 725,000 American dollars.[49] These were used to kill a little over half of the

49 Melvern L. (2006): *Conspiracy To Murder – The Rwandan Genocide*, London-New York: Verso, 56.

victims of the Rwandan genocide.[50] Organisations dealing with early warning and the protection of human rights in general are particularly critical of the sale of arms to non-democratic states that have historically used weapons against their populations and are likely to re-use them.

However, military sanctions prove ineffective due to the abundant supply of weapons. It is worth noting that all the Permanent Members of the Security Council, responsible for maintaining peace and international security, feature on the list of top arms exporters, including to non-democratic countries.[51] An embargo can also generate imbalances in the access to weapons enjoyed by combatants, and this can translate into crime on a yet-greater scale. This is one of the conclusions to be drawn from the conflict in the former Yugoslavia.[52]

In countries facing a serious threat of mass crimes, a preventative role may be played by the very presence of international forces, which may be invited by the government, or as a result of UN Security Council authorisation. Irrespective of the mandate of the operation, the outbreak of mass violence directed against civilians is considered a failure of international forces, or at least proof of their ineffectiveness. Deployed troops are an important link within early-warning systems if they share information about security in the field. However, they also play a stabilising role, dissuading perpetrators and supporting civil protection. They inform the local population of dangers, and help organise the provision of humanitarian aid in crisis situations.[53]

Examples of military operations that have played a preventative role relate to UN forces deployed in the 1990s in Macedonia, initially under the United Nations Protection Force in the Balkans (UNPROFOR), and then the United Nations Preventive Deployment Force in Macedonia (UNPREDEP), with a

---

50 Verwimp P. (2006): 'Machetes and Firearms: The Organization of Massacres in Rwanda,' *Journal of Peace Research*, No. 43(1), 16, http://jpr.sagepub.com/content/43/1/5.full.pdf+html.

51 See ranking of SIPRI: https://www.sipri.org/databases/armstransfers.

52 Comras V. D. (2011): 'Pressuring Milosevic: Financial Pressure Against Serbia and Montenegro, 1992–1995' in: Asher D. L., Comras V.D., Cronin P.M., *Pressure Coercive Economic Statecraft and U.S. National Security*, Center for a New American Security, 55–74.

53 See more: D. Raymond (2016): 'Military Means of Preventing Mass Atrocities' in: Rosenberg S.P., Galis T., Zucker A. (eds.), *Reconstructing Atrocity Prevention*, Cambridge University Press, 299–310.

view to a "spillover" conflict being prevented.[54] Similar tasks were discharged by the UN Operation in Cote d'Ivoire in 2004. Operations set up to monitor agreements on the cessation of hostilities or peace treaties have also played preventative roles, for example in Eastern Slavonia, Barania and Western Syrmia (UNTAES) in 1996–1998, East Timor (UNTAET / UNMISET) in 1999–2005 or Kosovo (UNMIK) since 1999.

Despite the mistakes and unfulfilled expectations characterising UN forces in Srebrenica in 1995 and Sri Lanka in 2009, research has shown that their presence works to reduce both levels of violence and numbers of victims.[55] An in-depth June 2015 report from the International Peace Institute concerning mistakes made in the context of atrocity crimes prevention listed such challenges to the effectiveness of UN military involvement in civil protection and prevention as the gap between expectations and capabilities, the tendency to avoid force, intelligence weaknesses, competing priorities and insufficient political support.[56]

The UN's 2005 adoption of the concept of Responsibility to Protect provided an impetus for reflections on the role armed forces may play in preventing mass cruelty. The negative experiences and consequences of the humanitarian interventions in Somalia and Kosovo have strengthened the conviction that the use of force is a definitive means that can be applied in both the prevention and reaction spheres. Every armed intervention, especially of a preventative nature, is a source of dilemmas, and distrust regarding the actual intentions of the intervening bodies.[57] In particular, US inclusion of the right to pre-emptive strike in its National Security Strategy has raised fears regarding the possible use of armed forces for political purposes other than those associated with civil protection.[58]

---

54 On the preventative role of peacekeeping operations and UN observers, and especially the relevant Macedonian experience, see Ramcharan B. (2008): *Preventive Diplomacy at the UN*, Bloomington-Indianapolis: Indiana University Press, 138–144.

55 See especially the UN report: Evaluation of the Implementation and Results of Protection of Civilians Mandates in United Nations Peacekeeping Operations, UN Doc. A/68/787, March 7, 2014, as well as: Hoeffler A. (2014): 'Can International Interventions Secure the Peace,' *International Area Studies Review*, No. 1, 75–94; Hultman L., Kathman J., Shannon M. (2014): 'Beyond Keeping Peace: United Nations Effectiveness in the Midst of Fighting,' *American Political Science Review*, No. 4, 737–753.

56 Bellamy A.J., Lupin A. (2015): *Why We Fail: Obstacles to the Effective Prevention of Mass Atrocities*, New York: International Peace Institute, 13–17.

57 For more, see: Zajadło J. (2005): *Dylematy humanitarnej interwencji*, Gdańsk: Arche.

58 Helal M.S. (2012): 'Middle East' in: Genser J., Cotler I., *Responsibility to Protect. The Promise of Stopping Mass Atrocities in our Time*, New York: Oxford University Press, 214.

By definition, the launching of an armed intervention prior to the onset of mass murder would tend to mean a lack of hard evidence justifying intervention.[59]

Concerns are more limited where the use of force is in accordance with the Charter of the United Nations, and meets the criteria for military interventions developed by the International Commission on Intervention and State Sovereignty, which is to say right authority, just cause, right intention, last resort, proportional means and reasonable prospects.[60] However, even assuming an intervention meets R2P criteria, its implementation is always associated with huge costs and the risk of negative, unpredictable effects.[61] Naturally, the dilemma of whether to intervene is also augmented by the key further dilemma of how to do so. The prospect of mass atrocities being prevented should be taken into account even at the stages of planning and the preparation of armed forces.

A valuable proposal in this area is the concept developed by the Carr Centre for Human Rights Policy, the Harvard Kennedy School and the 2010 US Army Peacekeeping and Stability Operations Institute on Mass Atrocity Response Operations (MARO).[62] This came in response to the recommendation of the Genocide Prevention Task Force (GPTF), as co-chaired by Madeleine Albright and William Cohen, which was addressed to the Secretary of Defence and military commanders, and had as its aim the drawing up of a military guide on preventing and responding to genocide, as well as that guide's incorporation into the policy, plans, doctrine and training of the Department of Defense and other relevant institutions.[63]

The MARO proposal was addressed primarily to the US Armed Forces, though possibly also those of its allies. Its main premise is that, just as armed forces prepare for traditional military operations or the fight against terrorism, so they must also have developed procedures for involvement in the prevention

59 See Feinstein L., Slaughter A.-M. (2004): 'A Duty to Prevent,' *Foreign Affairs*, 136–137.

60 Evans G., Sahnoun M. (2002), 'The Responsibility to Protect. Revisiting Humanitarian Intervention,' *Foreign Affairs*, Vol. 81, No. 6, 99–110.

61 Raymond D. (2016): 'Military Means of Preventing Mass Atrocities' in: Rosenberg S.P., Galis T., Zucker A. (eds.), *Reconstructing Atrocity Prevention*, Cambridge University Press, 314–317.

62 Sewall S., Raymond D., Chin S. (2010): *MARO – Mass Atrocity Response Operations: a Military Planning Handbook*, The President and Fellows of Harvard College, https://www.ushmm.org/m/pdfs/MARO-Handbook-091117.pdf.

63 Albright M., Cohen W. (2008): *Preventing Genocide: A Blueprint for US Policymakers, Genocide Prevention Task Force (GPTF)*, Washington: United States Holocaust Memorial Museum, recommendation 5.1, 87, 65–69, 120–127.

and combating of the most serious crimes. However, as the purpose of operations aiming to react to mass acts of cruelty is to stop genocide or other crimes, activation is foreseen once killings have already begun.

Equally, the authors of the concept agree that the use of force is the ultimate means by which the so-called Flexible Deterrent Options (FDOs) should be used. These entail diplomatic, information-related, military and economic activities aimed at interrupting the escalation of violence and preventing mass crimes. They include: crisis management; demonstration of power; pressure; the building of a coalition, as well as credibility of its being deployed on an international military intervention; media information campaigns; efforts to isolate perpetrators and discourage them from using violence; and civil protection.

If the given crisis is still not resolved, a full MARO operation is planned, with the aim of acts of violence being stopped and control in selected areas (re)established. The situation is to be stabilised, and responsibility delegated to local structures. Prevention and suppression of crimes should be achieved, among others, by securing large areas through the presence of armed forces; creating buffer zones between perpetrators and victims, or demilitarised zones; protecting civilian concentration zones, e.g. refugee camps; and exerting pressure on perpetrators through armed action, in order to overcome difficulties completely.[64]

The use of military instruments should mean the use of armed force only as a last resort. Each intervention causes losses in the civilian population and can be condemned as lacking humanity. All the more, if it is indispensable, it should be best prepared to match the given population. The usefulness of all these military instruments, both confrontational and positive, may be greater if they are better correlated with other instruments used in a given case.

---

64 The "Will to Intervene" (W2I) project, led by the Montreal Institute for Genocide and Human Rights Studies, was also significant for the discussion. However, it focused mainly on the issue of leadership and the mobilisation of political will to intervene: Chalk F., Dallaire R., Matthews K., Barqueiro C., Doyle S. (2010): *Mobilizing the Will to Intervene. Leadership to Prevent Mass Atrocities*, Montreal&Kingston-London-Ithaca: McGill-Queen's University Press.

Part Two: Case Studies

VII. Chechnya: An Attempt at Self-Determination

7.1. Background: Chechen independence aspirations and the first Russian-Chechen war

Chechnya came under the rule of Tsarist Russia in 1859, as a result of the Russian conquest of the Caucasus in 1817–1864. Since then, the Chechens have struggled for their independence repeatedly,[1] and have therefore been repressed by the Russian authorities and later by the Soviets. The dissolution of the Soviet Union awakened movements seeking independence. On 27 November 1990, following the other Soviet republics, the Chechen-Ingush Republic adopted a "Declaration of State Sovereignty" in which it defined itself as a sovereign state reflecting self-determination among the Chechen and Ingushian peoples.[2] One year later, Chechnya's newly elected President Dzhokhar Dudayev issued a decree "On the State Sovereignty of the Chechen Republic,"[3] which was to be an executive act to the Declaration adopted previously.[4] This act, confirmed the next day by the Parliament, was the equivalent of the declaration of independence adopted by the Soviet Republics.[5]

As a consequence of the proclamation of independence on 12 March 1992, a Constitution was adopted and, on 31 March, the Parliament passed a Resolution "On Chechnya Republic jurisdiction over military units". In May 1992, Chechnya refused to sign a federation agreement. However, Russia did not accept the Republic's right to self-determination and Chechnya was included in

1 Over the previous 150 years the Chechens had raised a total of 14 insurrections, Przełomiec M. (1997): *Czeczenia – niepodległość czy ograniczona suwerenność?*, Warsaw: Centrum Stosunków Międzynarodowych Instytutu Spraw Publicznych.

2 *Rossiya i Chechnya (1990–1997 gody). Dokumenty svidetelstvuyut,* Moscow 1997, 7.

3 Presidential and parliamentary elections were not held in Ingushetia, which decided to remain in Russia. In the referendum of 30 November – 1 December 1991 on the establishment of the Republic of Ingushetia in the RSFSR and the recovery of lost territories in favour of North Ossetia, 90% of the voters votes positively, P. Grochmalski, Chechnya. *Rys prawdziwy*, Wrocław 1999, 118–120.

4 On 12 March 1992, the Constitution was adopted, and on 31 March the Parliament passed a Resolution "On Chechnya Republic jurisdiction over military units."

5 Among the independent republics belonging to the Russian Soviet Federative Socialist Republic, Tatarstan also announced its independence at one point.

the Constitution of the Russian Federation as a component part.[6] As early as in November 1991 it introduced a state of emergency in Chechnya and then an economic blockade of the Republic. After unsuccessful attempts to subjugate Chechnya, the Russian authorities launched military action on 11 December 1994, with a view to ensuring control over its territory.[7] The mission was accompanied by serious violations of human rights and international humanitarian law, including direct attacks on civilians and torture, as NGOs including Human Rights Watch and Amnesty International reported.[8] They claimed that Russia, as the state controlling Chechnya, has the capacity to halt and prevent human-rights violations.

Chechnya's proclamation of independence was not recognised by the international community and the conflict itself was treated by the majority of states as an internal matter for Russia. However, the war in Chechnya aroused the considerable interest of the international community, as well as the world, and the Russian public.

The OSCE was the international organisation that tried to resolve the conflict. First of all, the Organisation, following the outbreak of the conflict, sent a Mission of the Personal Representative of the Hungarian Foreign Minister, Laszlo Kovacs – Ambassador I. Gyarmati. His task was to gather information on the development of human-rights issues and explore the possibilities for peace to be restored in the region. The report prepared by the mission called the situation in Chechnya a "humanitarian catastrophe" and appealed to states and international organisations for humanitarian aid. It also called for reconstruction of constitutional order and free elections in the Republic. The report presented at the Permanent Council meeting in Vienna on 3 February 1995 became the basis for a Resolution in which participating countries expressed their deep concern over violations of humanitarian law and human rights in Chechnya, and called for a ceasefire.[9]

---

6 Missala M. (2000): 'Bariery samostanowienia Czeczenii,' *Polityka Wschodnia*, No. 2, 89–91.

7 Modrzejewska-Leśniewska J. (1996): 'Konflikt rosyjsko-czeczeński (1994–1996)' in: Bartnicki A. (ed.), *Zarys dziejów Afryki i Azji 1869–1996*, Warsaw: Wydawnictwo Książka i Wiedza, 469–485.

8 See e.g. *Russia. Russia's War in Chechnya: Victims Speak Out*, Human Rights Watch Report, January 1995; *Russia. Three Months of War in Chechnya*, Human Rights Watch Report, February 1995; *Russian Federation: Armed Conflict in the Chechen Republic: Seeds of Human Rights Violations Sown in Peacetime*, Amnesty International, 31 March 1995.

9 *PC Decision No. 10, 6th Plenary Meeting*, OSCE Decisions 1995, Reference Manual.

A conviction as to the need for a permanent presence in the conflict region has been felt in the OSCE. However, negotiations on the establishment of the aforesaid Mission and its mandate were relatively brief, given Russia's sceptical attitude to the proposal.[10] On the Organisation's side, the talks were chaired by the OSCE President and his Personal Representative. They resulted in the adoption by the Permanent Council (on 11 April 1995) of the mandate of the OSCE Assistance Group to Chechnya.[11] That mandate was established for an indefinite period of time, covering the promotion of respect for human rights and fundamental freedoms, the identification of violations thereof, the strengthening of democratic institutions and processes, the restoration of local authorities, the development of new constitutional arrangements, and the conducting and observation of an election. The Mission was also to facilitate the provision by international and non-governmental organisations of humanitarian aid to the victims of the crisis, as well as to assist the authorities of the Russian Federation and international organisations in ensuring the return of refugees and displaced persons to their places of residence as soon as possible. It was also tasked with supporting the peaceful resolution of the crisis and stabilising the situation in the Chechen Republic, in accordance with the principle of territorial integrity of the Russian Federation and OSCE principles, with dialogue and negotiation engaged in, where appropriate, through participation in "Round Tables" to establish a ceasefire and remove sources of tension, as well as support for the establishment of mechanisms to guarantee the rule of law, security and public order.

The OSCE Assistance Group launched its activities on 26 April in Grozny,[12] with the initial focus being on the peaceful resolution of the Chechnya conflict. Under its auspices, a military agreement was signed in July seeking the withdrawal of Russian troops and the disarming of Chechen militants, as well as the release of persons detained unlawfully.[13] However, this agreement was not respected by any of the parties and the war was aggravated. The work of the OSCE Assistance Group was thus carried out under very difficult security conditions. For many months, it simply acted as an "international witness" of events, including mass human-rights abuses and war crimes, providing systematic reports on this subject. At the same time, it tried to maintain constant contact with the parties to the

10 H. F. Hurlburt (1995): 'Russia Plays a Double Game,' *Transition*, 30 June, Vol. 1, No. 11.

11 *PC Decision No. 35, 16th Plenary Meeting*, OSCE Decisions 1995, Reference Manual.

12 At first the group consisted of six persons, then twelve.

13 *First Round of OSCE Talks Concluded in Grozny*, OSCE Newsletter, May 1995, Vol. 2, No. 5.

conflict, with a view to this leading to talks in the fullness of time. Negotiations in Nazran with representatives of the Group (on 4–6 and 9–10 June 1996) led to the signing of two Protocols. The first of these concerned the ceasefire and the cessation of hostilities, as well as the conduct of free elections in the Republic under international supervision, while the second set up a Commission to release unlawfully detained prisoners and search for missing persons.

However, the above arrangements were not implemented. It was not until 6 June 1996, when Chechen fighters organised an attack on the capital and the two largest cities of Chechnya: Argun and Gudermes, that Russia made peace. On 31 August 1996, the newly-appointed Russian Security Council Secretary, A. Lebed, and the chief of the militants, A. Maskhadov, signed a political declaration in Khasavyurt on the principles of peaceful settlement of the conflict in Chechnya, as well as an agreement based on relations between the Russian Federation and the Chechen Republic. The settlement of the most controversial issue – Chechnya's status – was postponed until the end of 2001. The first Chechen War was settled on the battlefield.[14] The truce of Khasavyurt was replaced by the peace treaty concluded in Moscow on 12 May 1997.

The first war in Chechnya was very brutal. Over 100,000 people were killed in it, with the vast majority, probably no less than 80,000, from within Chechnya's civilian population. During the war, more than 500,000 people left their homes.[15] The capital Grozny was devastated, as were many smaller towns.

7.2. Institutions involved and instruments applied

The Peace Treaty of Moscow was treated by many scholars,[16] and especially by the Chechen side, as a *de facto* recognition of Chechen independence – the consequence of which was the withdrawal of Russian troops from Chechnya. However, in the absence of *de jure* recognition, the states decided not to recognise Chechnya. Such a scenario was also precluded for the Russian Federation, while

---

14 Przełomiec M. (1997): *Czeczenia – niepodległość czy ograniczona suwerenność?*, Warsaw: Centrum Stosunków Międzynarodowych Instytutu Spraw Publicznych, 3.

15 First Chechnya War: 1994–1996, Federation of American Scientists, Military Analysis Network, December 2, 2002, https://www.globalsecurity.org/military/world/war/chechnya1.htm.

16 Boyle F.A. (1998): 'Independent Chechnya: Treaty of Peace with Russia of 12 May 1997,' *Journal of Muslim Minority Affairs*, Vol. 18, No. 1; Kuźniar R. (1998): 'Prawa człowieka i stosunki międzynarodowe,' *Sprawy Międzynarodowe*, No. 3, 43–44; Missala M. (2000): 'Bariery samostanowienia Czeczenii,' *Polityka Wschodnia*, No. 2, 93–102.

leaving the issue of Chechnya suspended raised the threat of further civil conflict and suffering.

The organisation that naturally had the opportunity to engage was the OSCE, which continued its mission in Chechnya. The way to address the situation was to organise free and fair elections in which the Chechen people could express their will. The date of the presidential and parliamentary elections was set for 27 January 1997. The OSCE Assistance Group, with the help of the Centre for Conflict Prevention, guaranteed the technical side of the elections. Ballot boxes, ballot papers and special spray which marked the hands of voters to prevent repeat-voting were all brought in from abroad.[17] The registration of candidates and voters, as well as the election campaign, were also supervised. The Office of Democratic Institutions and Human Rights (ODIHR) sent 72 observers to the polls, and these visited a majority of the 437 polling stations, and monitored the vote count. The OSCE dedicated 600,000 USD from voluntary contributions from the participating countries.[18] Both the Russian and Chechen sides demanded the presence of international observers.

The election was evaluated positively, and the only complaint concerned the fact that refugees abroad were not allowed to participate in the vote. The winner of the presidential election turned out to be the main author of the Chechen victory, Aslan Maskhadov, who had already received 60% of votes in the first round of the presidential election. The parliamentary elections were not without their problems, however. In the first round, only five new MPs were elected and in the second thirty-eight. Thus, only two thirds of the Parliament – consisting of independent members in the main – were completed.[19] Strengthening the position of the parliament as a moderate, secularist body represented a significant challenge for the OSCE in the context of the building of democratic institutions, and at the same time an opportunity (unused) to delegate democratic values by, among others, facilitating contacts between its members and the outside world, as well as educational activities.

---

17 OSCE Prepares for Elections in Chechnya, OSCE Newsletter, December 1996, Vol. 3, No. 12.

18 OSCE Assists with Chechnya Elections, OSCE Newsletter, January 1997, Vol. 4, No. 1.

19 One of the reasons for the failure of the parliamentary elections lay in the presence of too many candidates – 784 for 63 seats. Most of these were independent candidates, while the rest represented as many as 36 different parties and groups. These were not Western-type parties, and their constitutions were not favoured by the Dudayev rule, or by the subsequent war.

After the election, the OSCE President stated that they had reflected the free will of the voters, and so legitimised the new authorities. In the meantime, two weeks before the swearing-in ceremony of A. Maskhadov, the previous Chechnyan authorities requested that the President of the Assistance Group, T. Guldimann, should leave Chechnya as persona non grata. As the reason, they gave the recognition of Chechnya by the OSCE as part of the Russian Federation. They demanded the changes in the mandate of the Group and the Chechen authorities' consent to its functioning.[20] Although the newly-elected President did not accept the decision of the previous authorities, and T. Guldimann participated in the ceremony of the swearing-in as one of the few international representatives, the incident augured badly for future difficulties.

In the months that followed, the activities of the OSCE Assistance Group focused mainly on the human dimension of the OSCE. One of the tasks was to assist the Russian-Chechen Commission responsible for locating and identifying the victims of the war. The staff of the OSCE Group helped in locating graves. It also bought the right equipment for groups dealing with the exhumation. The OSCE group also facilitated the exchange of prisoners and the search for persons lost during the war. According to the Chechen side, the Russians held about 1400 prisoners, 95% of them civilian, detained illegally in so-called filtering camps. On the other hand, the Russian authorities claimed that there were 1300 Russian combat veterans in Chechnya. The chief of the Chechen fighters, A. Maskhadov, admitted the presence of about 250 prisoners, but in reality most of the Russians were detained as hostages with Chechen families whose relatives were in the hands of the Russian authorities.[21] The OSCE Assistance Group set up a special office to collect information on the missing persons.

A large share of OSCE activity in Chechnya was concerned with humanitarian aid for inhabitants. This was important as most of the aid organisations, for security reasons, following such incidents as the murder of six employees of the International Committee of the Red Cross at New Atagach in December 1996, or the abduction of the UNHCR President in Vladikavkaz, Vincent Cochetel, on 29 January 1998, withdrew from Chechnya. The Assistance Group was, in fact, the only point of contact for organisations and institutions wishing to provide humanitarian aid. It prepared specific projects and then sought sponsors for their

20 Bloed A. (1997): 'The OSCE Response to Conflict in the Region,' *Helsinki Monitor*, Vol. 8, No. 2.

21 Report to the OSCE: The International Helsinki Federation for Human Rights Fact-Finding Mission to Chechnya, 1–11 October 1996, Vienna 16 October 1996, 3.

implementation.[22] Humanitarian projects were also implemented by the Assistance Group after its withdrawal to Moscow in December 1998. The most important ones included the Wheat Flour Programme,[23] rehabilitation programmes for children and deaf and blind people, funding the supply of medicines to hospitals and the reconstruction of heating systems in hospitals and schools. To alleviate the consequences of the withdrawal of humanitarian organisations from Chechnya, the OSCE Group provided local NGOs with support by coordinating their work and providing material support and know-how.

A difficult area for the OSCE Assistance Group concerned the implementation of the last point relating to the strengthening of the rule of law and public security. The issue of Islam and, consequently, religious Islamic law or Sharia, which has been the basis for legislative acts issued, was of great importance. Chechnya's Criminal Code was seen to contain a number of rules inconsistent with the Universal Declaration of Human Rights, the Final Act and the International Convention for the Prevention of Torture. Sharia law was introduced permanently in February 1999, with this tending to undermine both the Constitution and the legitimacy of the democratically-elected government, i.e. the Parliament and President.[24] It also contributed to an increase in numbers of human-rights abuses committed by the Chechen authorities, especially in relation to non-Muslim communities.

Progressing internal instability, including the development of criminal structures, was one of the consequences of the country's poor economic situation. A specific problem that affected perceptions of Chechnya abroad was kidnapping for ransom. The OSCE Assistance Group has repeatedly been involved in the release of abducted foreigners. The terrorist threat, the growing importance of radical Wahhabi groups and the fight between the President and the Opposition have had a major impact on the deterioration of the situation across the entire North Caucasus region.

As the only representative of the international community in Chechnya, the Assistance Group was the likely target of a terrorist attack, so OSCE President

22 Among other things, projects concerned the setting-up of children's homes, providing financial support and organising the delivery of medicines to the children's hospital and maternity home, as well as financing the supply of building materials, Annual Report on OSCE Activities 1997, 15.

23 Humanitarian Aid Activities of the Assistance Group to Chechnya after the Evacuation on 16 December 1998, Report of OSCE Assistance Group to Chechnya.

24 *Analysis of OSCE Long-Term Field Activities*, June 1999. 27–32.

Bronisław Geremek decided to transfer OSCE staff from Grozny to Moscow[25] in December 1998, due to the deteriorating security situation.[26] From that time on, the activities of the Assistance Group, apart from organising humanitarian aid, have been limited to monitoring developments in Chechnya (including as regards the state of human rights), as well as preparing reports. This was the beginning of the marginalisation of the Mission, and the importance of the entire OSCE, for the situation in Chechnya.

In September 1999, Russia resumed its armed operations in Chechnya, thereby prompting the OSCE to transfer local staff and remaining equipment from Grozny to the neighbouring Ingushetia, with this in fact paralysing any action.[27] The period from December 1999 to May 2000 was the time of practical inactivity on the part of the OSCE Mission, the staff of which remained in Moscow, with tasks confined to the preparing of "distance" reports only.

During the second Russian-Chechen War, the OSCE states were limited to exerting verbal pressure on Russia. At meetings of organs of this Organisation, they called upon Russia to respect human rights in Chechnya, to cease hostilities and to settle the conflict peacefully. The OSCE emphasised each time that the conflict in Chechnya was an internal affair of Russia, while the United States and the United Kingdom expressed their understanding of the methods inherent in the "fight against terrorists" used by Putin in Chechnya. The negotiations on the return of the OSCE mission to Chechnya were ongoing for months, but the lack of conditions to work on site prompted the OSCE to close it.[28]

Meanwhile, in 2001, the Committee on Conscience of the United States Holocaust Memorial Museum put Chechnya on the Genocide Alert list, giving a warning of potential crime. Such factors as the demonising of Chechens as a

---

25 It was on 16 December 1998, http://www.osce.org/ag-chechnya-closed.

26 The motives behind the withdrawal of the Assistance Group for Chechnya were not entirely clear. This decision could have been wrong and consequently could have had a negative impact on further developments. See Sammut D., Shields J. (1999): *An Assessment of the work of the OSCE in the Caucasus*, LINKS Report for the OSCE Review Conference, Istanbul 8–10 November 1999, 4–5.

27 OSCE *Annual Report on OSCE Activities 1999*, 29–30.

28 The group was placed in Znamienskoje, a small village in northern Chechnya, 8 km from the Russian border. This area was not war-torn and the main military base and headquarters of the Russian military was located nearby. The staff of the mission consisted of 2–3 people, while 24 security guards attended to their security. The mission did not have means of transport, and so had none of the freedom of movement necessary for its work.

social group in Russia, the level of Russian violence targeted against civilians, and historical experience were listed.[29] During the war, Russian troops used methods similar to those from 1996, i.e. mass bombing and artillery attacks on civil settlements, torture and filtering camps. The new pro-Russian Chechen authorities were also accused of violations of human rights, including mass disappearances, mainly of men. Chechen militants were also accused of using terrorist methods. International opinion was particularly shaken by the terrorist attacks on the Dubrovka Theatre in Moscow on 23 October 2002, during which a total of 173 people were killed; and at a school in Beslan on 1 September 2004, the result of which was the deaths of 334 hostages, including children.

The Council of Europe was another international organisation interested in the situation in Chechnya. Russia has been a member of the Council since 1995, and it ratified the latter's European Convention on Human and Fundamental Freedoms in 1998. Given the doubts concerning the fulfilment of criteria by Russia as it joined the Council, human-rights violations in Chechnya were crucial from the standpoint of the organisation's reputation. Unfortunately, the Council only took an interest in the problem after the Second Russian-Chechen War had begun.

Rudolf Bindig, Chairman of the Committee on Legal Affairs and Human Rights of the Parliamentary Assembly, put forward the idea that a procedure for the suspension of Russia from the Council be launched under Art. 8 of the Statute of the Council of Europe. However, states were not convinced that application of this measure would affect Russia's policy, bring an end to human-rights violations in Chechnya and prevent other ones, so they did not choose to deploy this measure. The Parliamentary Assembly only briefly suspended Russia's right to vote – in the period from April 2000 through to January 2001. It is thus possible to talk about very weak involvement of the Council of Europe in the face of mass human-rights abuses in Chechnya. None of the states decided to file a State complaint against Russia to the European Court of Human Rights. The lack of political pressure made it unlikely that the actions of independent and expert institutions would be effective.

The Secretary General of the Council, under Art. 52 of the European Convention on Human Rights, sent a letter to the authorities of the Russian Federation asking about the situation in the Chechen Republic. Referring the matter to the Committee of Ministers, he stated that the reply from Minister of Foreign Affairs,

---

29 Jones A. (2006): *Genocide. A Comprehensive Introduction*, London-New York: Routledge, 144–145.

Sergei Lavrov, was not satisfactory, and that a group of independent experts considered that Russia had breached the standards contained in the Convention. In response, the Committee of Ministers merely adopted a general statement (of 10 October 2000) asking the Secretary-General to provide regular information on the subject.[30]

The Commissioner for Human Rights of the Council of Europe, Alvaro Gil-Robles, effectively demanded the opening of a permanent office in Chechnya that would monitor the human-rights situation. In response, Russia set up the post of Special Representative for Human Rights in Chechnya, Vladimir Kalamanov. However, no exhaustive procedures were developed to deal with victims in a comprehensive way. The Representative's work was supported periodically by three experts of the Council of Europe who started work on 23 June 2000, as well as local staff. In practice, the experts did not have the opportunity to comprehensively monitor the human-rights situation, only acting in a technical role, supporting and training local staff. Despite the difficult working conditions and high costs of securing the safety of international staff, 12 local offices have been set up to report infringements. Through to the end of 2000, the office met 12,167 people and collected 5485 complaints and notices.[31] They concerned disappearances, arbitrary detention, destruction or confiscation of property, lack of payment, bribes and other problems. However, no further complaint procedure was established. The office could not count on civilian or military prosecutors. Abdul-Khakim Sultygov, the successor of Kalamanov, who took office in July 2002, denied human-rights abuses, such as the use of torture, and worked to ensure the marginalisation of the office and its closure in January 2004. By that time 9952 notifications had been filed.[32]

Another initiative of the Council of Europe entailed the establishment of a Joint Working Committee on Chechnya of the Parliamentary Assembly of the Council of Europe and the Russian Duma, which was to deal with the political arrangements in Chechnya. The first meeting was held on 14 March 2001, but since it did not assume the presence of the Chechen side, it proved unacceptable to it and its work could be considered controversial. The Parliamentary Assembly adopted numerous resolutions and recommendations on the situation in Chechnya. The most detailed document was Resolution 1315 (2003) of 29

30 Compliance with Member States' Commitments: The Committee of Ministers' Monitoring Procedures, Monitor/Inf (2004)3, April 29, 2004.

31 Council of Europe, SG/Inf (2000) 51, "Information Document", January 16, 2001.

32 Council of Europe, SG/Inf (2004): 3, "Information Document", January 16, 2004.

January 2003. It condemned the massive human-rights violations in Chechnya, and the lack of prosecution and punishment of war criminals; and it called upon the Russian authorities to solve the conflict. It also called upon Chechen fighters to lay down their arms.[33]

In a Resolution adopted in June 2005, the Parliamentary Assembly of the Council of Europe arrived at an assessment that Russia had made very little progress in meeting commitments made in connection with its accession to the Council of Europe in 1996, as regards the obligation that those responsible for human-rights violations should be brought to justice. The Resolution therefore called on the Russian authorities to take effective action to immediately put an end to disappearances, torture, arbitrary arrests and unlawful killings.

After 1999, Chechnya received regular visits from Commissioners for Human Rights of the Council of Europe Alvaro Gil-Robles, and Thomas Hammarberg.[34] They met with the main politicians and officials on the Russian and Chechen sides. In their reports, they pointed to mass human-rights abuses (even in 2007[35]), unwarranted bombings, torture, disappearances, kidnappings, and unlawful killings of civilians and human-rights activists. They levelled accusations against both the Russian side and the Chechen extremists, though such a "symmetrical" approach aroused the mistrust of non-governmental organisations. In consequence, The Human Rights Conference organised in Grozny in 2007 at the end of Thomas Hammarberg's three-day visit was boycotted by the most prominent non-governmental organisations in Russia, Memorial and the Helsinki Group, with these seeing the organisation of the conference as a legitimisation of Ramzan Kadyrov, a Russian-backed Chechen President himself accused of human-rights violations.[36]

From October 2004 onwards, the European Court of Human Rights begun processing complaints against Russia in connection with its activities in

---

33 Evaluation of the prospects for a political solution of the conflict in the Chechen Republic, Parliamentary Assembly, Resolution 1315 (2003), http://assembly.coe.int/nw/xml/XRef/Xref-XML2HTML-en.asp?fileid=17075&lang=en. See other Resolutions: Resolution 1323 (2003), Resolution 1402 (2004), Resolution 1403 (2004), Recommendation 1678 (2004), Recommendation 1679 (2004).

34 Report by Mr Alvaro Gil-Robles, Commissioner for Human Rights, on his visit to the Russian Federation, (in particular Chechnya, Daghestan and Ingushetia), December 7–10, 1999, CommDH(1999)1 / 10 December 1999.

35 Wingfield-Hayes R., 'Torture "Systematic" in Chechnya,' *BBC News*, 1 March 2007.

36 Kilner J., 'Rights Groups Boycott Conference in Chechnya,' *Reuters*, March 1, 2007.

Chechnya. Their scope attested to mass human-rights violations, for example, the unreasonable bombing of the Grozny refugee convoy in October 1999, the kidnapping and subsequent extrajudicial execution of five people in Grozny in January 2000, and disproportionate air attacks on Katyr-Jurt in February 2000. In its rulings, the Court found that the Russian government had violated many relevant articles of the European Convention on Human Rights, including in respect of the right to life, the right to property, and the prohibition of torture and inhuman or degrading treatment. It is difficult to judge how much such rulings could have a preventative effect on the Russian authorities. In many cases, the latter did not pay the indemnity required of them, while the unexplained disappearances of applicants in the cases continued.

The fact that the Reports of the Commissioner for Human Rights, as well as the Committees created by the Parliamentary Assembly of the Council inevitably suffered from a lack of co-operation with the Russian authorities that stood in the way of the investigation and prosecution of criminals prompted Rudolf Bindig to promote (from March 2003 onwards) the idea that an international tribunal be set up, and resemble those relating to Rwanda and the former Yugoslavia, in that it would investigate the crimes committed in Chechnya. The Assembly supported the initiative by adopting Resolution 1600, by 92 votes against 27, stating that it was proposing to the international community that an ad hoc tribunal for the war crimes and crimes against humanity committed in Chechnya be set up.[37] This initiative was unrealistic, in practice impossible to pursue, and it met with a negative reaction from Russia. Nevertheless, the Parliamentary Assembly also called on the Russian authorities to ratify the Statute of the International Criminal Court.

The European Union mobilised the UN Commission on Human Rights to address human-rights violations in Chechnya. In 2000 and 2001, for the first time in history, the Commission adopted Resolutions on the human-rights situation in a Permanent Member of the Security Council.[38] It related to the unreasonable and disproportionate use of force by Russian troops. It called on Russia to investigate crimes committed, and to use peaceful means and special Commission procedures: sending invitations to the Special Rapporteurs on extrajudicial,

---

37 *The Human Rights Situation in the Chechen Republic*, Parliamentary Assembly, Recommendation 1600 (2003).

38 Resolution of the UN Commission on Human Rights, E/CN.4/RES/2000/58, April 25, 2000, Resolution of the UN Commission on Human Rights, E/CN.4/RES/2001/24, April 20, 2001.

summary and arbitrary executions, torture and other cruel, inhuman or degrading treatment or punishment, and others. Under pressure from Russia, the Commission did not succeed in setting up an international committee of inquiry, which provided for the first motion for a resolution. Russia explained that it was conducting a national investigation that raised doubts about non-governmental organisations.[39]

In 2002, the majority of the Member States voted against the Resolution, accepting Russia's arguments on its fight against terrorism, which coincided with the sentiment following the attacks of 11 September 2001. The European Union attempted to adopt new Resolutions in 2003 and 2004. Provisions condemning Russia for serious violations of international human-rights standards, and calling for preventative action against torture and other human-rights violations were envisaged. In 2004, the Russian representative took the opportunity provided by the debate at the Human Rights Commission to call the motion seeking a Resolution an unfriendly act that favoured terrorists and those against Russia, as well as the entire anti-terrorist coalition, given that Chechen terrorists were said to be active, for instance, in Afghanistan.[40]

UN High Commissioner for Human Rights, Mary Robinson, was very critical of the situation in Chechnya. She paid a visit there in 2000, but did not have the freedom to move around its territory. For example, she was not allowed into villages outside Grozny where civilians were massacred, or to places of her choice.[41] However, she was able to visit the Sleptsovskaia camp in Ingushetia for internal refugees. On the basis of the talks, she came up with a conclusion regarding gross human-rights violations, such as mass killings and executions, torture, rape and plundering.[42] The Special Representative of the UN Secretary-General on internally displaced persons, Francis Deng, and the Special Rapporteur on Violence

---

39 'Chechnya: A UN Commission Resolution on Chechnya. Another Missed Opportunity to Guarantee Accountability and Justice, *Press Release*, Amnesty International UK, April 26, 2000.

40 Statement by the Russian Ambassador at the 60th UN Commission on Human Rights on the Draft Resolution "Situation Of Human Rights In Chechnya", Geneva, April 15, 2004, http://www.radicalparty.org/en/content/statement-russian-ambassador-60th-un-commission-human-rights-draft-resolution-%E2%80%9Csituation-hum.

41 Traynor I., 'UN Chief Ends Futile Chechnya Trip,' *The Guardian*, April 4, 2000.

42 Statement by Mary Robinson, High Commissioner for Human Rights, on the situation of human rights in Chechnya in the Russian Federation, UN Commission on Human Rights, Geneva, April 5, 2000.

against Women, its causes and consequences, Yakin Ertürk, visited Russia in September 2003 and June 2004 respectively.

The problem of Chechnya was also dealt with during the examination of Russian reports by the UN Treaty bodies. They called on the Russian authorities to allow in independent experts who could honestly investigate the violation of law. The Committee on the Elimination of Racial Discrimination expressed its concern about the ethnic conflict in Chechnya in 1998, calling for the perpetrators of violations of international humanitarian law to be punished and for the indemnities to be paid.[43] In 2002, the Committee against Torture classified the violations of human rights as severe, paying particular attention to the illegal temporary closure sites and filtering camps at which severe torture was taking place.[44] The Human Rights Committee expressed regret that the Report came with a four-year delay, and called on Russia to clarify the situation as regards major human-rights violations and mass killings of civilians taking place in 1999 and 2000 in Alkhan Yurt, Novye Alda and Grozny.[45]

7.3. Results and evaluation

Officially, the second war in Chechnya (known as the anti-terrorist operation) ended on 15 April 2009. Most of the Russian troops were withdrawn and the burden of further fighting with the rebels was taken on by local forces subordinated to Ramzan Kadyrov. Russia's victory was fuelled by a media blockade, the propaganda success entailing the war in Chechnya being put in the context of the fight against terrorism, and the successful internalisation of the conflict. A split in the Chechen independence movement was not without significance. Nevertheless, the second war was no less violent, and in some respects even more violent, than the first. According to various, divergent estimates, between 30,000 and 100,000 civilian inhabitants of Chechnya died. The number of refugees was similar to in the first war. Shortly after the commencement of hostilities, the

43 Concluding observations of the Committee on the Elimination of Racial Discrimination, Russian Federation, CERD/C/304/Add.43, March 30, 1998.

44 Conclusions and recommendations of the Committee against Torture, Russian Federation, CAT/C/CR/28/4, June 6, 2002.

45 Concluding Observations of The Human Rights Committee, Russian Federation, CCPR/CO/79/RUS, December 1, 2003.

number of Chechen refugees in Ingushetia alone exceeded that area's 300,000 inhabitants.[46]

Despite experience with the first war's brutality, and the awareness that the postponement of the regulation of Chechnya's status would result in further military action, the international community did not opt for adequate preventative measures. It emerged that the OSCE mission was too weak to play a major role in post-conflict reconstruction, and to restore dialogue between Chechnya and Russia. There was a lack of political support from participating countries. The decision to withdraw the mission from Chechnya to Moscow in 1998 deprived Russia's military action of any international control.

In fact, no other instruments were used, except for weak political and diplomatic ones. For example, at the OSCE Summit in Istanbul in November 1999, states criticised Russia for mass violations of human rights, but did not denounce it officially. No consideration of economic sanctions and military measures was engaged in (the latter of course being impossible given the risk of gigantic costs). States have not seen the need to expose their interests in relations with Russia. The media's lack of interest in the situation in Chechnya likewise combined with an indifferent public opinion to fuel this approach. Had it not been for the largest non-governmental organisations like Human Rights Watch, information on mass human-rights abuses in Chechnya would "never have seen the light of day" at all.

The example of the gross human-rights abuses in Chechnya has shown that, in a situation involving armed conflict with a Permanent Member of the Security Council, the international community emerges as very ineffective. In this particular case there was not even coordination between the various European institutions like the OSCE and Council of Europe. Neither did the European Union use its economic and political opportunities in direct relations with Russia.

Russia has always sought to play the role of sole arbitrator in conflicts involving the CIS. It referred with reluctance to any attempts on the part of international bodies to have an involvement on its own territory. It has also shown itself far more clever than the international community in its deployment of diplomatic instruments. With deliberate half-hearted cooperation with representatives of the Council of Europe, Russia could afford to perceive international

46 War Crimes in Chechnya and the Response of the West, Human Rights Watch, February 29, 2000, https://www.hrw.org/news/2000/02/29/war-crimes-chechnya-and-response-west.

standards of human-rights protection as no kind of constraint on its plans for – and in – Chechnya.

VIII. Rwanda – Prevention After Genocide

8.1. Background: causes and consequences of genocide in 1994

The 1994 genocide in Rwanda represented one of the most tragic failures of the international community. That was all the more the case given that mass murders had been taking place there systematically, especially in 1959, 1963, 1966, 1973, 1990, 1991, 1992 and 1993,[1] and that the main cause was as basic as ethnic divisions and the struggle for power. Colonial powers proceeding in line with the principle of "divide et impera," had divided the population into Hutu, Tutsi and Twa, as an entry in an identification document from 1932 confirms. As years passed, the privileged position the Tutsi managed to achieve in political and economic life contributed to growing antagonism.[2] And, as noted above, the first mass murder of Tutsis perpetrated in the history of Rwanda took place in 1959, following the death of King Mutara Rudahigwa. At that time, some 20,000 died, while nearly 100,000 elected to leave Rwanda.[3]

Following victory in the 1961 elections, Prime Minister Grégoire Kayibanda, founder of the Hutu People's Emancipation Party (PARMEHUTU) took office. He and his party had improvement of the Hutus' social standing as their key goal. In the 1960s, a policy of resettlement of the Tutsis to Bugeswar was pursued, with a view to their being separated from the rest of the population. Pogroms were again organised, with the effect that some 200,000 lost their lives between 1963 and 1972, while Rwanda was left behind by some 700,000 emigrants.[4] In 1973, a moderate representative of the Hutu, Juvénal Habyarimana, took over as President.

---

1 Preliminary report of the Independent Commission of Experts established in accordance with Security Council resolution 935 (1994), S/1994/1125, October 4, 1994, 12.

2 On the causes of genocide in Rwanda, see Forges A. des., Leave None to Tell the Story. The Genocide in Rwanda, Human Rights Watch, 1999, 31–140.

3 Zins H. (1986): *Historia Afryki Wschodniej*, Wrocław: Zakład Narodowy im. Ossolińskich, 304–305.

4 Zins H. (1986): *Historia Afryki Wschodniej*, Wrocław: Zakład Narodowy im. Ossolińskich, 306.

In 1985, Rwandan refugees in Uganda set up a Rwandan Patriotic Front. This sought to take power in the homeland from October 1990 onwards. It demanded equal treatment for the Tutsis and power-sharing. The Peace of Arusha, signed in 1993 in the presence of the representative of the Organisation of African Unity and the representative of Tanzania as a mediator, represented an opportunity to end the conflict.[5] Members of the Akazu clan opposed the agreement, declaring "the final solution to the Tutsi problem" and in *Kangura* magazine publishing ten Hutu decrees seeking to achieve extreme discrimination against the Tutsis in society.[6] Due to the radicalisation of one part of the Hutu, the implementation of the Arusha agreement encountered some problems. The downing of the aircraft transporting President Habyarimana then became a pretext for the extermination of the Tutsis, as well as any Hutu not wanting to participate in that action.

General Roméo Dallaire, Head of the United Nations Mission for Aid to Rwanda (UNAMIR), the mission of which was to implement the Arusha agreement, warned in October 1993 about the threat of civil war, and asked for support. He maintained that increasing the UNAMIR mission to 5000 soldiers would help to control the situation. The rising tensions were also signalled by, among others, the UN Special Rapporteur on extrajudicial executions (in February 1994), and the UNDP Mission.[7] Reports were ignored by the most involved on-site states (Belgium and France), as well as by UN institutions. After an incident in which Belgian soldiers were killed in Kigali, decisions were taken to withdraw international personnel and reduce the mission to 270 volunteers from Ghana. The mandate of UNAMIR was also limited.[8] Most non-governmental organisations also withdrew from Rwanda. Humanitarian aid was provided by the International Committee of the Red Cross and Doctors without Borders. On 22 June,

---

5 Peace Agreement between the Government of the Republic of Rwanda and the Rwandese Patriotic Front, January 9, 1993, http://www.incore.ulst.ac.uk/services/cds/agreements/pdf/rwan1.pdf.

6 'Appeal to the Bahutu Conscience (With the Hutu Ten Commandments),' *Kangura*, No. 6, December 1990, http://hrlibrary.umn.edu/instree/loas2005.html?msource=UNWDEC19001&tr=y&auid=3337655.

7 Davis R., Majekodunmi B., Smith-Hohn J. (2008): 'Prevention of Genocide and Mass Atrocities and the Responsibility to Protect: Challenges for The UN and International Community in the 21st Century,' *Responsibility to Protect. Occasional Papers*, 9; Feil S. (1998): *Preventing Genocide. How the Early Use of Force Might Have Succeeded in Rwanda*, A Report to the Carnegie Commission on Preventing Deadly Conflict, New York.

8 Resolutions of the UN Security Council, S/RES/912, April 21, 1994.

the French-led Turkus Operation was launched by the United Nations, aiming to provide humanitarian protection for civilians in the south of the country. It also allowed some of the perpetrators of genocide to withdraw. Only on 17 May did the Security Council decide to establish UNAMIR II, with 5500 soldiers, giving this a mandate to use force.[9] In practice, the mission was only deployed after the massacre in August 1994.[10]

Approximately 800,000 people died in Rwanda as a result of the genocide between 6 April and 17 July 1994,[11] while tens of thousands survived torture and rape. The genocide left 300,000 orphans and 500,000 widows. About 500,000 women were raped, with many later dying of AIDS.[12] As a result of the actions of the Rwandan Patriotic Front, approximately 25–30,000 Hutus were killed.[13] At the time of the genocide, one third of the Rwandans were displaced and about 3 million fled to camps in Burundi, Tanzania, Uganda and Zaire, among them Hutu fleeing vengeance. Material devastation of the state was a further consequence of the genocide. The theft of private and public property accompanied the massacres. About 100 million dollars in gold[14] was stolen from the state treasury.

Violence was finally reined in by the Rwandan Patriotic Front, which entered Rwanda from Uganda and took power in the state. In July 1994, Pasteur Bizimungu became President of the state, as followed in 2000 by Paul Kagame. Rwanda then had to deal with the problems of a traumatised, fragmented society, bring to justice about 120,000 suspects who were in jails, repair a destroyed economy and infrastructure, and rebuild the state administration. In 2003, a new Constitution was adopted, which contained solutions based on Western legislation.[15] The Constitution defined Rwanda as a multi-party republic with features

9 Resolutions of the UN Security Council, S/RES/918, May 17, 1994.

10 J. Bar (2013), *Rwanda,* Warsaw: Wydawnictwo Trio, 176.

11 Barnett M., *The United Nations Security Council and Rwanda*, Expert Opinion Paper "International Decision-Making in the Age of Genocide: Rwanda 1990–1994", June 1, 2014, 3 and sub.

12 Data from the Genocide Museum in Kigali and the National Commission on Unity and Reconciliation in Rwanda.

13 Forges A. des (1999): 'Leave None to Tell the Story. The Genocide in Rwanda,' Human Rights Watch, 1118–1119.

14 Kinzer S. (2008), *A Thousand Hills: Rwanda's Rebirth and the Man Who Dreamed It*, Wiley 181.

15 Constitution of the Republic of Rwanda dated June 4, 2003 https://www.parliament.gov.rw/fileadmin/Images2013/Rwandan_Constitution.pdf.

of the presidential system, and among that system's principles, account was taken of the fight against the ideology of genocide. Among other things, a ban on the creation of parties whose programmes are subject to racial, ethnic or tribal expectations was established. The prevention of genocide was to be assured by the National Unity and Reconciliation Commission created by Parliament in March 1999, as well as the National Commission for the Fight against Genocide established in 2007.

The Rwandan model of unity and reconciliation, which was intended to prevent crimes in the future, referred to common cultural values and assumed internal conflict resolution mechanisms, the building of Rwanda's sense of citizenship, good governance and the strengthening of the economy. The spread of a Rwandan consciousness was emphasised, as evidenced by the absence of personal identification of Hutu and Tutsi. Solidarity (*ingando*) camps, especially for students, returning refugees, former prisoners and local leaders, taught people to reconcile the Rwandan history adopted by the authorities and visions of the future. In addition, a traditional *gacaca* justice system was set up in which residents participated, with a view to the perpetrators of the genocide being judged, and local communities brought closer to reconciliation. Common public works (*umuganda*) were implemented, such as road cleaning, tree planting or house construction. A (*Girinka*) programme for the poorest families was also launched, involving support in the form of cattle. The aim was to reduce poverty and malnutrition by delivering 350,000 cows to Rwandan families by 2017.[16]

The mission of the National Commission for the Fight against Genocide was to prevent and combat genocide and its ideology, and to overcome its consequences. The Commission focused on genocide research, including data collection, documentation, debate and education. It was tasked with managing memorial sites and coordinating commemorations of the anniversary of genocide in Rwanda. In 2003, Rwanda adopted an Act on the Prevention of Genocide, Crimes against Humanity and Crimes of War, which lays down definitions of crimes, penalties and a ban on the denial of genocide.

Since 1994, the Rwandan government has been consistent in its pursuance of centralisation, the subjugation of all areas of life in the state, and the elimination of opponents and critics. This also involves narratives regarding the genocide and its commemoration, as well as history lessons failing to recall the victims of the Hutu. In practice, "the advocacy of genocide ideology" or "denial

16 Mudingu J., *Girinka Programme Transforms Livelihoods, Reconciles Communities*, http://rab.gov.rw/fileadmin/user_upload/documentss/article_about_Girinka.pdf.

of genocide" has been interpreted broadly, with individuals and organisations criticising the Rwandan authorities being accused themselves. This process affected, among others, the late Alison Des Forges – author of one of the most thorough studies on genocide in Rwanda, some-time employee of the BBC and Human Rights Watch activist.

The Rwandan state has also reduced the independence of non-governmental organisations, put an end to media freedom, and manipulated and subordinated the electoral process. However, the strong leadership of President Paul Kagame, elected to office three times (in 2000, 2010 and 2017) was designed to prevent ethnic violence and to promote the economic development of the state.[17]

8.2. Institutions involved and instruments applied

United Nations Secretary-General Kofi Annan, referring to the passivity of the international community in the face of the 1994 genocide in Rwanda used the term "the sin of omission", in this way giving his assessment of the many international institutions and states that failed to respond to the tragic events.[18] In 2000, Guy Verhofstadt, Prime Minister of Belgium, who coordinated the withdrawal of international personnel from Rwanda, recognised the responsibility of the state and international community, notably the United Nations, for the genocide.[19] This "sin of omission" has ensured a special place for Rwanda in the policies of states and international institutions. Can instruments developed following the genocide prevent another massacre?

In the first period after the genocide, it was essential that the situation be stabilised and the security of the remaining population assured. Resort to the military and diplomatic spheres was essential. States and non-governmental organisations remained concerned about a resurgence of violence, and appealed to the United Nations for on-the-spot involvement. Security monitoring was the task of the UNAMIR mission on the basis of the May Security Council decision. Its total deployment was of 5500 soldiers and 320 military observers in so-called north-eastern, south-eastern, southern, south-western, north-western and capital-city sectors, and was ongoing from October 1994 onwards. The first

17 Longman T. (2011), 'Limitations to Political Reform. The Undemocratic Nature of Transition in Rwanda' in: Straus S., Waldorf L., (eds.), *Remaking Rwanda. State Building and Human Rights after Mass Violence*, The University of Wisconsin Press, 25–43.

18 *UN Secretary-General's speech at a conference commemorating genocide in Rwanda organised by the governments of Canada and Rwanda*, New York, March 26, 2004.

19 'Belgian Apology to Rwanda,' *BBC News*, April 7, 2000.

task was to participate in the disarmament of Hutu fighters. The mission also had the duty of caring for the safety and protection of displaced persons, refugees and civilians. It established safe humanitarian zones, protected humanitarian supplies, and supported the laborious repatriation of refugees. In the following months it helped create police and military police forces.[20]

In the autumn of 1994, the government of Rwanda warned of the threat posed by armed formations loyal to the previous government. It also expressed dissatisfaction with the continuation of the arms embargo imposed by the Security Council on Rwanda in April 1994, while its reports indicated that weapons were easily accessible to Hutu operating in neighbouring countries. It also accused the international community of coming forward too late with economic help (donors were spending more on refugee camps in Zaire or Tanzania than in Rwanda itself – 2.5 billion USD as opposed to 572 million USD in the years to 1995[21]); and of being sluggish towards the perpetrators of genocide who had conspired from abroad against the new Rwandan authorities. Formally for security reasons, the government limited UNAMIR's ability to move freely around Rwanda. Cases of searches and acquisitions of UNAMIR equipment, propaganda against the mission on Rwandan radio and even demonstrations and attacks on UN personnel were numerous.

The Organisation for African Unity also saw refugee camps as the most major problem, capable of causing further destabilisation. At a meeting in Addis Abeba in September 1994, representatives from the OAU and UNHCR, as well as regional leaders and representatives of non-African donor countries recognised that priority should be given to security in refugee camps, that attacks by former FAR soldiers on Rwanda were likely, and that the presence of armed "refugees" in Rwanda's neighbouring states posed a danger to the entire region.[22] Despite this correct assessment of the situation, no further steps have been taken.

In April 1995, the Government of Rwanda decided to close the camps for internally displaced people (IDPs) in the Gikongoro region in the south of the country without consulting UNAMIR. Seven were closed in a peaceful way, but violence was applied on a large scale in Kibeho, where about 80,000 people were resettled. According to Doctors without Borders, about 4000 people could have

20 Resolution of the UN Security Council, S/RES/965, November 30, 1994.

21 Human Rights Watch World Report 1996, Rwanda.

22 See Report of the Organisation of African Unity: *Rwanda: The Preventable Genocide International Panel of Eminent Personalities*, July 2000, 229, http://www.refworld.org/pdfid/4d1da8752.pdf.

died at that stage, though the exact number is not known and could be much higher.[23] The mission of UNAMIR, representatives of which visited Kibeho, as well as the Special Representative of the Secretary General, tried to exert pressure on the government, organise transport for IDPs, and provide medical assistance. The civilians in the camps, being deprived of the trust of all sides, felt intimidated and were exposed to violence at the hands of both Hutu armed groups and government forces. An independent international inquiry committee consisting of representatives from Belgium, Canada, France, Germany, The Netherlands, the United Kingdom, the United States, the Organisation of African Unity, the United Nations and the Government of Rwanda stated that the Kibeho tragedy could have been avoided.

The closure of the camps necessitated organising humanitarian aid for some 70,000 people, over which the many organisations collaborating with the authorities included UNAMIR, the United Nations Rwanda Emergency Office, UN agencies, the International Organisation for Migration (IOM) and non-governmental organisations. Key challenges related to transport, access to water, food and the opening of medical points. The World Food Program distributed food to 420,000 people in May 1995 alone.

After the events in Kibeho, Rwanda began demanding that the presence of UNAMIR be limited, in the wake of an improved security situation. In June 1995, in this connection, the Secretary General proposed that the mission indeed be reduced in scale, with the mandate changed from a peacekeeping to a confidence-building operation. In Resolution No. 997 of 9 June 1995, the Council authorised a reduction in troop strength to 1800 over four months. It preserved the level of observers and police personnel.[24] Under the new mandate, it was supposed to provide good offices, assist the government in facilitating the return of refugees, support the distribution of humanitarian aid, train the police and secure international staff.

Refugees in neighbouring countries remained a major problem. The Security Council also called on Rwanda's neighbours to ensure that no arms would be provided to refugee camps for Rwandans. It recommended that the Secretary-General begin to consult with states over whether the deployment of international observers in camps was feasible. Both Secretary-General Boutros-Ghali, who visited the countries in 13–14 June, and his Special Envoy Aldo Ajello

23 'The Hunting and Killing of Rwandan Refugees in Zaire-Congo: 1996–1997,' *MSF Speaking Out*, April 2014, 229.

24 Resolutions of the UN Security Council: S/RES/997, June 9, 1995.

confirmed the uncontrolled flow of weapons, which could have a negative impact on Rwanda and Burundi. It was recognised that any destabilisation in any Central African country could have dramatic consequences for all states, so the S-G proposed to convene a regional conference on this issue. States proved sceptical as regards the ideas of the UN, however. The Bujumbura Action Plan embarked upon in early 1995 to resolve the refugee problem was augmented by a mission (ultimately ending in failure) comprising a group of "wise men", i.e. former US President Jimmy Carter, former leader of Mali Amadou Toumani Touré, former President of Tanzania Julius Nyerere and South African Archbishop Desmond Tutu.

Particular distrust prevailed between Rwanda and Zaire. It was in the camps managed by the United Nations Refugee Agency near the border with Rwanda that a large part of the majority-Hutu Rwanda Armed Forces was located (with about 230 political leaders, 50,000–70,000 former soldiers and about 10,000 former members of pro-government militias[25]). These all counted on regaining power in Rwanda, and their return threatened a continuation of the previous genocide. Furthermore, these forces organised expeditions into the western territories of Rwanda. The UN had no idea how to react to this problem. In defiance of the recommendation of the Secretary-General and the OAU, attempts were not made to separate civilians from militants and to effectively demobilise soldiers. States were not willing to expose themselves to armed confrontation with Hutu, while the UNHCR lacked relevant competencies.

When the Security Council decided (on 16 August 1995) that the arms embargo in relation to Rwanda would be lifted from 1 September 1996, the Prime Minister of Zaire warned that he would begin dismantling the camps and sending refugees back to their country of origin, at their expense. The compulsory expulsion of refugees began on 19 August; however, following the visit of High Commissioner for Refugees Sadako Ogata, the Prime Minister backed down from this policy on 24 August. During this time, Zaire managed to expel 13,000 people, and cause the escape of 170,000 refugees from the camps to nearby hills. The UNHCR was talking, not only with Zaire but also with Burundi and Tanzania. In these three countries, as of mid-1995, about 1 million, 155,000 and 600,000 refugees respectively were located. Their repatriation was a gigantic challenge,

---

25 Rwanda – UNAMIR – Background, https://peacekeeping.un.org/en/mission/past/unamirS.htm.

and took place slowly in practice. For example, in September and October 1995 only 32,190 refugees returned to Rwanda.[26]

The Rwandan authorities reacted positively to the abolition of the embargo, which for them denoted a possibility of armed Hutu formations in Zaire being dealt with. They decided to carry out attacks on refugee camps using the pretext of the outbreak of the Banyamulenge rebellion and the Alliance of Democratic Forces for the Liberation of Congo (AFDL) in Zaire. The report of the UN investigation team presented to the Security Council on 29 June 1998 revealed widespread cases of war crimes and crimes against humanity committed by refugees from the Rwandan army. According to the UNHCR, about 200,000 people may have died.[27] The refusal to grant humanitarian aid to some areas, especially Goma, contributed to the tragic situation. In November 1996, the Secretary-General of the United Nations called the Hutu situation genocide through famine.[28] Around 600,000 refugees – including armed Hutu – returned to Rwanda in this period.[29] They embarked upon another fight against the Tutsi.

Rwanda also engaged militarily in the Democratic Republic of the Congo, during the so-called Great African War of 1998–2008 (which involved eight states and left behind some 2.7–5.4 million victims, together with hunger and disease).[30] It organised rebellions against Congolese power and Hutu militias. This situation was exploited by Hutu fighters, who invaded the north-western part of Rwanda. The rebellion was suppressed at the end of 1999. Non-governmental organisations were tardy in reporting on mass killings of civilians. Data collection was hampered by the lack of freedom of movement in the area, and by the abstention of witnesses who were afraid to tell of the massacres. According to Human Rights Watch, tens of thousands of people, including civilians, were killed in the fighting, and hundreds of thousands of refugees returning to Rwanda were

---

26 Rwanda – UNAMIR – Background, https://peacekeeping.un.org/en/mission/past/unamirS.htm.

27 Emizet F.K., Bobb S. (2010): *Historical Dictionary of the Democratic Republic of the Congo*, Playmouth: Scarecrow Press, lxxviii.

28 Reyntjens F. (2009): *The Great African War: Congo and Regional Geopolitics, 1996–2006*, New York: Cambridge University Press, 96.

29 Human Rights Watch Report 1999, Rwanda.

30 Coghlan B., Brennan R. J., Ngoy P. et al. (2006): 'Mortality in the Democratic Republic of Congo: a Nationwide Survey,' Lancet, Vol. 367, 44–51, http://conflict.lshtm.ac.uk/media/DRC_mort_2003_2004_Coghlan_Lancet_2006.pdf. The first estimates from the International Red Cross even suggested 5.4 million victims, *BBC News*, January 20, 2010, http://news.bbc.co.uk/2/hi/africa/8471147.stm.

placed in special government-created villages in which security forces were to guard the newly created local security forces.[31]

The second area of international-community involvement entailed the monitoring of the human-rights situation in Rwanda, and the identification of violations of the law with a view to the perpetrators being punished. It was well-known that without this, permanent reconciliation and peace would not be possible. It was here that the first UN Human Rights Field Operation was commenced with, on the basis of an agreement with the government. It had the task of not only observing the situation but also assisting the people and authorities in the field of human-rights standards. Among the objectives and functions of the mission, there were the prevention of human-rights violations, monitoring of the current situation, investigation of human-rights violations and humanitarian law, including possible acts of genocide, cooperation with other international agencies to restore confidence and facilitate the return of refugees and internally-displaced persons, the rebuilding of civil society and the implementation of technical cooperation programs. It was also about helping Rwanda to rebuild justice and provide human-rights education at all levels of Rwandan society. Collection of evidence for the future tribunal was handled by a special investigation unit.

Many countries responded positively to mission demands. The Netherlands, Norway, Spain, Switzerland and the United States, the European Union and non-governmental organisations sent specialised staff, i.e. investigators, prosecutors, police officers and forensics experts, who professionally protected the evidence of the crime. However, the mission faced financial problems. At the end of January 1997, there were 130 observers working in the 11 offices throughout Rwanda. After the tragic murder of five people on 4 February 1997, observers were temporarily withdrawn to Kigali.[32]

In addition to the human-rights observers in Rwanda, there was a Commission of Experts appointed by the Secretary-General to the Security Council. Its task was to gather evidence of serious violations of international humanitarian law and cases of genocide. In a Resolution adopted on 1 July, the Security Council also called on all states and humanitarian organisations to collect information on

31 Human Rights Watch Report 2000, Rwanda.

32 United Nations Human Rights Field Operation in Rwanda, Report of the Office of the UN High Commissioner for Human Rights, April 4, 1997. See also: Howland T. (1999): 'Mirage, Magic, or Mixed Bag? The United Nations High Commissioner for Human Rights' Field Operation in Rwanda,' *Human Rights Quarterly*, Vol. 21, No. 1, 1–55.

crimes and cooperate with the Commission of Experts. A similar obligation was imposed on the Special Rapporteur on Rwanda appointed by the Commission on Human Rights, whose task was to investigate the causes of genocide.[33]

The Commission cooperated with countries bordering with Rwanda, as well as the United States, France, Spain and Ireland, as well as numerous non-governmental organisations, for example Amnesty International, the Regional Council of Non-Governmental and Development Organizations of Southern Kivu, Droits de l'Homme sans Frontières, the International Federation of Human Rights, Médecins sans Frontières, Nord-Sud XXI, the World Organization Against Torture, OXFAM and, as well as many others. Information, including lists of perpetrators and victims, was also provided by the parties to the conflict.

In the report, the Commission of Experts stated that persons on both sides of the conflict violated international humanitarian law and committed crimes against humanity. However, it called Hutu actions against the Tutsi genocide within the meaning of Art. 2 of the Convention on the Prevention and Punishment of the Crimes of Genocide. It called on the Security Council to ensure that perpetrators responded to their actions in an independent international criminal court.[34]

The appointment of the Arusha International Criminal Tribunal for Rwanda took place on 8 November 1994, pursuant to Resolution 955.[35] On 27 February 1995, the Security Council adopted a resolution requiring all Member States to arrest suspects.[36] The court was supposed to judge those responsible for genocide, crimes against humanity and serious violations of international humanitarian law on the territory of Rwanda; as well as Rwandan citizens responsible for such crimes on the territories of neighbouring states between 1 January and 31 December 1994.

The initiative of setting up a tribunal came from the Rwandan government, who believed that this body would guarantee a fast, impartial processes, and contribute to peace and reconciliation in the country. As a Non-Permanent Member of the Security Council, Rwanda had the opportunity to participate actively in

33 Resolutions of the UN Security Council, S/RES/935, July 1, 1994; Resolution of the Commission on Human Rights S-3/1, May 25, 1994.

34 Preliminary report of the Independent Commission of Experts established in accordance with Security Council resolution 935, S/1994/1125, October 4, 1994.

35 UN Security Council Resolution, S/RES/955, November 8, 1994.

36 UN Security Council Resolution, RS/RES/1970, February 27, 1995.

the drafting of the statute, which influenced some of the provisions, including the *tempore ratione*[37] of the Tribunal and its seat. However. when the Resolution was voted on, the Rwandan representatives voted against it. Their decision was justified, among others, by the exclusion of the Tribunal's ability to rule the death penalty against the leaders of the crime of genocide. The expectation of the Rwandan government for all detainees under the jurisdiction of the international tribunal to surrender was not met either. Since there was a division of responsibilities between the Tribunal and the national courts, it was considered unacceptable that thousands of ordinary citizens, mostly manipulated by their leaders, would be subject to the death penalty, while the greatest culprits would be punished with life imprisonment in the worst case. Despite these divergences, Rwanda agreed to cooperate with the Tribunal, which indicted 95 people and sentenced 61. Among these individuals was Prime Minister of Rwanda Jean Kambanda.

States sought to cooperate with the Tribunal in prosecuting perpetrators. Many of them, like Belgium, Germany, Sweden, Switzerland and New Zealand, extended their jurisdiction to deal with genocide, regardless of where or by whom it was committed. NGOs, notably Human Rights Watch and the International Federation of Human Rights, were playing an important role in this process, they consistently monitored human-rights violations both during and after the genocide, and mobilised the press, governments and the public to engage in recognition and the prevention of the genocide. They provided evidence and witnesses of the crimes committed.

In 2002, Prosecutor Carla del Ponte announced her intention to accuse RPF soldiers of war crimes committed in 1994. This met with major criticism by Rwandan survivors' organisations, as well as call for the Tribunal to be boycotted. The government imposed restrictions on travel by witnesses to Arusha, with the effect that 3 meetings were cancelled. The Court issued indictments against 93 people, sentenced a total of 62 people and sent 10 cases for the national procedure.[38] This was the first international tribunal to condemn people for genocide (Jean-Paul Akayesu was the first such person condemned), and the first to

37 The Rwandan government was of the opinion that the jurisdiction of the Tribunal should be extended to the period from 1 October 1990, so as to judge the perpetrators of the 1991, 1992 and 1993 massacres; and to 17 July 1994, when a Tutsi government took power.

38 The ICTR in Brief, http://unictr.unmict.org/en/tribunal.

recognise rape as an instrument of genocide. It was also the first to condemn the politician of the government, Prime Minister Jean Kambanda.

Rwandan courts have faced serious problems. There were about 130,000 people waiting for a trial and detained on prison premises intended for 12,000 people. As of December 1996, conventional courts had commenced with trials of only 1292 people. In 1999, there were 150,000 retained, of which 135,000 were accused of genocide, with 2000 sentenced. In 2001, in turn, the authorities decided to implement a system of *gacaca* folk courts.[39] The trials carried out by these courts have been criticised by some non-governmental organisations such as Human Rights Watch and Amnesty International. They pointed to the lack of a professional staff of lawyers (most people had basic education), politicised processes and bad conditions in prisons. The Tutsi-dominated courts were accused of bias. Cases of sudden death among judges were reported. Non-governmental organisations understanding the approach and supporting the training of the staff involved included Lawyers Without Borders, the Citizens' Network and Penal Reform International.[40]

Interest in the human rights situation in Rwanda, including the issue of justice following the genocide, was expressed by the United Nations Commission on Human Rights. In addition to the establishment of the mandate of the Special Rapporteur on 25 May 1994,[41] the Commission adopted a total of 8 Resolutions related to crimes and their consequences. From the outset, it was recognised that the central role of the UN's involvement in Rwanda should be for effective action to be taken to prevent further violations of human rights. It called on the states neighbouring Rwanda to prevent their territories from being used to destabilise Rwanda.[42]

In its Resolutions, the Commission referred to the consequences of genocide and related actions. It did not refer to new human-rights problems in Rwanda. The 1998 Resolution was an exception, in which the Commission not only condemned "continued violence and genocide in Rwanda by former members of the Rwandan Armed Forces, Interahamwe and other insurgent groups" but also

39 *Justice Compromised. The Legacy of Rwanda's Community-Based Gacaca Court*, Human Rights Watch, May 31, 2011; Clark P. (2010): *The Gacaca Courts, Post-Genocide Justice and Reconciliation in Rwanda* Cambridge University Press.

40 Chakravarty A. (Winter/Spring 2006): 'Gacaca Courts in Rwanda: Explaining Divisions within the Human Rights Community,' *Yale Journal of International Affairs*, 132–143.

41 Resolution of the UN Commission on Human Rights, S-31, May 25, 1994

42 Resolution of the UN Commission on Human Rights, E/CN.4/RES/1995/91, March 8, 1995

called upon Rwanda to hold liable "individual members of the armed forces" who, in carrying out military operations, committed violations of human rights and international humanitarian law.[43] The Commission regularly called on the international community to provide Rwanda with financial and technical assistance.

In 2001, the Rwandan authorities requested that the Commission end the mandate of the Special Rapporteur. However, on 27 June 2011, Rwanda issued a permanent invitation to UN special procedures. Among other things, an independent expert on minority issues, a special rapporteur on adequate housing and a special rapporteur on the rights to freedom of peaceful assembly and of association paid a visit.

After 2006, the UN Human Rights Council undertook a comprehensive review of human rights in Rwanda. The situation was dealt with in 2011 and 2015. Rwanda accepted almost all of its recommendations for the first time. In 2015, the HRC gave a positive evaluation of Rwanda's efforts to achieve economic and social development. However, it was concerned about the lack of freedom of expression and the weakness of independent media, political pluralism, the independence of the judicial system, civil society and other human-rights problems.[44]

It is worth noting that, after the genocide, Rwanda expanded its international obligations in the area of human rights significantly. Before 1994 it was merely a party to the International Covenant on Civil and Political Rights, the International Covenant on Economic, Social and Cultural Rights, the Convention on the Elimination of All Forms of Discrimination against Women and the Convention on the Rights of the Child. After the genocide, it ratified the Convention against Torture (2008) with the Optional Protocol (2015), the Protocol on the abolition of the death penalty (2008), the Protocols to the Convention on the Rights of the Child (2002) and the Convention on the Rights of Persons with Disabilities (2008).

However, Rwanda avoided the ratification of legal instruments that included the possibility of notices being submitted to treaty bodies, including the Optional Protocol to the 1966 Covenant on Civil and Political Rights. After a break largely related to the genocide and policy of the previous authorities, it slowly entered into cooperation with the treaty bodies. The Committee on Combating Racial

---

43 Resolution of the Commission on Human Rights, E/CN.4/RES/1998/69, April 21, 1998.

44 Reports of the Working Group on the Universal Periodic Review. Rwanda. Human Rights Council, Universal Periodic Review, A/HRC/17/14, March 14, 2011 and A/HRC/31/8, December 18, 2015.

Discrimination, as the first body after the tragic events, evaluated the Rwandan report from No. 8 to No. 12 in March 2000. It pointed out that the government focused in its report on the legislative and institutional aspects of the fight against racial discrimination and did not present examples of discrimination. The Committee assessed positively the efforts of the authorities to not refer to ethnic origin in speeches, official texts and identification documents. However, it was of the opinion that impunity was prevalent in Rwanda, especially in connection with violations of law by members of the security forces. It criticised the conditions in prisons, and expressed concern over the resettlement policy and the development of poorly-trained local defence forces armed with firearms and machetes. It warned against the possibility of a new ethnic conflict. It expressed concern over the intimidation of courts expressing a willingness to investigate cases of human-rights violations after 1994.[45] In 2000, the Rwandan report was also verified by the Committee on the Rights of the Child. It expressed particular concern about the situation of children – refugees, and cases involving minors under the age of 18 conscripted into local defence forces.[46]

In 2009 and 2016, the Human Rights Committee examined reports on the implementation of the International Covenant on Civil and Political Rights. The first one was delivered with a 15-year delay. It was acknowledged that the government had provided too little detail to enable the Committee to assess the situation fairly. The Committee acknowledged that Rwanda was still in a post-genocide reconstruction phase, and stated that a lack of sufficient success in social reconciliation threatened to destabilise the state. Among other things, it expressed concern about cases of forced disappearances, arbitrary arrests and the execution and impunity of police forces responsible for such violations. The Committee also expressed concern about the "large number of people, including women and children" killed by the Rwandan National Front after 1994, and the lack of wider judicial proceedings in these cases. It pointed out that the *gacaca* courts did not function in line with appropriate standards of judicial independence and the presumption of innocence. It stood up for the Batwa.[47] In 2012,

---

45 Concluding observations of the Committee on the Elimination of Racial Discrimination, Rwanda, Fifty-sixth session, CERD/C/304/Add.97, March 6–24, 2000.

46 Consideration of Reports Submitted By States Parties under Article 44 Of The Convention, Concluding observations: Rwanda, Committee on The Rights of the Child, CRC/C/15/Add.234, July 1, 2004.

47 Consideration of reports submitted by States parties under article 40 of the Covenant Concluding observations of the Human Rights Committee Rwanda, Human Rights Committee, Ninety-fifth session, CCPR/C/RWA/CO/3, New York, May 7, 2009.

the Committee Against Torture was considering Rwanda's first report. It in turn expressed concern about the existence of secret closure sites.

The UN treaty bodies have always expressed their understanding for the fact that Rwanda is in a post-genocide reconstruction phase, but at the same time it never passed over omissions and human-rights abuses after 1994. The UN expert panel recommendations do not have the force of law, however, and their impact on Rwanda has been moderate. Nevertheless, the authorities have made efforts to meet their reporting obligations. Equally, in recent years they have actually tried to loosen ties with the international system of human rights. In 2015, Rwanda adopted an amendment to its Constitution that prescribes the supremacy of the Constitution and organic laws over international law.[48] One year later, it withdrew its declaration recognising the competence of the African Court of Human and Peoples' Rights to handle complaints filed by individuals and non-governmental organisations. This was related to the complaint to the Tribunal by opposition politician Victoire Ingabire, who considered imprisonment for the negation of genocide unreasonable.[49]

Assessing the importance of international instruments applied in Rwanda, it is impossible not to recall the enormous financial support it received after 1994. This was based on a conviction that, with a higher standard of living, the likelihood of a repeat of conflict and mass crimes is smaller, with the effect that such aid therefore aims at restoring order, developing the state and preventing destabilisation.

Even before 1994, Rwanda was one of the poorest countries in the world; and the genocide simply caused economic collapse. That left Rwanda dependent on external aid for many years. As of 2008, international aid accounted for about 50% of the state budget, though in subsequent years this was down to some 25–40%.[50]

The largest donors included the World Bank, the European Union, the African Development Bank, the USA, Germany, Belgium and the United

48 Concluding observations on the fourth periodic report of Rwanda, Human Rights Committee, May 2, 2016

49 Bekele D., *Dispatches: Rwanda Turns the Clock Back on Access to Justice*, Human Rights Watch, 11 March 2016.

50 Zorbas E. (2011): 'Aid Dependence and Policy Independence. Explaining the Rwandan Paradox' in: Straus S., Waldorf L., (eds.), *Remaking Rwanda. State Building and Human Rights after Mass Violence*, The University of Wisconsin Press, 103.

Kingdom.[51] Most funds were donated through the UN and NGOs. The first need after the genocide was for humanitarian aid to be organised. In July 1994, the United Nations estimated the sum needed to conduct humanitarian programs at 552 million USD. However, a total of 762 million USD was in fact raised.[52] Non-governmental organisations played an enormous role where this aid was concerned, with notable NGOs here being the International Committee of the Red Cross, Save the Children, Médecins Sans Frontières, Oxfam, the Catholic Church, and the American and Norwegian Refugee Committees.

In the later period, funding was provided for the reconstruction of the state and the restoration of human rights. The Paris Club's decision to write off 67% of Rwanda's debt and allow a 20% conversion to investment and aid in 1995 was important as well. Through the United Nations Development Program (UNDP), funds were allocated for training, transport and the construction of prisons. The United Nations Development Fund for Women (UNIFEM) also funded refugee programs for female refugees. The initiative *African Women in Crisis* likewise served to combat trauma and improve the living conditions of women. The United Nations Children's Fund (UNICEF), in partnership with the Rwandan Ministry of Justice, took care of minors and pregnant women.

The European Union provided humanitarian aid via the European Commission's Humanitarian Aid Department (ECHO) – about 277 million USD up to 1995. Money was also provided to support the functioning of the International Criminal Tribunal for Rwanda and the UN Human Rights On-Site Operation.[53] Between 1995 and 2000, the European Union ran a financial support programme in Rwanda, supporting the development of macroeconomic structures, decentralisation, increased institutionalism, trust in public mechanisms and the rule of law. A similar programme in the years 2002–2007 involved electoral processes and the strengthening of civil society. There were also projects in support of agriculture.

The United Kingdom was one of the most important state donors to Rwanda. In 2006, it signed an official Memorandum of Understanding with the Rwandan government, in which it pledged to provide Rwanda with at least 46 million

51 Department for International Development, Operational Plan 2011–2016: DFID Rwanda, 2014, https://www.gov.uk/government/uploads/system/uploads/attachment_data/file/389305/Rwanda.pdf.

52 Progress Report of The Secretary-General on the United Nations Assistance Mission For Rwanda, S/1994/1133, October 6, 1994.

53 Human Rights Watch World Report 1996, Rwanda.

pounds a year for the next 10 years.[54] It implemented several projects, mainly supporting the development of the economy, education and refugees.[55]

In the first year, the United States provided assistance mainly to refugees in neighbouring countries – 408 million USD, for Rwanda itself – 243 million USD; and 100 million USD to Burundi;[56] then also aid for the functioning of the Tribunal and the courts. They provided Rwanda with development aid and military aid. For example, US soldiers trained Rwandan soldiers just before the invasion of 1996 and 1998.

Critical views on Rwanda's involvement in the conflicts in Zaire and Congo hardly affected the behaviour of donors at all, especially since Rwanda was included in the Millennium Development Goals programme in the year 2000. Between 2000 and 2007, Rwanda received about 3.7 billion USD in aid.[57] The World Bank, the International Monetary Fund (IMF), the African Development Fund and the International Fund for Agricultural Development decided to write off 25 million USD of the Rwandan debt. China allocated 3.6 million USD to Rwanda for development aid and redeemed 16 million USD of its debt. Germany gave 16.6 million USD, then the USA – $14 million in development aid and another 1.5 million USD for the Great Lakes Justice initiative. The IMF also allocated 12 million USD for a three-year plan to combat poverty.[58]

The European Union decided to give Rwanda 100 million USD, but eventually the sum did not go to Rwanda in its entirety. 1.2 million passed to NGOs and the National Commission on Human Rights, with a view to the *gacaca* court trials being monitored. Over time, the EU increasingly focused on human-rights issues. In 2002, it donated 155 million USD under the European Initiative for Democracy and Human Rights, an additional 4 million USD for local and international non-governmental organisations, and 1.28 million USD for the National Commission on Human Rights to monitor *gacaca* court trials. The

54 Hayman R. (2011): 'Funding Fraud?: Donors and Democracy in Rwanda' in: Straus S., Waldorf L., (eds.), *Remaking Rwanda. State Building and Human Rights after Mass Violence*, The University of Wisconsin Press, 121–122.

55 Department for International Development, Operational Plan 2011–2016: DFID Rwanda, 2014, https://www.gov.uk/government/uploads/system/uploads/attachment_data/file/389305/Rwanda.pdf.

56 Department for International Development, Operational Plan 2011–2016: DFID Rwanda, 2014, https://www.gov.uk/government/uploads/system/uploads/attachment_data/file/389305/Rwanda.pdf.

57 OECD data, http://www.oecd.org/dac/stats.

58 Human Rights Watch World Report 2002, Rwanda.

United Kingdom systematically provided much financial support, spending it for budgetary purposes, and sporadically also on human-rights projects. While still somewhat critical of Rwanda's intervention in Congo (in 2004, it even suspended aid), it occasionally referred to human-rights issues, as did the United States, which avoided taking public positions on the issue. Human Rights Watch thus accused the US Embassy in Rwanda of supporting no international organisation dealing with this issue.[59]

The African Union was also involved in the reconstruction of Rwanda. It supported the development of agriculture, which had a practical effect in improving the situation of the population; contributed to a calming of the hostile moods among ethnic groups and mitigated difficulties with the process of political and economic transformation. In 2001, Rwanda was included in the New Africa Development Partnership (NEPAD), which aimed at increasing agricultural productivity, economic growth in African countries and their contribution to the global economy.[60]

Criteria for development assistance include respect for human rights and democratic standards, but the Rwandan authorities had serious problems with human-rights violations, while standards of practice diverged considerably from democratic principles. States and international institutions practically failed to exert pressure through financial and economic instruments, although taking into consideration the degree to which Rwanda's development was dependent on the external aid, it could have been effective. Sporadic decisions were made to criticise the authorities openly and suspend assistance.

Thanks to international aid and the reforms and actions undertaken by the Rwandan government in 2000–2013, the annual GDP growth was 7.7%, which represented a threefold increase from 207 to 633 USD per capita. The Human Development Index for Rwanda rose by 17 places to 151st place among 187 countries surveyed. No other country in the world improved its position so much. Despite these unquestionable achievements, 63% of the population still had to survive on less than 1.25 USD a day, while 45% lived below the poverty line and 24% in extreme poverty.[61]

---

59 Human Rights Watch World Report 1999, Rwanda.

60 Bar, J. (2013): *Po ludobójstwie. Państwo i społeczeństwo w Rwandzie 1994–2012*, Cracow: Księgarnia Akademicka, 96.

61 Department for International Development, Operational Plan 2011–2016: DFID Rwanda, 2014, https://www.gov.uk/government/uploads/system/uploads/attachment_data/file/389305/Rwanda.pdf.

According to Eugenia Zorbas, four factors contributed to the high level of aid: the guilt and the unique character of the genocide, language friendly to the donor government, the need for a success story in Africa, and the support for the RPF in the United Kingdom and the United States, which acknowledged the concerns of Hutu militants as justified.[62] Rwanda made impressive progress post-1994. Centralisation of power translated into political stability, and there was consistent implementation of a plan to reduce poverty, achieve economic development and improve living conditions, as included, among others, in the document "Vision 2020" outlining the transition strategy of a state from a low-income economy based on agriculture to a middle-income knowledge-based and service-oriented economy.[63] It invested systematically in education, women's rights, environmental protection and infrastructural development. It was significantly different in this respect from other Central African countries.

8.3. Results and evaluation

The shock and guilt associated with the passivity of the international community before and during the genocide in Rwanda contributed to the significant involvement of states and institutions in restoring human rights and preventing renewed genocide. The scale of crimes and misfortunes largely outweighed the imagination and capabilities of international institutions. The United Nations failed to address the challenge of ensuring the security of a large number of refugees who were in neighbouring countries. Nor did it deal effectively with the problem of ex-Rwandan soldiers from the Hutu tribe hiding among refugees, Interahamwe and other paramilitary groups. They were not stopped or disarmed, and no monitoring of arms transfers was implemented. The UN was unlikely to be able to handle such tasks in this kind of complex conditions. States were not willing to face up to a military confrontation. The European Union believed that Africa itself should solve its problems and recommended support for the OAU

62 Zorbas E. (2011): 'Aid Dependence and Policy Independence. Explaining the Rwandan Paradox' in: Straus S., Waldorf L., (eds.), *Remaking Rwanda. State Building and Human Rights after Mass Violence*, The University of Wisconsin Press, 104.

63 *Rwanda Vision 2020*, Republic of Rwanda. https://www.greengrowthknowledge.org/sites/default/files/downloads/policy-database/RWANDA%29%20Rwanda%20Vision%202020.pdf.

over conflict prevention and resolution.[64] It preferred to provide humanitarian and development aid.

Similarly, the UN has been involved in humanitarian aid to a significant degree. The UNAMIR mission also provided on-site assistance, while it was less able to perform security tasks. UNHCR was involved in helping refugees, and the human rights operation in the field carried out specialised tasks primarily related to the monitoring of human rights. It can be said that there was a disruption in the proportion of humanitarian efforts at the expense of diplomatic, political and military instruments. Although the threat of destabilisation of the entire region was recognised in the case of the problem of mass refugees, there was no prevention of atrocity crimes during the war in Congo (which also reached the territory of Rwanda temporarily). Neither the UN nor the EU nor the OAU have had an adequate response.

Regional institutions in Africa, especially the OAE, did not have mechanisms in place to prevent and respond to serious human-rights violations. The OAE long avoided defending one or other of the parties in the 1994 Rwandan conflict, and never condemned the genocide. In June 1994, the Hutu authorities represented Rwanda at the OAE Summit in Tunis, where they met with no criticism. These moves caused a high level of distrust, which has plagued efforts in years following on from the genocide, and has hindered the implementation of diplomatic agreements.

The lack of interest in the region or the pursuit of particular objectives by countries such as France also hindered joint ventures and international cooperation. The Rwandan Patriotic Front has rather arrived at a conviction that, wherever possible, international institutions must deal with dangers independently. The international community respected the Rwandan authorities' competence to ensure security, and the concerns raised by the new authorities as regards the threats posed by the Hutu formation and the threats of continued genocide were justified.

In the long run, a hard time has been had in dealing with the Rwandan Patriotic front's violations of international law, and its destabilising action of the region. It proved difficult to work out a common approach for countries offering Rwanda financial assistance. The latter recognised the need to account for the

64 Council Decision on the common position adopted by the Council on the basis of Art. J.2 Treaty on European Union on the objectives and priorities of the European Union in relation to Rwanda, L 283/1, October 29, 1994, http://eur-lex.europa.eu/legal-content/PL/TXT/PDF/?uri=CELEX:31994D0697&from=EN.

serious and massive human-rights violations committed by the RPF; but the development and stabilisation of Rwanda were ultimately seen as the priority. In any case, no single approach could be agreed on, while it was not considered legitimate or morally right to make financial assistance conditional on Rwanda's policies, especially since its authorities proved successful in the sphere of economic and state development.

It is difficult to assess the contribution of the international community to the process of reconciliation after genocide. Rather, it is appropriate to recognise the limited capacity of the international community in this area, given its striving to provide assistance to survivors, while paying little attention to the issue of reconciliation. The International Criminal Tribunal for Rwanda was a more-concrete contribution to this process, and, although controversial, it was in many respects ground-breaking. However, the Tribunal's temporal jurisdiction was limited to 1994, so it could not deal with people involved in the earlier planning of genocide, or address the issue of war crimes or crimes against humanity in 1995 or 1996 as committed by both Tutsi and Hutu groups. Not everyone could have had the feeling that justice had been dispensed. The Tribunal's slowness was also criticised. It is difficult to assess the impact of the Rwandan reconciliation on the future, especially as regards the broad interpretation of denial of genocide. The lack of open debate on the causes and course of the genocide, on political exclusion and the instrumentalisation of memory may be a problem. What remains beyond doubt is that the institutions of human-rights protection still have to prove themselves.

Economic instruments applied were undeniably successful, while the level of international assistance was relatively high. The Rwandan anti-corruption policy and the introduction of good-governance solutions have made it well-suited, and have indeed contributed to the development of the economy and the improvement of the social situation in Rwanda.

IX. Côte d'Ivoire's Elections of 2010

9.1. Background: the fight for power

Côte d'Ivoire achieved independence in 1960, having earlier been a French colony. For more than 30 years, it was governed by President Félix Houphouët-Boigny (1960–1993),[1] who was replaced by Henri Konan Bédié after the election. He was the creator of the concept of pure Ivorianism. "The True Ivorian," both the candidate and the voter, could be a person of whom both parents were Ivorians.[2] This concept hit the Muslim minority in the North, representing 35% of the population, most of all; but also other ethnic groups living in Côte d'Ivoire for hundreds of years. Many Muslims came from neighbouring countries, mainly from Burkina Faso. They were treated like foreigners, did not have the right of citizenship, did not have documents confirming their nationality. They also had a worse economic position than the predominant group of Christians, or other ethnic groups.[3]

Electoral law eliminating a large part of society from voting was an incentive for power to be seized by means of a coup. On 24 December 1999, President Bédié was overthrown and power was seized by Robert Guéï, leader of a military junta. In 2000, as a result of partially-free elections (only 5 out of 19 candidates were registered),[4] Laurent Gbagbo became the President. He was another follower of pure Ivorianism, and led a policy of discriminating against minorities. Ethnic tensions, xenophobia and violence motivated by this all increased in the country. In 2002, due to an attempted coup, a civil war erupted. In December, anti-presidential forces united and formed the Forces Nouvelles (FN) under the command of Guillaume Soro. They occupied the northern part of the state,

---

1 See Ipinyomi F. (2012): 'Is Côte d'Ivoire a Test Case for R2P? Democratization as Fulfilment of the International Community's Responsibility to Prevent,' *Journal of African Law*, Vol. 56, No. 2, 151–160.

2 Klaas B. (2008): 'From Miracle to Nightmare: An Institutional Analysis of Development Failures in Côte d'Ivoire,' *Africa Today*, Vol. 55, No. 1, 109–126; Bah A.B. (2010): 'Democracy and Civil War: Citizenship and Peacemaking in Côte D'Ivoire,' *African Affairs*, Vol. 109, No. 437, 597–615.

3 About sixty ethnic groups lived in Côte d'Ivoire, Chirot D. (2006): 'The Debacle in Cote d'Ivoire,' *Journal of Democracy*, Vol. 17, No. 2, 65–66.

4 Freedom House Report 2006, Côte d'Ivoire.

causing its actual division. The southern part was controlled by the loyal forces of President Gbagbo.[5]

Battles then ensued to varying degrees. By the end of 2003, 700,000 people had left their homes.[6] There were cases of killings, collective executions, disappearances, torture and sexual violence. What is more, an atmosphere of impunity prevailed. There was no free media or independent judiciary. The country was heavily corrupted.[7] The Special Rapporteur on Contemporary Forms of Racism, Racial Discrimination, Xenophobia and Related Intolerance of the United Nations drew attention to the possibility that ethnic tensions might transform into a regular conflict.[8]

An interested in the situation was shown by the UN, AU and ECOWAS, as well as France. On 13 May 2003, the Security Council took the view that the situation in Côte d'Ivoire threatened international peace and security, and decided to send the United Nations Mission in Côte d'Ivoire (MINUCI) to facilitate the implementation of the Linas-Marcoussis agreement adopted by the conflicting parties; and to support the ECOWAS and French peacekeeping operations. In April 2004, this was replaced by the United Nations Operation in Côte d'Ivoire (UNOCI). Following the death of 9 French soldiers as a result of the government's attack on the New Forces in November 2004, the Security Council imposed an arms embargo.[9] Many African countries involved in the peace process included Togo, Mali, Angola, Nigeria, South Africa, Ghana, Senegal and Burkina Faso.

On 13 March 2007, a Peace Agreement was signed in Ouagadougou,[10] with this envisaging the creation of a Government of National Unity. Laurent Gbagbo continued to serve as President, while Guillaume Soro, the leader of the New Forces, became the Prime Minister. The parties agreed to hold democratic elections in 2008. The demilitarisation process and integration of the armed forces

---

5 Toungara J.M. (2001): 'Ethnicity and Political Crisis in Côte d'Ivoire,' *Journal of Democracy*, Vol. 12, No 3, 63–72.

6 'Côte d'Ivoire: 'The War Is Not Yet Over,' *International Crisis Group Africa Report*, No. 72, New York, 28 November 2003.

7 Transparency International in 2005 ranked Côte d'Ivoire 152 out of 159 countries surveyed.

8 *Racism, Racial Discrimination, Xenophobia And All Forms Of Discrimination, Mission to Côte d'Ivoire*, Report by Mr. Doudou Diène, Special Rapporteur on Contemporary Forms of Racism, Racial Discrimination, Xenophobia and Related Intolerance, E/CN.4/2004/18/Add.4, March 4, 2004.

9 Resolution of the UN Security Council, S/RES/1572, November 15, 2004.

10 Ouagadougou Political Agreement, 13 March 2007.

into the state, together with the identification and registration of all persons entitled to vote, were to be a *sine qua non* condition. According to the plan, the government's control over the northern part of Côte d'Ivoire was to be restored. The opening of the border between south and north was a positive event for the conflicted country. The process of registering and assigning identification cards started. It was the disarmament process that encountered the greatest difficulties, accounting for the rescheduling of the election in line with a modified deadline.

In June 2009, the Electoral Commission announced that over 6 million voters had been registered successfully, as opposed to the expected 8.6 million. In turn, less than 12,000 of some 30,000 New Force soldiers had undergone the process of reintegration.[11] The pro-government militia was not involved in this process. In February 2010, President Gbagbo unilaterally suspended the registration of voters in the north of the state, dissolving the government and the Electoral Commission, and in this way prompting mass demonstrations. As a result of clashes with the police, 5 people were killed. In April 2010, a new Electoral Commission chair and new Prime Minister were appointed.

Despite the incomplete implementation of the 2007 agreement, the first round of elections took place on 31 October. Foreign observers considered these relatively free and fair. The incumbent President Gbagbo received the greatest support, with 38% of the vote, while the second-placed Alassane Ouattara, from the *Rassemblement des Républicains* (RDR), was supported by 32% of voters who turned out.[12] Prior to the second round of the election, armed incidents occurred between units subordinated to Gbagbo and Ouattara. And, while the day of the second round of the elections (28 November) went smoothly enough, government forces and militias controlled by Gbagbo had attacked the Ouatarra quarters in Abidjan even before results were announced.[13]

It thus came as rather little surprise when, on 2 December, the Independent Election Commission announced Ouatarra's victory with 54.1% support. And, needless to say, President Gbagbo chose not to recognise his defeat. The loyal Constitutional Council then declared the elections in the districts where

---

11 *Freedom House Report 2010*, Côte d'Ivoire.

12 *Twenty-sixth progress report of the Secretary-General on the United Nations Operation in Côte d'Ivoire*, S/2010/600, 23 November 2010.

13 *Côte D'ivoire: Ensure Security, Protect Expression, Movement. Constitutional Council's Overrule Of Election Results Raises Risk Of Violence*, Human Rights Watch, 4 December 2010, https://www.hrw.org/news/2010/12/04/cote-divoire-ensure-security-protect-expression-movement.

Ouatarra won null and void. Both Gbagbo and Ouatarra were sworn in as President during separate ceremonies. Subsequent days then brought an escalation of the violence, a curfew was introduced and foreign media coverage banned.

Ethnic conflict overlapped with this power struggle. Persons from neighbouring countries and Ivorians belonging to the Malinke, Dioula and Senoufo groups supported Alassane Ouattara, while Guéré and Bété people supported former President Gbagbo. Troops under Gbagbo led a blockade of the hotel in which Ouatarra was staying, albeit protected by French and the UN forces. There was a clash between the forces subordinated to the two candidates which turned into civil war. There were also attacks on the UN forces that supported Ouatarra when the New Forces, subordinated to him, took control of the territory. Finally, Gbagbo was detained on 11 April, and the inauguration ceremony for the Ouatarra Presidency took place on 21 May 2011.[14]

9.2. Institutions involved and instruments applied

Due to the presence of international organisations and the systematic monitoring of the dynamics of events, the international community had a good grasp on the internal situation in Côte d'Ivoire. Regular reports were presented by the Secretary-General of the United Nations and the High Commissioner for Human Rights. The UNOCI mission, which was authorised by the Security Council and included a division on human rights and the French army, was present on site. It was considered that a fair election process and full implementation of the Ouagadougou Agreement could have stabilised the situation in the state. The president of Burkina Faso, Blaise Compaoré, was the moderator of the electoral process, which was observed by 300 observers from the African Union, Carter Centre, Economic Community of West African States, West African Economic and Monetary Union and International Organisation of La Francophonie. They appreciated the course of the second round of the election, noting the few incidents that in their opinion did not affect the final result.

At a press conference on 3 December, the Special Representative of the UN Secretary-General confirmed the election results according to the announcement of the Independent Election Commission.[15] In October 2011, the

14 *Twenty-eighth Report of the Secretary-General on the United Nations Operation in Côte d'Ivoire*, S/2011/387, June 24, 2011.

15 *Twenty-seventh Progress Report of the Secretary-General on the United Nations Operation in Côte d'Ivoire*, S/2011/211, 30 March 2011. Other reports by the UN

Secretary-General warned that militias would threaten the electoral process and announced the need for the UNOCI Mission to cooperate with state institutions to ensure the security of Ivorians.[16]

As Gbagbo contested the election results, an unsuccessful mediation attempt was made by South African President Thabo Mbeki. On 7 December, the Economic Community of West African States, invoking Art. 45 of the Protocol on Democracy and Good Governance, imposed sanctions on Côte d'Ivoire, including suspension of its participation in the decision-making process. It also issued a declaration of recognition of the results of the election in line with the announcement of the Independent Election Commission. On 10 December, the African Union Peace and Security Council acted in a similar way. It suspended Côte d'Ivoire from all activities within the organisation until Alassane Ouattara took power.

Both organisations undertook diplomatic initiatives. The UA decided to entrust mediation to previously-involved South African President Thabo Mbeki. The ECOWAS leaders, who did not rule out the use of force if Gbagbo did not give up peacefully, were also involved in a peaceful resolution of the dispute.[17] President Gbagbo maintained that he was ready to negotiate and share power, but Alassane Ouattara rejected the possibility of embarking upon talks before Gbagbo resigned from office. Further initiatives by the AU failed as well: the appointment of the AU Special Representative, Prime Minister of Kenya Raille Odinge, and the establishment of the High-Level Panel on the Resolution of the Crisis in Côte d'Ivoire, set up on 28 January.[18] The Panel was to negotiate a division of power between the Gbagbo and Ouattara camps and the establishment of a Government of National Unity. Despite an amnesty with security and preservation of property being offered to Gbagbo (the US was among those offering a place to stay), his position remained virtually unchanged.

Secretary-General on the Côte d'Ivoire: https://peacekeeping.un.org/en/mission/past/unoci/reports.shtml.

16 *Progress Report of the Secretary-General on the United Nations Operation in Côte d'Ivoire*, S/2010/537, October 18, 2010.

17 ECOWAS Press Releases (2011) *Press Statement by the President of the ECOWAS Commission on the Current Crisis in Cote d'Ivoire URL*: http://news.ecowas.int/presseshow.php?nb=015&lang=en&annee=2011.

18 See the Report of the High-Level Panel on the Resolution of the Crisis in Côte d'Ivoire, 31 January 2011, http://allafrica.com/stories/201101311908.html; Cook N. (2011): 'Cote d'Ivoire Post-Gbagbo: Crisis Recovery,' *International Reactions*, 30–45.

The European Union also responded to the events. The High Representative of the Union for Foreign Affairs and Security Policy, Baroness Catherine Ashton, called for a peaceful transfer of power. On 13 December 2010, the Council of the European Union decided to impose sanctions. These included a ban on entry into the EU and the freezing of financial assets in respect of Laurent Gbagbo and his associates. The Council called on all parties to resolve the crisis peacefully and ensure the security of the population. It warned that the violent would be held accountable for their actions.[19] The United States, the Central Bank of West African States and the West African Monetary and Economic Union also joined in with the sanctions, and blocked President Gbagbo and his associates from accessing assets, and from representing their state in institutions.

In the absence of cooperation from Gbagbo, international sanctions were sharpened. The Council of the European Union tightened visa sanctions for another six persons and also cut off the financing of the state administration controlled by Gbagbo by freezing the financial assets of two banks (the Savings Bank of Cote d'Ivoire and Housing Bank of Cote d'Ivoire). The sanctions were backed by Alassane Ouattara. He also suggested that large trading companies introduce an embargo on cocoa and coffee from Côte d'Ivoire.

The difficulties in the transfer of power resulted in clashes between the forces loyal to Gbagbo and Ouatarra. The situation regarding human rights deteriorated. The United Nations High Commissioner for Human Rights Navanethem Pillay sounded the alarm. On 19 December, it was reported that hundreds of people had been abducted from their homes by strikers in uniforms. The Commissioner referred to some 50 people being killed, and more than 200 injured, and also reported evidence of massive human-rights violations.[20] The UN Human Rights Council convened a special session on 23 December chaired by a group of African countries. It condemned human-rights abuses, including abduction, extrajudicial killings, arbitrary detentions, sexual violence, violation of freedom of assembly, and destruction of property.[21] On 28 December UNHCR reported 20,000 Ivorian refugees in Liberia, and three days later the presence of

---

19 *Council Conclusions on Côte d'Ivoire*, 3058th Foreign Affairs Council meeting Brussels, December 13, 2010, http://www.consilium.europa.eu/uedocs/cms_data/docs/pressdata/EN/foraff/118442.pdf.

20 'Hundreds Abducted' in Ivory Coast Election Unrest – UN,' *BBC News*, December 19, 2010.

21 Resolution of the UN Human Rights Council A/HRC/RES/S-14/1, January 4, 2011.

mass graves in the vicinity of Abidjan and Gangoa.[22] The Ambassador of Côte d'Ivoire to the UN Youssouf Bamba called for action to prevent violence. On 29 December 2010, he called upon the organisation to "be credible". He claimed that mass human-rights violations were being committed in the state, and that there was a threat of genocide.[23]

The Global Centre for the Responsibility to Protect issued a December alert regarding the threat of mass crimes.[24] Special Adviser on the Prevention of Genocide, Francis Deng, and Special Adviser on the Responsibility to Protect, Edward Luck, highlighted serious violations of human rights, the use of hate speech, and incitement to violence for political purposes. They stated that, in the light of the recent conflict, the above-mentioned approach was irresponsible. They were extremely worried about reports of the destruction of the homes of political opponents of Gbagbo in Abidjan. The Special Advisers reminded the parties to the conflict of their responsibility to protect all people, irrespective of their ethnicity, nationality and religion.[25]

The second press conference of 19 January 2011 warned explicitly against possible genocide, crimes against humanity, ethnic cleansing or war crimes. These possibilities were suggested by the hasty recruitment to the armed forces and groups of militia of members of different ethnic groups, as well as incidents of hate speech, the encouragement of attacks and refugee flows: 23,500 inhabitants had apparently fled to neighbouring countries, while a further 16,000 were identified as internal refugees. The Advisers called on all parties to the conflict to uphold their responsibility to protect, and warned about criminal liability in the cases of all involved in crimes.[26]

The Special Advisers' warnings produced no breakthrough vis-à-vis involvement of the international community, which had long been monitoring events

---

22 UN High Commissioner for Refugees, *UNHCR to establish new camp in Liberia for refugees from Côte d'Ivoire*, December 31, 2010, https://www.unhcr.org/news/press/2010/12/4d1dd09b9/unhcr-establish-new-camp-liberia-refugees-cote-divoire.html.

23 'Ivory Coast UN Ambassador Warns of Genocide Risk,' *BBC News*, December 30, 2010.

24 *Open Statement on the Situation in Côte d'Ivoire,* Global Centre for the Responsibility to Protect, December 17, 2010.

25 *UN Secretary-General's Special Advisers on the Prevention of Genocide and the Responsibility to Protect on the Situation in Côte d'Ivoire*, UN Press Release, December 29, 2010 and January 19, 2011.

26 *Statement attributed to the UN Secretary-General's Special Advisers on the Prevention of Genocide and the Responsibility to Protect on the Situation in Côte d'Ivoire*, Geneva, January 19, 2011.

in Côte d'Ivoire and trying to stabilise the situation. However, they provided an impetus for the correction of the instruments used, in particular sanctions and military instruments.

The UN Security Council dealt with the situation in Côte d'Ivoire on a regular basis. On 20 December, it adopted a Resolution calling on all parties to recognise Alassane Ouattara as the winner of the election, and instructed the Secretary General, also through his Special Representative, to facilitate political dialogue. It condemned the violence against civilians and called on all parties to ensure their protection and to lead the perpetrators of breaches to liability. The resolution also mentions stopping violence, and preventing and protecting civilians from all forms of sexual violence.

The military instruments resorted to prove to be of key importance. A decision was made to extend UNOCI's mandate and reinforce the deployment of three United Nations Infantry Divisions from the United Nations Mission in Liberia (UNMIL), two helicopters and 500 personnel (400 soldiers and 100 policemen).[27] UNOCI was to support the peace process, including work to complete the electoral process; and to engage in the implementation of the 2007 Peace Agreement concerning the reunification of the state, restoration of state power throughout the territory, disarmament, demobilisation and reintegration of former militants, strengthening the institution of law, reforming the security sector, and promoting and protecting human rights with particular regard to the situation of children and women. What was important, UNOCI was authorised to use all necessary means to perform its tasks, including the protection of civilians.[28] On 19 January, it was decided to increase the number of UNOCI soldiers from 9000 to 11,000, and to transfer two military helicopters and three helicopter crews from Liberia.[29] In subsequent months, the mandate of the operation was adjusted to the changing situation, including monitoring of the border with Liberia, supporting power in the demobilisation of militants and monitoring compliance with the arms embargo.[30]

To prevent mass human-rights violations, the Security Council also demanded a cessation of the use of the media, especially RTI (*Radiodiffusion Télévision Ivoire*) in hate speech, incitement to violence and the dissemination of false

27 Resolution of the UN Security Council S/RES/1951, November 24, 2010.

28 Resolution of the UN Security Council S/RES/1962, December 20, 2010.

29 Resolutions of the UN Security Council S/RES/1967, January 19, 2011, S/RES/1967, February 16, 2011.

30 Resolutions of the UN Security Council S/RES/1980, April 18, 2011.

information. The Security Council also applied the threat of imposing sanctions on people who did not recognise the results of the presidential election, as was finally done with respect to Laurent Gbagbo and his closest associates under Resolution 1975 of 30 March 2011.[31]

From the beginning of the post-election crisis, numerous institutions had warned Parties as to their liability for violations of human rights and international humanitarian law. Among them there were the Security Council, the Human Rights Council and UN High Commissioner for Human Rights. Proof regarding crimes was thus collected by the Committee on Human Rights formed in March 2011, the UN Expert Group and UNOCI. On 1 January, President Ouattara asked the International Criminal Court to investigate cases of mass crimes.

9.3. Results and evaluation

The takeover of Côte d'Ivoire by troops under Ouattara, and the detainment of Gbagbo, made it possible to end the conflict and stabilise the situation. On 11 December 2011, free and fair legislative elections were held, as an important step in restoring law enforcement in the state.

According to UN estimates, the post-election conflict cost the lives of at least 3000 people. The Secretary-General, in a Report to the Security Council dated 24 June 2011, reported half a million refugees;[32] while – on 1 July 2011 – the International Commission of Inquiry presented the Human Rights Council with a figure of 700,000.[33]

While as of February 2011, only the troops loyal to Laurent Gbagbo were using violence, in the following months massacres were carried out by both parties.[34] Militia and militant groups under Gbagbo carried out attacks against civilians from Ouattara support groups. For example, the Secretary General reported that 130 people had been killed in Bloléquin and Bédi-Goazon. According to Freedom House, the Ouattara forces were responsible for the largest single crime, which was perpetrated in Duékoué in March 2011, and involved the killing of no fewer than 1000.[35]

---

31 Resolution of the UN Security Council No. 1975, March 30, 2011.

32 *Twenty-eighth Report of the Secretary-General on the United Nations Operation in Côte d'Ivoire*, S/2011/387, June 24, 2011.

33 *Report of the International Commission of Inquiry on Côte d'Ivoire*, A/HRC/17/48, July 1, 2011.

34 Human Rights Watch World Report 2012, Côte d'Ivoire.

35 Freedom House Report 2012, Côte d'Ivoire.

The International Commission of Inquiry considered the violations of human rights in Côte d'Ivoire to be mass and serious. It did not preclude certain acts – especially FDS attacks on the districts of Abidjan – being qualified as crimes against humanity and war crimes. It reported on killings, collective executions, torture, rape, arbitrary detentions, looting and the involvement of child soldiers. It noted that, even after Gbagbo's detention, violations continued, mostly against his followers.

The Commission called on the authorities to guarantee liability for infringements that had occurred. On 13 September 2011, a Commission of Inquiry was launched to investigate the crimes committed; and on 28 September the Commission for Dialogue, Truth and Reconciliation began its work. Both Commissions were set up and controlled by President Ouattara, which raised doubts as regards independence and integrity. Research into the possibility of crimes having been committed was also initiated by the International Criminal Court. It then indicted former President Laurent Gbagbo, who was transferred to The Hague in November 2011, as well as Charles Blé Goudé, a military commander, and Simon Gbagbo, the former President's wife. This was done despite the existence of a process domestically.

The international community's efforts to stabilise the situation in Côte d'Ivoire have been very long lasting. International institutions drew conclusions from the short history of the state characterised by the constant struggle for power, especially after the death of President Félix Houphouët-Boigny, ethnic tensions, land disputes, a high level of corruption, and constant human-rights violations. Côte d'Ivoire was a country proving moderately cooperative with the UN human-rights institutions. It was selective in providing reports to treaty bodies, and proved only a reluctant implementer of recommendations received.[36]

Considering that during the 2000 elections, 200 people were aware that the next difficult-to-organise elections could be a factor that would cause massive human-rights violations and would trigger another long civil war, reaction to the crisis associated with Gbagbo's unwillingness to hand over power was actually rather rapid. The staunchness of states and international institutions also reflected a lack of satisfactory results with bringing about the rule of law and respect for human rights, as well as significant delays with the organisation of elections. The international community was determined to enforce the election

36 In January 2010 the UN Human Rights Council published a Report on the human rights situation in Côte d'Ivoire. 108 recommendations were issued: *Report of the Working Group on the Universal Periodic Review*, A/HRC/13/9, January 4, 2010.

results, and also took seriously the warnings from non-governmental and intergovernmental organisations regarding likely mass violations of human rights and atrocity crimes.

Numerous diplomatic instruments were used, so President Gbagbo received many opportunities for peaceful submission and the avoidance of sanctions. However, he remained impassive in his position. Greater African unity (as opposed to countries like Gambia supporting Gbagbo's position) might have combined with better coordination between the AU, ECOWAS and the UN to bring greater efficiency where diplomatic initiatives were concerned.[37]

The Security Council played a positive role in this case, for it responded quickly and flexibly to the changing situation. The UNOCI operation under Resolution 1975 can be considered of key importance when it comes to possible means by which civil protection might be safeguarded. It was primarily about the destruction of heavy weapons being sued against civilians, and UNOCI played an important role in that, while also helping with the evacuation of civilians and providing medical care. At the end of the conflict, its local involvement continued, thereby contributing to the stabilisation of the situation and a slow rise in human-rights standards.

The regional and UN organisations' willingness to take one side in the conflict, both politically and militarily, was quite controversial, as it resulted in accusations of partiality of the international community. The International Criminal Court also charged only one party – the former President and his co-workers, but finally Gbagbo was acquitted in 2019. For, despite the UN declaration, Ouattara supporters responsible for serious human-rights violations and crimes were not punished.[38]

---

37 'Responsibility to Protect after Libya and Côte D'Ivoire,' *Background Briefing*, Global Centre for the Responsibility to Protect, 5.

38 Bmeki T. (2011): 'What the World Got Wrong in Côte D'Ivoire,' *Foreign Policy*; Ipinyomi F. (2012): 'Is Côte d'Ivoire a Test Case for R2P? Democratization as Fulfillment of the International Community's Responsibility to Prevent,' *Cardiovascular Journal of Africa*, Vol. 56, No. 2; Bellamy A., Williams P.D. (2011): 'The New Politics of Protection? Côte d'Ivoire, Libya and the Responsibility to Protect, *International Affairs*, Vol. 87, No. 4, 2011, 829–838.

X. The Conflict in Libya and the Intervention of International Force

10.1. Background: the collapse of the dictatorship and the outbreak of the civil war

The revolutions in Arab countries ongoing since December 2010 were the background to the Libyan conflict of 2011. It was under their influence that protests against Colonel Muamar Gaddafi, who had ruled the authoritarian state of Libya since 1969, began in January 2011.[1]

Libya had long failed to meet democratic standards, and civil rights and freedoms were not respected. There were no political parties or independent media in the state, no elections were held and political opponents were sent to jail arbitrarily. Outside the Human Rights Society controlled by the Gaddafi Foundation, there were no independent NGOs and international organisations, and foreign journalists had very limited access, so monitoring of the situation was quite difficult. The Berbers were the biggest and most persecuted national minority; they could not even use their language publicly.[2]

However, the country remained relatively stable and peaceful. Libya ranked first in Africa in terms of the Human Development Index[3] and has the highest GDP per capita on the continent, primarily due to its large oil revenues. However, the public could not fully feel the benefits of the good economic situation. The unemployment rate was 20.74% in 2010 and even educated Libyans were facing labour-market barriers.

After a period of sanctions triggered by Libya's support for terrorism, normalisation of relations with the United States and European Union states which has sold arms to Libya on a large scale was ongoing from 2003 onwards. Western companies also benefited from Libyan natural resources, while European states have seen Libya as a security net against refugees.

1 Danecki J., Sulowski S. (eds.) (2011): *Bliski Wschód coraz bliżej*, Warsaw: Dom Wydawniczy Elipsa, 25; Dzisiów-Szuszczykiewicz A. (2008): 'Arabska Wiosna – przyczyny, przebieg i prognozy,' *Bezpieczeństwo narodowe*, 41–56.

2 Human Rights Watch World Report 2011, Libya; Freedom House Freedom in the World Report 2011.

3 United Nations Development Reports 1990–2015, http://hdr.undp.org/en/data.

In the case of Libya it is possible to talk about the weak influence of international human-rights mechanisms. Libya has been party to relevant UN conventions, i.e. the Covenant on Civil and Political Rights, the International Convention on the Elimination of All Forms of Racial Discrimination, the Convention on the Elimination of All Forms of Discrimination against Women and the Convention against Torture and Other Cruel, Inhuman or Degrading Treatment or Punishment. As far as human-rights control mechanisms are concerned, Libya has accepted individual notifications to the Human Rights Committee, the Committee on the Elimination of All Forms of Discrimination against Women and the Committee against Torture. At regional level, Libya was a party to the African Charter on Human and Peoples' Rights and the Protocol on the Rights of Women in Africa.

However, the state frequently refrained from providing reports on the implementation of Conventions, or else delayed submitting them. It likewise failed to respond to requests from treaty bodies and other human-rights institutions.[4] In June 2010 it removed the Office of the UN High Commissioner for Refugees without any formal justification. The strong position of Libya in Africa had led to its election as UN Human Rights Commissioner in 2003, and to election as a member of the Human Rights Council in 2010. Just before the outbreak of the conflict, Libya was subjected to a Universal Periodic Review of Human Rights at the November 2010 Human Rights Council. It accepted 66 recommendations and declined 25, including the publication of a list of missing persons.[5]

In Benghazi in 2010 demonstrations were organised by families of political prisoners, in particular the 1200 killed in the pacification of the rebellion taking place in 1996 at the Abu Salim prison. The assemblies were not suppressed, but the organisers were arrested and Gaddafi threatened violence against a possible revolt.[6] The escalation occurred after Egypt's president Hosni Mubarak, ruling uninterruptedly since 1981, stepped down on 15 February, and the lawyer representing the above-mentioned families, Fethy Tarbel, was arrested. In many cities, demonstrators appeared on the streets, demanding, among others, an improved

---

4 See e.g. *Report of The Special Rapporteur for Follow-Up on Concluding Observations*, March, 2009.

5 *Report of the Working Group on the Universal Periodic Review, Libyan Arab Jamahiriya*, A/HRC/16/15, January 4, 2011.

6 Waal A. de (2013): African Roles in the Libyan Conflict of 2011, *International Affairs*, Vol. 89, No. 2, 369.

financial situation and civil liberties. The response of government forces to that took the form of mass arrests and attacks.

On 17 February, the so-called "Day of Wrath" took place, with large-scale demonstrations organised in many cities. The authorities used force against the demonstrators, with Human Rights Watch claiming a consequent death toll amounting to 49 people.[7] The organisation documented the treatment of protesters by fire, arrests and the disappearance of hundreds of those suspected of involvement in anti-government demonstrations.[8] Revolutionary Committees then took shape among armed civilians, and the regular Libyan Army was deployed to fight the demonstrators on 21 February. The situation was transformed into an armed conflict between government forces and rebels. The President of Libya then made speeches resorting to the language of hatred, and threatening all those who would turn out to be disloyal. He dehumanised his opponents by calling them cockroaches and rats, thereby evoking an association with the situation in Rwanda just before the genocide.[9]

10.2. Institutions involved and instruments applied

The civil war in Libya met with a fairly quick reaction from states and international organisations. On 22 February 2011, human-rights violations were condemned by the League of Arab States,[10] which suspended Libya's membership in the work of all organs, in protest against the violence.[11] Special Advisers to the UN Secretary-General on the Prevention of Genocide and Responsibility to Protect identified events in Libya as broad and systematic attacks against civilians, with the use of armed forces, mercenaries and combat aircraft constituting violations of human rights and international humanitarian law. They did not

7 *Human Rights Watch, Libya: Security Forces Kill 84 Over Three Days*, February 18, 2011; *Libya: Commanders Should Face Justice for Killings. Reports Of "Random" Fire in Tripoli, At Least 62 Dead*, Human Rights Watch, February 22, 2011.

8 Human Rights Watch World Report 2012, Libya.

9 'Gaddafi: 'I Will not Give Up,' 'We Will Chase the Cockroaches,' *Times of Malta*, February 22, 2011.

10 LAS Council Statement No. 136, February 22, 2011

11 Membership was restored on 27 August 2011, when the Libyan Transition Council was recognized as a representative of Libya, LAS Council Resolution No. 7370, August 27, 2011.

exclude the classification of acts as crimes against humanity if they were confirmed.[12] The condemnation of excessive use of violence against demonstrators was also expressed by the Secretary-General of the Organisation of the Islamic Conference[13] and the following day by the African Union.[14] Some Libyan diplomats complained about the escalation of violence and many have resigned from their functions.[15]

Navi Pillay, UN High Commissioner for Human Rights, speaking at a special session of the UN Human Rights Council on 25 February, called on Libya to cease violent human-rights violations immediately.[16] In a Resolution on the human-rights situation in Libya, the Human Rights Council expressed its deep concern about the deaths of hundreds of civilians and the lack of response to the incitement to hostility and violence by the highest state authorities. It called on the authorities to take responsibility for the protection of citizens and the deterrence of attacks on them, for the release of arbitrary detainees, the security of citizens and foreigners and the establishment of a dialogue that would lead to the aspirations of Libyan society being met. The Council decided to send to Libya an independent international investigative committee to investigate human-rights violations, to establish the facts and circumstances of the infringements and, where possible, to identify the persons responsible for them. It also obliged the High Commissioner to provide information on the human-rights situation in Libya, and to organise an interactive dialogue at the next session.[17] The Human Rights Council also recommended to the UN General Assembly the suspension of Libyan membership of the Council, which was achieved by unanimous

---

12 *UN Secretary-General Special Adviser on the Prevention of Genocide, Francis Deng, and Special Adviser on the Responsibility to Protect, Edward Luck, on the Situation in Libya*, February 22, 2011.

13 'OIC General Secretariat Condemns Strongly the Excessive Use of Force against Civilians in the Libyan Jamahiriya,' *Press News*, February 22, 2011.

14 Message from the 261st African Union Peace and Security Council meeting, PSC/PR/COM (CCLXI), February 23, 2011.

15 Adams S. (2012) 'Libya and the Responsibility to Protect,' Global Centre for the Responsibility to Protect *Occasional Paper Series*, No. 3, 6.

16 *Situation of Human Rights in the Libyan Arab Jamahiriya:* Statement by Navy Pillay, UN High Commissioner for Human Rights (Human Rights Council – 15th Special Session – February 25, 2011).

17 UN Human Rights Council Resolution, A/HRC/RES/S-15/1, February 25, 2011.

decision of the GA on 1 March 2011.[18] Efforts to respond to the situation in Libya were also made by UN treaty bodies, in the shape of the Committee on the Elimination of Racial Discrimination[19] and the Committee for the Protection of the Rights of Migrant Workers and Members of Their Families,[20] through special declarations. Human-rights violations were also reported by non-governmental organisations.[21]

On 26 February, the UN Security Council held a debate on the situation in Libya. It adopted Resolution No. 1970, in which it regretted the brutal and systematic violations of human rights, including repression of peaceful demonstrators and the death of civilians. It acknowledged that the broad and systematic attacks on civilians in Libya could be considered crimes against humanity.

It decided to use a number of instruments. It called on the Libyan authorities to stop violence, respect human rights and international humanitarian law, and ensure the security of humanitarian aid. It recommended investigation of the situation by the Prosecutor of the International Criminal Court. It introduced an embargo, urging all Member States to prevent the sale and transfer of arms to Libya, including weapons, ammunition, military vehicles, paramilitary and non-lethal equipment; and it also banned all military aid. It also put in place a travel ban in respect of sixteen representatives of the Libyan authorities, as well as freezing the assets of six of them.[22] These were people involved in planning, controlling and issuing decisions that resulted in serious human-rights abuses, or else the bombing of civilian targets.

On 10 March, the problem of Libya was taken up by the African Union Peace and Security Council, at the level of the highest representatives of states. The majority of representatives claimed that Gaddafi could not remain in power, in connection with the Arab Spring and the postulates of insurgents. It was nevertheless feared that his departure would entail huge destabilisation in the region.[23] The final communiqué underlined the legitimate aspirations of the Libyan people

---

18 *General Assembly Suspends Libya from Human Rights Council*, Report of the UNGA meeting, GA/11050, March 1, 2011; http://www.un.org/press/en/2011/ga11050.doc.htm.

19 Statement under CERD's Early Warning and Urgent Action Procedure, March 2, 2011.

20 Statement on the Situation of Migrant Workers in Libya, April 8, 2011.

21 *Ivory Coast: Call for the protection of civilians and respect of the population's fundamental rights*, Human Rights Watch, December 16, 2010.

22 UN Security Council Resolution, RS/RES/1970, February 26, 2011.

23 Waal A. de (2013): African Roles in the Libyan Conflict of 2011, *International Affairs*, Vol. 89, No. 2, 369–370.

to democracy, political reform, justice, peace and security, expressing firm condemnation for the disproportionate use of force that had led to the loss of civilian and military life. It was also noted that the situation in Libya required action aimed at hostilities being suspended immediately, as well as cooperation with the Libyan authorities over humanitarian aid, the protection of foreigners, including African migrants, and the implementation of reforms.[24]

As a result, the African Union launched a diplomatic initiative. It established an *ad hoc* High-Level Committee on Mediation between Colonel Gaddafi and the rebels. Its members included Mauritania, the Republic of Congo, Mali, South Africa, and Uganda. The aim was to achieve Gaddafi's peaceful resignation and the introduction of a peace restoration plan in Libya. The AU's diplomatic initiative was not taken seriously by Western states, the UN and other regional organisations. They did not believe in the effectiveness of the organisation, which was seen as favouring Muammar Gaddafi.[25] On 11 March, the UN Secretary-General also appointed a special envoy whose task it would be to seek out a lasting and peaceful solution in Libya. Abdel-Elah Mohammed Al-Khatib maintained contacts with both sides in an attempt to bring about a cease-fire and to bring Libyan parties closer to peace.[26]

Without waiting for the effects of diplomatic efforts, on March 12th the LAS Council addressed the UN Security Council with an appeal that a no-fly zone for Libyan military aviation be imposed, and security zones for Libyan citizens and foreigners established.[27] The Council dealt with the case on 17 March. In its adopted Resolution No. 1973, it stated that Libya had not been adhering to its recommendations. It condemned the brutal and systematic violations of human rights, including torture and collective executions, and expressed the belief that broad and systematic attacks against civilians could be perceived as crimes against humanity. It further stated that the situation in Libya threatened international peace and security. It called for a ceasefire and authorised all necessary measures to protect civilian populations and areas inhabited by civilians under threat of attack, as well as introducing a ban zone on the state and increased

24 Message from the 265th African Union Peace and Security Council meeting, PSC/PR/COM (CCLXI), March 10, 2011.

25 Adams S. (2012): 'Libya and the Responsibility to Protect,' Global Centre for the Responsibility to Protect *Occasional Paper Series*, No. 3, 9.

26 See an interview with special envoy to Libya Abdel-Elah Al-Khatib, UN News Centre, July 14, 2011, http://www.un.org/apps/news/newsmakers.asp?NewsID=37.

27 LAS Council Resolution No. 7360, March 12, 2011.

sanctions. At the same time, the Security Council ruled out armed occupation, emphasising respect for Libya's sovereignty and integrity. It also cited the responsibility to protect civilians, which was the main motto of the Resolution.[28] In voting on its adoption, no state objected, though there were abstentions from two Permanent Members of the Council (China and Russia), as well as Brazil, India and Germany.

On 19 March, France organised a summit to discuss the implementation of the UNSC Resolution. The Libyan authorities were called upon to adopt a ceasefire immediately, and agreed to take any necessary measures. Also scheduled for the same day was an African Union meeting on a diplomatic mission to Libya, hence a dilemma for many African countries as to which meeting to participate in. The AU decided to travel to Libya the following day, but international armed intervention had already begun, so the inbound flight by the negotiator could not be taken. No African leaders went to the meeting of Foreign Ministers in London on 29 March, attended by representatives of the UN, the LAS, the Organisation of the Islamic Conference, the EU and NATO. Thus the Contact Group for Libya created at the time had no AU involvement. The Contact Group called on Gaddafi to surrender, and endorsed the National Transitional Council (NTC).[29]

Were there any special events between 26 February and 17 March that prompted the UN Security Council (with such significant support from states) to allow military intervention in Libya before any diplomatic measures had been taken? There were still ongoing reports of serious human-rights violations. On 1 March, an article was published in *The Guardian*, describing the hundreds of deaths that had occurred in the preceding two weeks, as well as the need for an investigation to confirm whether crimes against humanity had been committed.[30] On 13 March, Human Rights Watch reported on mass arrests of government opponents in Tripoli, as well as incidents of murders, arbitrary detentions, disappearances and torture.[31] The media also provided information on the detention and the beating of two BBC reporters, the detention of a correspondent from *The*

28 Resolution of the UN Security Council, S/RES/1973, March 17, 2011.

29 Waal A. de (2013): African Roles in the Libyan Conflict of 2011, *International Affairs*, Vol. 89, No. 2, 371.

30 Baldwin C., 'Libya: What the Security Council Has Done for Justice,' *The Guardian*, March 1, 2011.

31 *Libya: End Violent Crackdown in Tripoli Disappearances and Torture Major Concerns*, Human Rights Watch, March 13, 2011.

Guardian, and the murder of an *Al Jazeera* journalist. The authorities also made it more difficult for foreign journalists to travel to Tripoli and the area in which there were clashes taking place between government forces and the opposition. In western Libya, the International Committee of the Red Cross and other humanitarian organisations were experiencing problems with gaining access to the needy.[32]

The key problem was the offensive mounted by government forces and hitting the most important cities of Ajdabiya, Bin Jawad, Brega, Ra's Lanuf and Zuwarah. Benghazi was to be the last step, as crimes reflecting acts of vengeance were feared. On national media, Gaddafi then announced that his troops would not show any pity for the city.[33]

The military coalition operation began on 19 March. In its first phase, it was focused on the Libyan air defence system. This was followed by attacks on Libyan forces, their equipment, artillery and vehicles. Initially, the Air Forces of France, Canada, the USA, United Kingdom and Italy took part. Four days later, NATO joined the forces and on 25 March assumed command of a military operation in Libya called *Unified Protector*.[34] The was latter was aimed primarily at strengthening the embargo on arms, and at enforcing compliance of the no-fly zone over Libya. International intervention, lasting formally until 31 October, allowed Libya's insurgents to gain the advantage in combat. It was in this way that Gaddafi came to be captured and killed on 20 October.

During the fighting, diplomatic efforts continued. On 10 March, Colonel Gaddafi met with representatives of the African Union, who persuaded him to negotiate with the NTC, and argued that any solution should be based on democratic standards and human rights. Gaddafi accepted the so-called AU road map, agreeing initially to a ceasefire and negotiations. On the following day, the leadership of the NTC rejected the AU proposal, believing that the commencement of talks had unconditionally to be preceded by Gaddafi's immediate

32 *Libya: Allow Relief Aid in And Refugees Out*, Human Rights Watch, March 8, 2011.

33 'Gaddafi Tells Benghazi His Army Is Coming Tonight,' *Al Arabiya News*, March 17, 2011.

34 The NATO states whose armed forces participated in the Operation *Unified Protector* were Belgium, Bulgaria, Denmark, France, Greece, Spain, The Netherlands, Canada, Norway, Romania, Sweden, Turkey, the USA, the United Kingdom and Italy, as well as three NATO partner countries – Jordan, Qatar and the UAE, as well as NATO AWACS, See Weissgerber R., Bierdziński S., Nawrocki M., Piłat Z. (2012): 'Operacja powietrzna "Zjednoczony Obrońca 2011"', *Przegląd Sił Powietrznych*, No. 3, 12–18.

resignation.[35] In the following months, the AU repeated its call for a ceasefire, but was divided as to Gaddafi's fate. In the light of the international intervention, it adopted an increasingly critical attitude towards the coalition's crossing of the mandate arising out of Resolution 1973.

In June 2011, after consulting with African leaders, Russia also sent its envoy Mikhail Margelow to Libya. Only the African Union had a comprehensive ceasefire plan including Gaddafi's resignation and the UN peacekeeping operation in Libya. In the opinion of many experts, states intervening in Libya were not (or no longer) interested in negotiations.[36] On 15 July, the Libyan Contact Group recognised the authority of the National Transitional Council and demanded that Gaddafi hand over power. The following day, the American delegation met with representatives of the Libyan government, agreeing that Gaddafi could remain in Libya, provided that he accepted the NTC.[37] As international intervention gathered pace, Gaddaf became much less ready to negotiate, all the more so as the International Criminal Court issued a warrant for his arrest on 27 June 2011, alleging that he had committed crimes against humanity – murders and persecutions – as well as warrants for the arrests of his son Saif al-Islam, and intelligence chief Abdullah al-Senussi.[38]

10.3. Results and evaluation

On 23 October 2011 in Benghazi, the National Transitional Council announced the liberation of the country from long-term dictatorship, and the beginning of a transition. The exact number of victims of the Libyan civil war is not known. According to the first summaries of insurgent forces, about 30,000 people were killed on both sides, while some 50,000 were injured.[39] A month later, the government of the insurgents verified this number to 25,000,[40] and after two years

35 'Libya: Opposition Rejects African Union Peace Plan,' *Daily Telegraph*, April 11, 2011.

36 Waal A. de (2013): African Roles in the Libyan Conflict of 2011, *International Affairs*, Vol. 89, No. 2, 375.

37 'Plan Would Keep Qaddafi in Libya, But Out of Power,' *New York Times*, July 27, 2011.

38 Muammar Gaddafi's arrest warrant was withdrawn on his death on 22 November 2011. The proceedings against Abdullah al-Senussi ended on 27 July 2014, when the Court of Appeal confirmed the decision of the Preparatory Chamber that the case was inadmissible before the ICC.

39 'Libyan Estimate: At Least 30,000 Died in The War,' *Associated Press*, November 7, 2011, https://archive.is/vgno#selection-1652.0-1720.2.

40 'Residents flee Gaddafi Hometown,' Sydney Morning Herald, October 3, 2011.

to about 10,000.[41] In their February 2011, condemnations of human-rights violations and the use of violence against demonstrators in Libya, international institutions themselves acknowledged the need for verification of the data. Indeed, some figures, e.g. those relating to numbers of mass rapes, have not been confirmed.[42]

The situation of the population in the context of violations of international humanitarian law was investigated in Libya by the International Commission of Inquiry for Libya established by the UN Human Rights Council, as well as an independent non-governmental investigation mission established by NGOs in the Middle East, plus others such as Human Rights Watch and Amnesty International.[43]

The International Commission of Inquiry for Libya presented two reports: on 31 May 2011 and 2 March 2012. It pointed to the excessive use of force against demonstrators in the early days of the protests, and then also to unlawful killings and executions, arbitrary detentions, torture, abduction and sexual violence. Government troops used anti-personnel mines and cassette bombs, causing disproportionate loss and suffering, as well as rockets and heavy ammunition in cities, causing enormous damage. Gaddafi's individual role as a perpetrator of war crimes and crimes against humanity was also recognised.[44] Allegations were also made against insurgent forces in the area of arbitrary killings, torture and looting.[45]

Furthermore, the NATO operation did result in victims, even though it was rated as highly precise, in line with the principle of proportionality and aimed at minimising the side effects of military action. In a few cases, unjustified attacks

---

41 'Libyan Revolution Casualties Lower Than Expected, Says New Government,' *The Guardian*, January 8, 2013.

42 During the first days of the conflict, 100–110 civilians were killed in Benghazi and 59–64 in Bayda. 'Amnesty Questions Claim that Gaddafi Ordered Rape as Weapon of War,' The Independent, June 24, 2011.

43 Independent Civil Society Fact-Finding Mission consisted of Palestinian Centre for Human Rights, Arab Organization for Human Rights, the International Legal Assistance Consortium.

44 *Report of the International Commission of Inquiry to investigate all alleged violations of international human*
rights law in the Libyan Arab Jamahiriya, June 1, 2011, A/HRC/17/2011, http://www2.ohchr.org/english/bodies/hrcouncil/docs/17session/A.HRC.17.44_AUV.pdf.

45 *Report of the Independent Civil Society Fact-Finding Mission to Libya*, January 2012, http://www.pchrgaza.org/files/2012/FFM_Libya-Report.pdf.

on civilians were found to have taken place. It was argued that NATO's offensive activities, i.e. the bombing of the cities in which Gaddafi's forces were stationed, could not be said to properly discharge the task of "protecting civilians," as set out in the Council's Resolution. The attack on Sirte on 15 September 2011, one of the last cities controlled by Gaddafi's forces, can serve as an example. According to witnesses, an attack aimed at supporting opposition forces caused the deaths of some 47 civilians,[46] or according to the Libyan government – 354 people. Human Rights Watch visited all areas in which civilians were killed as a result of NATO attacks (choosing to eschew research on wounded civilians and destroyed belongings). In total, the organisation counted at least 72 civilian victims of attacks organised for questionable purposes.[47]

In the long run, the results of the international engagement have come to be assessed rather negatively, also from the viewpoint of civil protection. The lack of a plan and the ability to restore order in the state and support its development led to a lasting destabilisation of the situation, not only in Libya but also in neighbouring countries. The rise of radical Islamic movements, uncontrolled migration, and the negative impact on the security situation in Mali or Niger are all indicated. In addition, the lack of a single centre of control over Libyan territory, the struggles between various groups, the dysfunction of the criminal justice system and the serious increase in crime all lead it to be concluded that a drastic deterioration in personal security in Libya took place.

In the case of Libya about it is possible to refer to the involvement of numerous universal or regional institutions with a view to mass human-rights violations being prevented. At all stages, relevant decisions were taken very rapidly by the standards of current practice. This is true of both the early warning and resort to diplomatic and military instruments. Although the international community has been accused of lack of action in the literature's most frequently-cited examples – of the Balkan Wars and the genocide in Rwanda. In the case of Libya, it is rather a question of whether such swift and consistent action was justified – and beneficial – in terms of responsibility to protect the population.

There was justification for condemnation of the use of violence against peaceful demonstrators in February 2011, as well as for concerns regarding the further course of the conflict and possible crimes. There was, however, no hard evidence

46 *Report of the Independent Civil Society Fact-Finding Mission to Libya*, January 2012, http://www.pchrgaza.org/files/2012/FFM_Libya-Report.pdf, 45.

47 *Unacknowledged Deaths. Civilian Casualties in NATO's Air Campaign in Libya*, Human Rights Watch Report, May 13, 2012.

about the mass crimes committed by Muammar Gaddafi's troops, particularly in relation to the period between the first UN Security Council Resolution and Resolution 1973, which was in essence the decision about a military intervention in Libya. In none of the reports of the International Commission of Inquiry set up by the Human Rights Council were there examples, or even additional evidence of, massive human-rights violations committed during the period. Still, the decision to intervene was taken as Muammar Gaddafi was approaching victory and stabilising the situation in the country, a situation that would probably have been accompanied by a policy of vengeance pursued against opponents.

Certainly, the decision was influenced by the figure of Gaddafi himself and the history of his dictatorship, which the international community judged very critically, even though this had not bothered it as it concluded various agreements with Libya, and pursued political cooperation. In addition, Gaddafi's threats to opposition forces, dehumanisation of opponents and the announcement of total revenge had to set the organisations dealing with the responsibility to protect and prevention of mass crimes in readiness. Even if some countries like France or the UK were involved on the basis of particular interests, many communities backed the need for armed intervention.

Nevertheless, a relatively quick decision on military intervention and its launch two days after the Council's Resolution did much to reduce possibilities for diplomatic initiatives. Similarly, Gaddafi's stiffening saw the case remitted to the International Criminal Court, which issued a summons for his arrest. The National Transitional Council was not willing to negotiate, not able to imagine conversations with the dictator who had decided to open fire on protesters.

The rapid take-up of military action contributed to the general escalation of violence and violations of international humanitarian law. Because the intervention was of an anticipatory nature, most victims died after it commenced. International military instruments were used extensively, not only to enforce the no-fly zone and protect civilians but also to provide direct support to Gaddafi's opponents. Insurgent forces were trained, provided with arms, and supported by Special Forces. The international coalition thus made an active contribution to the overthrow of the dictator and his regime, and hence to a changeover of power. This ensured that the mandate of the UN Security Council Resolution was exceeded.

Although the intervention in Libya offers important proof that many international organisations can work together in a situation where they are at risk of mass human-rights violations and atrocity crimes; and are able to turn to armed action effectively, it is also a warning to use the instruments available proportionately and appropriately to the situation.[48] Going beyond the mandate of the Security Council, as well as acting without its authorisation, as has also been the case in Kosovo in 1999, serves only to multiply doubts about the intentions underpinning intervention, while stiffening the positions of states (in the case of Libya: China and Russia) where similar cases have been concerned.[49]

48 'The Lessons of Libya,' *New York Times*, November 15, 2011.

49 Positive assessments of the intervention in Libya were included in: Weiss T. (2011): 'RtoP Alive and Well After Libya,' *Ethics & International Affairs*, Vol. 25, 287–292; Zifcak S. (2012): 'The Responsibility to Protect after Libya and Syria,' *Melbourne Journal of International Law*, Vol. 13, 1–35; Williams I. (2012): 'Applying "Responsibility to Protect" to Syria no Cakewalk,' *The Washington Report on Middle East Affairs*, Vol. 31, No. 4, 35–36; Borghard E.D., Pischedda C. (2012): 'Allies and Airpower in Libya,' *Parameters*, Vol. 42, No. 1, 63–74. See critical opinions: Hehir A. (2013): 'The Permanence of Inconsistency: Libya, the Security Council, and the Responsibility to Protect,' *International Security*, Vol. 38, No. 10, 137–159; Claes J. (2011) *Libya and the Responsibility to Protect*, United States Institute of Peace; http://www.usip.org/publications/libya-and-the-responsibilityprotect; Nuruzzaman M. (2013): 'The "Responsibility to Protect" Doctrine: Revived in Libya, Buried in Syria,' *Insight Turkey*, Vol. 15, No. 2, 57–66.

Concluding Remarks: Factors Contributing to the Prevention

Human-rights protection was rarely a priority for states in the past. Only after the tragedy of the Second World War did states incorporate human-rights issues into the international order, adopt international laws, and establish institutions and mechanisms by which to monitor the situation and facilitate cooperation in this area. The Convention on the Prevention and Punishment of the Crime of Genocide put in place a strong prohibition on killing and eliminating groups of people on a large scale. Another breakthrough came in 1989, when Communism – with its disregard for individual and political rights – collapsed in many states. While this transformation failed to produce democracy and the rule of law in each and every case, the end of the Cold War did bring about a new standard in cooperation in the area of human rights. The Office of the United Nations High Commissioner for Human Rights was established, a new Plan of Action was adopted in Vienna, and the Security Council acknowledged the relationship between the human-rights situation and security. The accession of new Member States to both the Council of Europe and the European Union resulted in a significant expansion of the area of observance of human rights and democratic standards. The capacity of these two organizations was further strengthened by the adoption of new regulations and mechanisms.

The immense tragedies that took place in the 1990s in Somalia, Rwanda, the Democratic Republic of the Congo and Sudan triggered a shift in the approach taken by international institutions to international crimes and to the need for prevention. Sixty years after the tragedy of the Second World War, an acknowledgment of the international community's inability to offer an effective response to suffering on a massive scale brought prevention into even sharper focus.

In the UN, the breakthrough materialised in the 2004 establishment of the first specialised institution, the Special Adviser on the Prevention of Genocide, as well as the 2005 adoption of *Responsibility to Protect*. The work of the Secretary-General and the General Assembly led to conceptual progress over the prevention of genocide, crimes against humanity, ethnic cleansing, and war crimes. When the Security Council later cited *Responsibility to Protect* with increasing frequency, it translated into international practice and raised the profile of R2P.

Sadly, reorientation in the direction of prevention has made few inroads into the UN bodies and institutions that focus on human rights, i.e. the Human Rights Council, treaty bodies, and the High Commissioner for Human Rights.

While these naturally play their important part in preventing individual and mass human-rights violations, there has been no more major shift that would enable treaty bodies to cooperate more successfully with countries in which signs of some impending mass violations and atrocity crimes are present.

Expert bodies often release opinions when there is a threat of mass violations, or when such violations do occur. These opinions tend to be worded radically and usually come closest to the truth. But they are hardly effective. The hands of these bodies are tied when it comes to taking action against states that, for example, fail to report on treaty implementation, or ignore opinions and recommendations. At the Human Rights Council (previously the Commission on Human Rights), political interests and support from stronger states often either make it impossible for resolutions condemning mass violations and atrocity crimes to be adopted, or else stop outright the implementation of previously-adopted procedures (e.g. in the case of Syria). Events such as the adoption of Resolutions on the human-rights situation in Russia – a Permanent Member of the Security Council – in relation to the war in Chechnya, or else the suspension of Libya's Security Council membership, were exceptional in the history of this institution.

The United Nations High Commissioner for Human Rights has a strong involvement in the protection of human rights, and uses his mandate to contribute to the structural prevention of mass human-rights violations. The High Commissioner influences the policies of states and the operations of international institutions by providing a strong response. However, the High Commissioner is not recognised within the UN as an institution that can make a more-major contribution to preventing atrocity crimes; and the role of this office is limited to at most 'serious' human-rights violations. As a result, its potential is not fully realised. Only very limited cooperation pertains between the Geneva-based UNHCR and the New-York based Special Adviser on the Prevention of Genocide as regards early warning is very limited. Appeals made by the Special Adviser warning of potential genocide and other atrocities fail to translate into specific actions of the UNHCR. This supports the sub-hypothesis that the shift has been insufficient, and that the potential of the UN human-rights institutions remains untapped.

The idea of preventing originated with the UN and has so far not had a great impact on regional organisation in Europe. The OSCE has continued to develop its own instruments, independently of the UN, on the basis of its experiences during the Cold War in Balkan conflicts, and in the face of the atrocities of the early 1990s. The adoption of R2P by the UN system, and the fact that has now gained relatively wide acceptance, has not changed the institutions and/or the measures the OSCE has at its disposal in the area of prevention.

The EU has little need to focus on preventing mass violations of human rights and atrocity crimes in its Member States, given that strong observance of human rights is a prerequisite for accession. Instead, the focus has been on foreign policy in that area, with the scope thereof gradually expanding post-1992. However, the EU has not adopted separate mechanisms to prevent mass violations of human rights and atrocity crimes, focusing instead on developing conflict-prevention instrumentation. When a threat of mass violations arises, the EU has a record of both individual diplomatic and economic initiatives. It has cooperated closely with the UN, in particular as regards the short-term use of the EU's military potential and humanitarian aid. Its involvement on the ground often depends on the interests of specific Member States, such as France – in the case of Chad or the Central African Republic.

On the other hand, African organisations have made quite significant changes to their laws, institutions, and mechanisms since the late 1990s. The documents of the AU and ECOWAS now include direct references to the need for conflicts and/or human-rights violations and atrocity crimes to be prevented. Both organisations allow for the option of armed intervention to prevent and stop atrocities covered by R2P. The AU has not resorted to this measure so far, despite mass-scale violence against the populations of Sudan (Darfur), the Democratic Republic of the Congo, South Sudan, and other African countries. Perhaps this instrument will remain outside practical application, just as the legal instruments relating to the African system of human rights are hardly ever used. ECOWAS places strong emphasis on respect for human rights, and views conflict prevention as safeguarding individual security. While ECOWAS may lack sufficient resources to pursue its ambitious goals in practice, it is not averse to applying its instruments where there is a risk of destabilisation. Another example of the emergence of new institutions and mechanisms for preventing atrocity crimes is provided by the International Conference on the Great Lakes Region in Africa, which was created in the aftermath of conflicts and the accompanying crimes. However, this form of cooperation has only a very limited practical dimension, and has failed in recent years to prevent the aggravation of the situation in Burundi and gross human-rights violations.

The Organization of American States has implemented a regional system of human-rights protection quite effectively. While there has been steady development in terms of instruments used in this area, and while the role of the Inter-American Court of Human Rights appears stronger, there is no particular focus on preventing atrocities. However, certain states – notably Brazil – are willing to engage in the development of the concept of R2P. The Latin American Network for Genocide and Mass Atrocity Prevention is an example of a move in the right direction.

The involvement of international organisations in the prevention of mass violations of human rights and atrocity crimes is largely dependent on state policy. This also applies to expert institutions, in which initiatives depend on the budget allocated to them by states. Implementation of specific recommendations is also dependent on the willingness of states to engage and cooperate. Experts believe that these recommendations are crucial in preventing human-rights violations. However, states are more inclined to use international institutions to address these problems than to use bilateral channels. Whether international institutions act, or remain inert, depends on the decision-making mechanisms, and on the positions of the countries with most significant standing therein. For example, it is the position of the Permanent Members that generally determines the position of the UN Security Council. In the case of the OSCE, the consensus-based approach to decision-making paralyses the organisation where the use of a confrontational instrument is appropriate. The organisation can only be effective if it uses cooperative instruments that are accepted by the country to which they are addressed.

The adoption of R2P provided an additional incentive for states to engage in preventative action. A new interpretation of the sovereignty of states – one that involves the crucial responsibility to protect the population – found support with proponents of the idea of humanitarian intervention, as popularised in the 1990s. Did it manage to convince its opponents? Countries that respect human rights are willing to engage in this area at international level, and those that are subject to international criticism are more likely to invoke arguments relating to national sovereignty and the principle of non-interference in internal affairs. However, the sovereignty argument is not decisive in whether or not a specific action is taken. Instead, humanitarian, security, economic and other considerations can prevail, including the pursuit of specific interests, and even just the pursuit of influence.

The foremost characteristic of policy of states in the area of preventing and stopping mass violations of human rights and atrocity crimes appears to be its inconsistency. This may be due to the fact that individual protection or civil protection as such are not foreign-policy priorities. States steer clear of this area, where resort to action would lead to excessive political, economic or security costs. Hence, the involvement of the international community in Chechnya, Rwanda (until 1994), and then also Darfur and Syria, has been weak. On the other hand, involvement intensifies if inaction would trigger the risk of high costs, or if additional interests can be promoted by becoming involved, as was the case in the 1990s in the Balkans, Libya, or Côte d' Ivoire. Inconsistent foreign policy may also result from frequent shifts in power, typically accompanied by a reorientation of foreign-policy priorities (the examples of the United States and Canada mentioned earlier in the paper offer a good illustration).

On a more positive note, various networks and fora have emerged to bring together countries interested in preventing genocide and other atrocity crimes, such as Global Action Against Mass Atrocity Crimes or the Global Network of R2P Focal Points. These make the international community more aware of the problem of mass suffering and, above all, serve as hubs for the exchange of ideas and sharing of good practice. This is very useful, because states are still in the process of developing concepts and principles for the prevention of mass atrocities and human-rights violations.

In the face of disinterest on the part of states and international organisations when mass violations of human rights occur, a lone voice 'crying out in the desert' is often that of NGOs with a mission to promote the protection of such rights. These NGOs often issue first warnings as to possible crimes, and make first attempts to mobilise the international community to take action. While there are several local and international early-warning, advisory, and education-oriented organisations, no strong sector of international NGOs with a focus on prevention in the field has yet emerged. This is related to the sensitivity of NGOs to security issues, and their inability to operate where there is a risk (or actual occurrence) of mass human-rights violations and atrocity crimes. However, when a humanitarian crisis strikes, NGOs and the International Committee of the Red Cross provide humanitarian aid, and at the same time keep an eye out for possible violations of human rights and international humanitarian law, which does to some extent contribute to prevention.

This paper analyses four cases in which there was either a high risk or actual occurrence of mass-atrocity crimes and human-rights violations. The focus is on the institutions involved in these cases, and on the instruments available to them in the effort to prevent or stop the violence. In the case of Chechnya, I demonstrated how little room for manoeuvre the international community had – or essentially, how completely helpless it was – in a scenario where the perpetrator of the violence was a superpower and a Permanent Member of the UN Security Council – a circumstance that rendered the forum useless as an instrument of resolution. The international community accepted the claim of the Russian Federation that the conflict in Chechnya was an internal matter; and acted with understanding for Russia's self-professed struggle to preserve its integrity and eliminate terrorism. The states were unwilling to complicate their relations with

Russia, mostly in the light of economic and security considerations. No economic or military instruments were used. The political and diplomatic pressure exerted must be assessed as insufficient, and the OSCE mission as inadequate, although it was likely the only viable solution. Any potential action of the international community was also hindered by the minimal presence of international staff on the ground in Chechnya and insufficient understanding of local conditions. During the second war there, only officials of the International Committee of the Red Cross were present on site. Since four of these were actually killed, engagement on the ground was yet further discouraged. Staff of the OSCE, the Council of Europe and the UN who visited Chechnya periodically were restricted in their ability to move around and take action, and proved unable to persuade the Russian authorities to accept the solutions these organisations had put forward.

The situation was quite different in Côte d'Ivoire in 2010. This was a smaller country in which power, and the situation of ethnic groups, were at stake for the parties to the conflict. There was no threat to the territorial integrity of the state. The conflict was protracted and a UN military operation had been in place for quite some time. A number of institutions were involved, including the UN Secretary-General and the UN High Commissioner for Human Rights, the African Union, the Economic Community of West African States, the European Union and others. The situation in Côte d'Ivoire had been monitored regularly by the UN Security Council, which had demonstrated flexibility in the face of changing circumstances in the country, and which had proved very perceptive in addressing the role of the media. A broad spectrum of instruments had been used, ranging from political pressure, via preventive diplomacy and sanctions, through to military instruments which ensured direct UN involvement in efforts to calm the situation. The key factor was the effectiveness of the Security Council, including its ability to adjust the mandate of its military operation, and to maintain an insightful analytical view of the internal situation, e. g. regarding the use of media in spreading hatred. France had a particularly strong interest in the situation in Côte d'Ivoire, but there was also much interest from neighbouring countries, which feared an influx of refugees, and for which Côte d'Ivoire served as a transit country by which the sea could be accessed. International companies that control cocoa and coffee cultivation were also involved.

Given the outbreaks of periodic fighting and numbers of casualties and refugees, it would be difficult to say that the preventative action taken in Côte d'Ivoire was entirely successful. It demonstrated that even a very good understanding of internal conditions, along with long-term involvement of the international institutions and states on the ground, can be insufficient to prevent massacres.

However, the situation stabilised relatively quickly, and the crisis of 2010 did not turn into a prolonged conflict.

As for the threat of mass killings in Libya in 2011, the analysis in this paper pertained mostly to the military intervention based on the historical Security Council Resolution which invoked R2P. In an unprecedented move, China and Russia abstained from voting, effectively green-lighting the intervention. Support also came from regional organisations and most Western countries, with a strong voice of France in favour of intervention. The decision to use a military instrument was made very quickly, at the moment when Muammar Gaddafi's troops were regaining control over Libya's territory. The diplomatic opportunities that emerged in particular from the African Union were disregarded. On the contrary, the rapid decision to use legal instruments (including the International Criminal Court) effectively torpedoed any diplomatic efforts, by ensuring that the position of the Gaddafi regime would become completely inflexible.

Most casualties were recorded after the start of international intervention, which went beyond its mandate to support coalition forces in their overthrow of the dictator's regime. Libya became a failed state and the security situation deteriorated significantly. The international community had no plan or an idea as to how to consolidate the state. Criticism of the intervention by China and Russia slowed discussions on the possibility of military instruments being used to prevent or stop mass human-rights violations. Criticism of the operation overall also contributed to the unwillingness to take strong action noted in Syria after 2011, even though armed conflict in that country caused one of the gravest humanitarian disasters in the post-WWII era.

The opposite stance was taken by the international community in Rwanda. There was no armed intervention in response to the 1994 genocide. Instead, there was heavy involvement in humanitarian, stabilisation and development efforts after the end of the main wave of atrocities. International institutions and their staff were unable to develop a solid understanding of the nuances of the internal situation in Rwanda and of the politics of the Rwandan authorities. It was difficult to assess the threat posed by the Hutu militias hiding in neighbouring countries, and to respond adequately to violations of human rights and international humanitarian law committed by the governing Rwandan Patriotic Front. In effect, Rwanda drifted towards dictatorship, while still doing better in terms of economic development than other countries in its region. Rwandan authorities achieved relative stability in the country at the expense of involvement in armed conflicts in Zaire / the Democratic Republic of Congo. Their responsibility for the atrocities committed there remains unclear.

The analyses engaged in demonstrate that states and institutions have so far failed to achieve consistent prevention of mass human-rights violations and atrocity crimes. The choice and use of instruments is largely unpredictable, as are the expected effects of their deployment. Whenever there is a threat of mass human-rights violations and atrocity crimes, the internal situation is always extremely complicated. Many factors contribute to this complexity, including ethnic conflict; power struggles; poverty and slow development. The international community is unable to fully grasp the details of the internal situation. To make matters worse, that situation is typically the subject of rapid change. Internationally, there are also the diverse – and often simply clashing – interests that affect decision-making.

Nevertheless, international institutions have a strong stabilising and facilitating role to play in the efforts in prevention, even if they are unable to offer consistent involvement in every case that might benefit from it, or have limited ability to exert pressure on potential perpetrators.

The following factors promote – but not guarantee – the effectiveness of international organisations and states in a given area:

1. Early involvement. Countries in which mass human-rights violations occur tend to avoid cooperating with the UN and regional human-rights institutions for years. The latter in particular can often be the first to realise that the state has a policy posing the threat of mass violations of human rights and atrocity crimes. Naturally, support for a state over the protection of individuals does not exhaust the potential for structural prevention. It is also necessary to offer support in terms of the building of democratic institutions, promotion of economic development, and response to specific needs, e.g. reconciliation between conflicted groups. Finally, it is equally important for operational prevention to be mobilised very quickly, especially when serious incidents have already been recorded.
2. Presence on the ground. This translates into better reporting to international institutions, with the consequence that better early-warning results are obtained. When states and international institutions are up to date with developments, they can react faster and more flexibly. Presence on the ground, even with the consent of the host country, is not synonymous with genuine willingness to cooperate on the part of local government and other local institutions. It nonetheless provides an opportunity to get to know these actors, and to discover potential partners with which the international community might work in its efforts to prevent mass-atrocity crimes. Without local partners, exerting an international impact is difficult. In addition, the

presence of civilian or military personnel on the ground tends to make perpetrators more cautious, allowing states and institutions to exert more pressure on the authorities with regard to the security of their personnel.

3. Strength of international pressure. This is where the media and public have an important role to play. The more countries and international institutions approve the use of specific instruments in a given situation, the more likely they are to be effective. This is particularly true with regard to countries and institutions which, due to their international position or relations with the country where there is a risk of violations, are able to mobilise the international community to act and exert pressure on potential perpetrators. The pressure is stronger in proportion to the following factors: agreement between parties in assessing the situation; agreement as to the selection of instruments to be used; cooperation; and finally, coordination.
4. Quality and adequacy of instruments. Depending on the situation, the choice is between instruments of a cooperative or confrontational nature. As the risk of atrocities rises, so does the preference for confrontational instruments (or the skilful application of instruments of both types). Moreover, the instruments should be genuinely matched to the situation in question, and targeted at potential perpetrators, particularly where sanctions are concerned. Most typically, in situations of mass human-rights violations and atrocity crimes, the instruments deployed are too weak and inadequate to truly change the situation. Declarations and announcements that criticise and condemn violations offer the best example here. However, when military instruments are used – in a particular, when a military intervention is launched – extreme caution is advisable, to avoid the risk of the intervention becoming yet another source of suffering for the population.
5. Consistency of interests and political will. The NGOs, researchers, activists and experts often employed in intergovernmental organisations may feel a passionate commitment to improving the effectiveness of institutions in the area of prevention. Yet it is states that have decision-making power. It is states that ultimately commit themselves to the use of specific mechanisms, provide funding, and implement decisions taken by the bodies of the relevant organisation. Respect for human rights as a measure that promotes security may be viewed as a common interest of the international community, but governments are not necessarily prepared to bear the associated costs and take the associated risks, even in the face of mass-atrocity crimes. Invoking additional security or economic interests promotes the mobilisation of political will, which is essential for the effective prevention of mass violations of human rights.

Bibliography

Books

Alfredsson G., Grimheden J., Ramcharan B., Zayas A. de (2009): *International Human Rights Monitoring Mechanisms. Essays in Honour of Jakob Th. Möller*, Leiden-Boston: Martinus Nijhoff Publishers.

Austin G., Koppelman B. (2004): *Darfur and Genocide: Mechanisms for Rapid Response, an End to Impunity*, London: Foreign Policy Centre.

Bacevich A.J., Cohen E.A. (eds.) (2001): *War Over Kosovo. Politics and Strategy in a Global Age*, New York.

Bachmann K., Heidrich D. (eds.) (2016): *The Legacy of Crimes and Crises Transitional Justice, Domestic Change and the Role of the International Community*, Frankfurt am Main – New York: Peter Lang.

Badescu C. (2010): *Humanitarian Intervention and the Responsibility to Protect: Security and Human Rights*, London – New York: Routledge.

Baehr P. (1996): *The Role of Human Rights in Foreign Policy*, London: Palgrave Macmillan.

Baehr P. (2009): *Non-governmental Human Rights Organizations in International Relations*, New York: Palgrave Macmillan.

Bar J. (2013): *Rwanda*, Warsaw: Wydawnictwo Trio.

Bar, J. (2013): *Po ludobójstwie. Państwo i społeczeństwo w Rwandzie 1994–2012*, Cracow: Księgarnia Akademicka

Barrs C.A. (2009): *Preparedness Support: Helping Brace Beneficiaries, Local Staff and Partners for Violence*, The Cuny Centre.

Bellamy A.J. (2009): *Responsibility to Protect: The Global Effort to End Mass Atrocities*, Cambridge – Malden: Polity Press.

Bellamy A.J. (2011): *Global Politics and the Responsibility to Protect: From Words to Deeds*, London – New York: Routledge.

Bellamy A.J. (2011): *Mass Atrocities and Armed Conflicts: Links, Distinctions and Implications for the Responsibility to Prevent*, Policy Analysis Brief, The Stanley Foundation.

Bellamy A.J., Lupin A. (2015): *Why We Fail: Obstacles to the Effective Prevention of Mass Atrocities*, New York: International Peace Institute.

Bellamy A.J., Dunne T. (2016): *The Oxford Handbook of the Responsibility to Protect*, Oxford: Oxford University Press.

Bieńczyk-Missala A. (ed.) (2017): *Civilians in Contemporary Armed Conflicts: Rafał Lemkin's Heritage*, Warsaw: Wydawnictwa Uniwersytetu Warszawskiego.

Biersteker T.J., Eckert S.E., Tourinho M. (ed.), (2016): *Targeted Sanctions – The Impacts and Effectiveness of United Nations Action*, Cambridge: Cambridge University Press.

Chalk F., Dallaire L.G.R., Matthews K., Barqueiro C., Doyle S. (2010): *Mobilizing the Will to Intervene. Leadership to Prevent Mass Atrocities*, Montreal – Kingston – London – Ithaca: McGill-Queen's University Press.

Clark P. (2010): *The Gacaca Courts, Post-Genocide Justice and Reconciliation in Rwanda*, Cambridge: Cambridge University Press.

Cooper R.H., Kohler J.V. (eds.) (2009): *Responsibility to Protect: The Global Moral Compact for the 21st Century*, New York: Macmillan.

Crossley N. (2016): *Evaluating the Responsibility to Protect: Mass Atrocity Prevention as a Consolidating Norm in International Society*, London – New York: Routledge.

Davies J.L., Gurr T.R. (eds.) (1998), *Preventive Measures: Building Risk Assessment and Crisis Early Warning Systems*, Oxford: Rowman & Littlefield Publishers.

Davies S.E., Glanville L. (eds.) (2010): *Protecting the Displaced: Deepening the Responsibility to Protect*, Leiden: Martinus Nijhoff.

Donnelly J. (1998): *International Human Rights*, Colorado-Oxford: Avalon Publishing.

Ercan P.G. (2016): *Debating the Future of the 'Responsibility to Protect': The Evolution of a Moral Norm*, London: Palgrave Macmillan.

Evans G. (2008): *The Responsibility to Protect: Ending Mass Atrocity Crimes Once and For All*, Washington DC: Brookings Institution Press.

Feris E.G. (2011): *The Politics of Prevention: The Limits of Humanitarian Action*, Washington DC: Brookings Institution Press.

Fiott D., Koops J. (ed.) (2014): *The Responsibility to Protect and the Third Pillar: Legitimacy and Operationalization*, New York – London: Palgrave Macmillan.

Flood P.J. (1998): *The Effectiveness of UN Human Rights Institutions*, London: Praeger Publishers.

Forsythe D.P. (1998): *Human Rights and U.S. Foreign Policy: Congress Reconsidered*, Gainesville: University of Florida Press.

Forsythe D.P., McMahon P.C. (2017): *American Exceptionalism Reconsidered: U.S. Foreign Policy, Human Rights and World Order*, London – New York: Routledge.

Gaeta P. (ed.) (2009): *The UN Genocide Convention. A Commentary*, Oxford: Oxford University Press.

Genser J., Cotler I. (eds.) (2012): *The Responsibility to Protect: The Promise of Stopping Mass Atrocities in Our Time*, Oxford – New York: Oxford University Press.

Genser J., Ugarte B.S. (2014): *The United Nations Security Council in the Age of Human Rights*, New York: Cambridge University Press.

E. Gilligan (2010): *Terror in Chechnya. Russia and the Tragedy of Civilians in War*, Princeton – Oxford: Princeton University Press.

Gillies D. (ed.) (2011): *Elections in Dangerous Places. Democracy and the Paradoxes of Peacebuilding*, Montreal – Kingston – London – Ithaca: McGill-Queen's University Press.

Grochmalski P. (1999): *Czeczenia. Rys prawdziwy*, Wroclaw: Atla 2.

Hamburg D.A. (2003): *No More Killing Fields: Preventing Deadly Conflict*, Lanham: Rowman & Littlefield Publishers.

Hehir A., Murray R. (2013): *Libya, the Responsibility to Protect and the Future of Humanitarian Intervention*, Chennai: Palgrave Macmillan.

Henkin L. (1978): *The Rights of Man Today*, Boulder: Westview Press.

Henkin L. (1979): *How Nations Behave*, New York: Columbia University Press.

Henriksen D., Larsse A.K. (ed.) (2016): *Political Rationale and International Consequences of the War in Libya*, Oxford: Oxford University Press.

Hinton A. (ed.) (2010): *Transitional Justice: Global Mechanisms and Local Realities after Genocide ad Mass Violence*, New Brunswick: Rutgers University Press.

Jarstad A.K., Sisk T. D. (ed.) (2008): *From War to Democracy. Dilemmas of Peacebuilding*, Cambridge: Cambridge University Press.

Jones A. (2006): *Genocide. A Comprehensive Introduction*, London – New York Routledge.

Kemp W., Popovski V., Thakur R. (2011): *Blood and Borders: The Responsibility to Protect and the Problem of the Kin-State*, Tokyo: United Nations University Press.

Knight W.A., Egerton F. (ed.) (2012): *The Routledge Handbook of the Responsibility to Protect*, London – New York: Routledge.

Korey W. (1993): The Promises We Keep. Human Rights, the Helsinki Process and American Foreign Policy, New York: St. Martin's Press.

Kuźniar R. (2000): *Prawa człowieka. Prawo, instytucje, stosunki międzynarodowe*, Warsaw: Wydawnictwo Naukowe Scholar.

Kuźniar R. et al. (2020): *Bezpieczeństwo międzynarodowe*, Warsaw: Wydawnictwo Naukowe Scholar.

Lemkin R. (1944): *Axis Rule in Occupied Europe. Laws of Occupation – Analysis of Government – Proposals for Redress*, Washington DC: Carnegie Endowment for International Peace.

Lillich R.B. (ed.) (1992): *Humanitarian Intervention and the United Nations*, Charlottesville: University Press of Virginia.

Lizak W. (2012): *Afrykańskie instytucje bezpieczeństwa*, Warsaw: Wydawnictwo Naukowe Scholar.

Łukaszuk L. (1995): *Międzynarodowe prawo humanitarne w systemie ochrony praw człowieka i humanizacji stosunków międzynarodowych*, Warsaw: Akademia Obrony Narodowej.

MacQueen N. (2011): *Humanitarian Intervention and the UN*, Edinburgh: Edinburgh University Press.

M. Madej (ed.) (2019): *Western Military Interventions After the Cold War*, London – New York: Routledge.

Mani R., Weiss T.G. (eds.) (2011): *Responsibility to Protect*, London – New York: Routledge.

McGovern M. (2011): *Making War in Côte d'Ivoire*, Chicago: Chicago University Press.

McLoughlin S. (2014): *The Structural Prevention of Mass Atrocities*, London – New York: Routledge.

Melvern L. (2006): *Conspiracy to Murder – The Rwandan Genocide*, London-New York: Verso, 2006.

Mertus J.A., Helsing J.W. (eds.) (2006): *Human Rights & Conflict. Exploring the Links between Rights, Law, and Peacebuilding*, Washington DC: United States Institute of Peace Press.

Michałowska G. (2007): *Ochrona praw człowieka w Radzie Europy i w Unii Europejskiej*, Warsaw: Wydawnictwa Akademickie i Profesjonalne.

Mosso D. (2009): *Early Warning* and *Quick Response: Accounting in the Twenty-First Century*, Bingley: Emerald Publishing Limited.

Nardin T, Williams M.S. (eds.) (2006): *Humanitarian Intervention*, New York: New York University.

Nijakowski L.M. (2014): *Rozkosz zemsty, Socjologia historyczna mobilizacji ludobójczej*, Warsaw: Wydawnictwo Naukowe Scholar.

Orford A. (2011): *International Authority and the Responsibility to Protect*, Cambridge: Cambridge University Press.

Pape M. (1997): *Humanitäre intervention: zur Bedeutung der Menschenrechte in den Vereinten Nationen*, Baden-Baden: Nomos Verlag.

Parzymies S., Zięba R. (ed.), (2004): *Instytucjonalizacja wielostronnej współpracy międzynarodowej w Europie*, Warsaw: Wydawnictwo Naukowe Scholar.

Pattinson J. (2010): *Humanitarian Intervention and the Responsibility to Protect: Who Should Intervene?*, Oxford: Oxford University Press.

Pradhan B., Buchroithner M. (eds) (2012): *Terrigenous Mass Movements: Detection, Modelling, Early Warning and Mitigation Using Geoinformation Technology*, Heidelberg – Berlin: Springer.

Przełomiec M. (1997): *Czeczenia – niepodległość czy ograniczona suwerenność?*, Warsaw: Centrum Stosunków Międzynarodowych Instytutu Spraw Publicznych.

Ramcharan B. (2002): *The Security Council and the Protection of Human Rights*, The Hague: Martinus Nijhof Publishers.

Ramcharan B. (2002): *The United Nations High Commissioner for Human Rights. The Challenge of International Protection*, Hague – London – New York: Martinus Nijhoff Publishers.

Ramcharan B. (2008): *Preventive Diplomacy at the UN*, Bloomington: Indiana University Press.

Ramcharan B. (2009): *The Protection Roles of UN Human Rights Special Procedures*, Leiden – Boston: Nijhoff Law Specials.

Ramcharan B. (2010): *Preventive Human Rights Strategies*, London – New York: Routledge.

Ramcharan B. (2011): *The UN Human Rights Council*, London – New York: Routledge.

Reyntjens F. (2009): *The Great African War: Congo and Regional Geopolitics, 1996–2006*, New York: Cambridge University Press.

Rosenberg S.P., Galis T., Zucker A. (eds.) (2016): *Reconstructing Atrocity Prevention*, Cambridge University Press.

Rotberg R.I. (ed.) (2010): *Mass Atrocity Crimes: Preventing Future Outrages*, Washington DC: World Peace Foundation.

Rotfeld A.D. (1990): *Europejski system bezpieczeństwa in statu nascendi*, Warsaw: Polski Instytut Spraw Międzynarodowych.

Rotfeld A.D. (2006): *Polska w niepewnym świecie*, Warsaw: Polski Instytut Spraw Międzynarodowych.

Rotfeld A.D., Symonides J. (1998): *Peace, Security and Conflict Prevention. SIPRI–UNESCO Handbook*, Oxford: Oxford University Press.

Semelin J. (ed.) (2011): *Resisting Genocide: The Multiple Forms of Rescue*, New York: Columbia University Press.

Serrano M., Weiss T.G. (eds.) (2014), *The International Politics of Human Rights: Rallying to the R2P Cause?*, London – New York: Routledge.

Shelton D. (ed.) (2013): *The Oxford Handbook of International Human Rights Law*, Oxford: Oxford University Press.

Simms B., Trim D.J.B. (2011): *Humanitarian Intervention: A History*, Cambridge University Press.

Steiner B.H. (2004): *Collective Preventive Diplomacy. A Study in International Conflict Management*, State University of New York Press.

Straus S., Waldorf L., (eds.) (2011): *Remaking Rwanda. State Building and Human Rights after Mass Violence*, Madison: The University of Wisconsin Press.

Symonides J. (ed.) (1998): *Human Rights: New Dimensions and Challenges*, Dartmouth: Ashgate.

Thakur R. (2006): *The United Nations, Peace and Security: From Collective Security to the Responsibility to Protect*, Cambridge: Cambridge University Press.

Thakur R. (2011): *The Responsibility to Protect: Norms, Laws and the Use of Force in International Politics*, London – New York: Routledge.

Twagilimana A. (2015): *Historical Dictionary of Rwanda*, London: Rowman & Littlefield.

Waleensteen P., Staibano C. (2005): *International Sanctions. Between Words and Wars in the Global System*, London – New York: Routledge.

Weiss T.G. (2004): *Military-Civilian Interactions: Humanitarian Crises and the Responsibility to Protect*, New York: Rowman & Littlefield Publishers.

Weiss T.G. (2007): *Humanitarian Intervention: War and Conflict in the Modern World*, Cambridge: Cambridge University Press.

Wilks A. (ed.) (2010): *Aid and Development Effectiveness: Towards Human Rights, Social Justice and Democracy*, Quezon: IBON Books.

Williams P.D. (2016): *War and Conflict in Africa*, Cambridge – Malden: Polity Press.

Zajadło J. (2005): *Dylematy humanitarnej interwencji: historia, etyka, polityka, prawo*, Gdańsk: Arche.

Zięba R. (2001): *Instytucjonalizacja bezpieczeństwa europejskiego: koncepcje – struktury – funkcjonowanie*, Warsaw: Wydawnictwo Naukowe Scholar.

Zins H. (1986): *Historia Afryki Wschodniej*, Wrocław: Zakład Narodowy im. Ossolińskich.

Zyberi G. (ed.) (2013): *An Institutional Approach of the Responsibility to Protect*, Cambridge: Cambridge University Press.

Articles and chapters

Adams S. (2012): 'Libya and the Responsibility to Protect,' Global Centre for the Responsibility to Protect *Occasional Paper Series*, No. 3.

Akhavan P. (2006): 'Report on the Work of the Office of the Special Adviser of the United Nations Secretary-General on the Prevention of Genocide,' *Human Rights Quarterly*, No. 28 Vol. 4, 1043–1070.

Alebeek R. van, Nollkaemper A. (2012): 'The Legal Status of Decisions by Human Rights Treaty Bodies in National Law' in: Keller H., Ulfstein G., *UN Human Rights Treaty Bodies. Law and Legitimacy*, Cambridge University Press, 356–413.

'Appeal to the Bahutu Conscience (with the Hutu Ten Commandments),' *Kangura*, December 1990, No. 6.

Arbour L. (2008): 'The Responsibility to Protect as a Duty of Care in International Law and Practice' in: *Review of International Studies*, No. 34(3), 445–458.

Ayoob M. (2002): 'Humanitarian Intervention and International Society,' *Global Governance* 2002, No. 7(3), 225–230.

Ayoob M. (2004): 'Third World Perspectives on Humanitarian Intervention and International Administration,' *Global Governance*, No. 10(1), 99–118.

Bah A.B. (2010): 'Democracy and Civil War: Citizenship and Peacemaking in Côte D'Ivoire,' *African Affairs*, Vol. 109, No. 437, 597–615.

Barbour B., Gorlick B. (2008): 'Embracing the "Responsibility to Protect:" A Repertoire of Measures Including Asylum for Potential Victims,' *International Journal of Refugee Law*, No 20(4), 533–566.

Bellamy A. J. (2008): 'The *Responsibility* to *Protect* and the Problem of Military Intervention,' *International Affairs*, No. 84(4), 615–639.

Bellamy A. J. (2010): 'Responsibility to Protect. Five Years on,' *Ethics and International Affairs*, No. 24(2).

Bellamy A.J. (2011): 'Mass Atrocities and Armed Conflict: Links, Distinctions and Implications for the Responsibility to Prevent,' *Policy Analysis Brief*, The Stanley Foundation.

Bellamy A.J., Griffin S. (2002): 'OSCE Peacekeeping: Lessons from the Kosovo Verification Mission,' *European Security*, No 11(1), 1–26.

Bellamy A.J., Beeson M. (2010): 'The Responsibility to Protect in Southeast Asia: Can ASEAN Reconcile Humanitarianism and Sovereignty?,' *Asian Security*, No 6(3), 262–279.

Bellamy A.J., Williams P.D. (2011): 'The New Politics of Protection? Côte d'Ivoire, Libya and the Responsibility to Protect,' *International Affairs*, No. 87(4), 829–838.

Bieńczyk-Missala A. (2000): '*The Human Dimension in CSCE/OSCE Missions,' The Polish Quarterly of International Affairs*, Vol. 9, No. 4.

Bieńczyk-Missala A. (2005): '*Cele i funkcje misji Organizacji Bezpieczeństwa i Współpracy w Europie,' Stosunki Międzynarodowe – International Relations*, No. 32(3–4), 53–74.

Bieńczyk-Missala A. (2015): 'Zapobieganie masowym zbrodniom jako realizacja koncepcji "Odpowiedzialność za ochronę"',*Stosunki międzynarodowe – International Relations*, Vol. 51, No. 3, 45–60.

Bieńczyk-Missala A. (2016): 'Early Warning and the Prevention of Atrocity Crimes. The Role of the United Nations' in: Bachmann K., Heidrich D. (eds.), *The Legacy of Crimes and Crises. Transitional Justice, Domestic Change and the Role of the International Community*, Frankfurt am Main: Peter Lang Edition, 199–207.

Bieńczyk-Missala A. (2016): 'Rola Rady Bezpieczeństwa w zakresie zapobiegania masowym zbrodniom, 'in: Gawrycki M. and others (eds.) *Tendencje i procesy rozwojowe współczesnych stosunków międzynarodowych*, Warsaw: Wydawnictwo Naukowe Scholar, 284–294.

Bieńczyk-Missala A. (2017): 'Cultural Determinants of the Development and Observance of Universal Human Rights' in: Michałowska G., Schreiber H. (eds.), *Culture(s) in International Relations*, Peter Lang Edition, 253–272.

Bieńczyk-Missala A. (2019): 'Kosovo: the First War for Human Rights' in: Madej M. (ed.), *Western Military Interventions After the Cold War*, London-New York: Routledge, 53–73.

Bieńczyk-Missala A., Grzebyk P. (2015): 'Safety and Protection of Humanitarian Workers' in: Gibbons P., Heintze H.-J., *The Humanitarian Challenge. 20 Years European Network on Humanitarian Action (NOHA)*, Switzerland: Springer, 221–251.

Black I.,'Libyan Revolution Casualties Lower Than Expected, Says New Government,' *The Guardian*, January 8, 2013.

Bloed A. (1995): 'The Human Dimension of the OSCE: More Words than Deeds?,' *Helsinki Monitor*, Vol. 6, No. 4, 23–29.

Bloed A. (1997): 'The OSCE Response to Conflict in the Region,' *Helsinki Monitor*, Vol. 8, No. 2, 49–55.

Borghard E.D., Pischedda C. (2012): 'Allies and Airpower in Libya,' *Parameters*, Vol. 42, No. 1, 63–74.

Boyle F.A. (1998): 'Independent Chechnya: Treaty of Peace with Russia of 12 May 1997,' *Journal of Muslim Minority Affairs*, Vol. 18, No. 1, 177–179.

Buchsbaum T. M. (1993): 'The Future of the Human Dimension of the OSCE,' *Helsinki Monitor*, Vol. 4, No. 2, 5–4.

Burke-White W.W. (2011): 'Adoption of the Responsibility to Protect,' *Public Law Research Paper*, University of Pennsylvania Law School, 33–34.

Caflish L. (2006): 'The Reform of the European Court of Human Rights: Protocol No. 14 and Beyond,' *Human Rights Law Review*, Vol. 6, No. 2, 403–415.

Chakravarty A. (Winter/Spring 2006): 'Gacaca Courts in Rwanda: Explaining Divisions within the Human Rights Community,' *Yale Journal of International Affairs*, 132–143.

Chirot D. (2006): 'The Debacle in Cote d'Ivoire,' *Journal of Democracy*, Vol. 17, No. 2, 63–77.

Chechnya: A UN Commission's resolution on Chechnya. Another missed opportunity to guarantee accountability and justice, Amnesty International UK Press Release, April 26, 2000.

Clarke G. (2012): 'The Evolving ASEAN Human Rights System: The ASEAN Human Rights Declaration of 2012,' *Northwestern Journal of International Human Rights*, Vol. 11, No. 1, 1–28, 1–28.

Coghlan B., Brennan R. J., Ngoy P. et al. (2006): 'Mortality in the Democratic Republic of Congo: a Nationwide Survey,' Lancet, Vol. 367, 44–51.

Cook N. (2011): 'Cote d'Ivoire Post-Gbagbo: Crisis Recovery,' *International Reactions*, 30–45.

Danecki J., Sulowski S. (eds.) (2011): *Bliski Wschód coraz bliżej*, Warsaw: Dom Wydawniczy Elipsa.

Davis R., Majekodunmi B., Smith-Hohn J. (2008): 'Prevention of Genocide and Mass Atrocities and the Responsibility to Protect: Challenges for The UN and International Community in the 21st Century,' *Responsibility to Protect. Occasional Papers*.

Dobriansky P. J. (Spring 1989): 'Human Rights and U.S. Foreign Policy,' *The Washington Quarterly*, 153–156.

Doyle N. (2014): 'The ASEAN Human Rights Declaration And The Implications of Recent Southeast Asian Initiatives In Human Rights Institution-Building And Standard-Setting,' *International and Comparative Law Quarterly*, Vol. 63, No. 1, 67–101.

Drzewicki K. (July-September, 1998): 'Prawa człowieka w Karcie NZ i w Powszechnej Deklaracji Praw Człowieka,' *Sprawy Międzynarodowe*, 9–16.

Dzisiów-Szuszczykiewicz A. (2008): 'Arabska Wiosna – przyczyny, przebieg i prognozy,' *Bezpieczeństwo narodowe*, 41–56.

Evans G., 'The Lessons of Libya,' *New York Times*, November 15, 2011.

Evans G., Sahnoun M. (2002), 'The Responsibility to Protect. Revisiting Humanitarian Intervention,' *Foreign Affairs*, Vol. 81, No. 6, 99–110.

Feinstein L., Slaughter A.-M. (2004): 'A Duty to Prevent,' *Foreign Affairs*, 136–150.

Finkel J. (2014): 'Atrocity Prevention at the Crossroads: Assessing the President's Atrocity Prevention Board After Two Years,' *Series of Occasional Papers*, Center for the Prevention of Genocide, No. 2.

First Chechnya War – 1994–1996, Federation of American Scientists, Military Analysis Network, December 2, 2002, https://www.globalsecurity.org/military/world/war/chechnya1.htm.

Ghanea N. (2006): 'From UN Commission on Human Rights to UN Human Rights Council: One Step Forwards or Two Steps Sideways? *International&-Comparative Law Quarterly*, Vol. 55, No. 3, 695–705.

Ghebali V.-I., Warner D. (eds.) (1999): 'The OSCE and Preventive Diplomacy,' *PSIO Occasional Paper*, No. 1.

Glanville L. (2012): 'The Responsibility to Protect Beyond Borders,' *Human Rights Law Review*, Vol. 12, 8–15, 1–32.

Goldstone J.A., Bates R.H., Gurr T.R., Lustik M., Marshall M.G., Ulfelder J., Woodward M. (2005): *A Global Forecasting Model of Political Instability*, Conference paper, Washington, 1–4 September.

Grzebyk P. (2014): 'Classification of the Conflict Between Ukraine and Russia in International Law (Ius ad Bellum and Ius in Bello),' *Polish Yearbook of International Law* 2014, Vol. 34, 39–60.

Grzebyk P. (2015): 'Miejsce interwencji zbrojnej w koncepcji "odpowiedzialność za ochronę",' *Stosunki Międzynarodowe*, No. 3, Vol. 51, 61–76.

Hałaciński A. (1995) 'Misje długoterminowe OBWE,' *Sprawy Międzynarodowe,* No. 2.

Hampson F.J. (2007): 'An Overview of the Reform of the UN Human Rights Machinery,' *Human Rights Law Review*, Vol. 7, No. 1, 7–27.

Harff B., Gurr T. R. (1988): 'Toward Empirical Theory of Genocides and Politicides: Identification and Measurement of Cases since 1945,' *International Studies Quarterly*, Vol. 37, No. 3, 359–371.

Hayman R. (2011): 'Funding Fraud?: Donors and Democracy in Rwanda' in: Straus S., Waldorf L., (eds.), *Remaking Rwanda. State Building and Human Rights after Mass Violence,* The University of Wisconsin Press, 118–131.

Hehir A., (2010), 'An Analysis of Perspectives on the Office of the Special Adviser on the Prevention of Genocide,' *Genocide Studies and Prevention: An International Journal*, No. 5, 258–276.

Hehir A. (2011): 'The Special Adviser on the Prevention of Genocide: Adding Value to the UN's Mechanisms for Preventing Intra-State Crises?' *Journal of Genocide Research*, No. 13, Vol. 1, 271–286.

Hehir A. (2013): 'The Permanence of Inconsistency: Libya, the Security Council, and the Responsibility to Protect,' *International Security*, Vol. 38, No. 10, 137–159.

Higgins R. (1987): 'Human Rights and Foreign Policy,' *Rivista di Studi Politici Internazionali*, 578–580.

Hoeffler A. (2014): 'Can International Interventions Secure the Peace,' *International Area Studies Review*, No. 1, 75–94.

Hultman L., Kathman J., Shannon M. (2014): 'Beyond Keeping Peace: United Nations Effectiveness in the Midst of Fighting,' *American Political Science Review*, No. 4, 737–753.

H. F. Hurlburt (1995): 'Russia Plays a Double Game,' *Transition*, 30 June, Vol. 1, No. 11, 10–17.

Ipinyomi F. (2012): 'Is Côte d'Ivoire a Test Case for R2P? Democratization as Fulfillment of the International Community's Responsibility to Prevent,' *Cardiovascular Journal of Africa*, Vol. 56, No. 2, 151–160.

Kingah S., Seiwert E. (2017): 'The Contested Emerging International Norm and Practice of a Responsibility to Protect: Where are Regional Organizations?' *North Carolina Journal of International Law*, Vol. 42, March 2017, 115–189.

Klaas B. (2008): 'From Miracle to Nightmare: An Institutional Analysis of Development Failures in Côte d'Ivoire,' *Africa Today*, Vol. 55, No. 1, 109–126.

Ku J., Nzelibe J. (2006): 'Do International Criminal Tribunals Deter or Exacerbate Humanitarian Atrocities?' *Washington University Law Review*, Vol. 84, 777–833.

Kuźniar R. (1998): 'Prawa człowieka i stosunki międzynarodowe,' *Sprawy Międzynarodowe*, No. 3, 25–58.

Maisonneuve M. (summer 2000), 'The OSCE Kosovo Verification Mission,' *Canadian Military Journal*, 49–54.

Miskel J.F., Norton R.J. (1998): 'Humanitarian Early-Warning Systems,' *Global Governance*, Vol. IV, 317–324.

Missala M. (2000): 'Bariery samostanowienia Czeczenii,' *Polityka Wschodnia*, No. 2, 89–91. 93–102.

Modrzejewska-Leśniewska J. (1996): 'Konflikt rosyjsko-czeczeński (1994–1996)' in: Bartnicki A. (ed.), *Zarys dziejów Afryki i Azji 1869–1996*, Warsaw: Wydawnictwo Książka i Wiedza, 469–485.

Moolakkattu J.S. (2010): 'The role of the African Union in Continental Peace and Security Governance,' *India Quarterly*, No 66(2), 151–165.

Morris J. (2013): 'Libya and Syria: R2P and the Specter of the Swinging Pendulum,' *International Affairs*, No. 89(5), 1255–1283.

Mucha W. (2014): 'The Next Spring is Certain to Come – and Certain to be Missed: Deficits in Conflict Prevention Research,' *Global Responsibility to Protect*, Vol. 6, No. 4, 2014, 382–406.

Nambiar S. (November 2011): 'The Emerging Principle of the Responsibility to Protect: An Asian Perspectives,' *Strategic Analysis*, Vol. 35, No. 6, 955–965.

Neier A. (Winter 1996–1997): 'The New Double Standards,' *Foreign Policy*, No. 105, 91–101.

Neuenkirch M., Neumeier F. (2014): 'The Impact of UN and US Economic Sanctions on GDP Growth,' *Joint Discussion Paper Series in Economics*, No. 24.

Nuruzzaman M. (2013): 'The "Responsibility to Protect" Doctrine: Revived in Libya, Buried in Syria,' *Insight Turkey*, Vol. 15, No. 2, 57–66.

Piiparinen T. (2012): 'Sovereignty-building: Three Images of Positive Sovereignty Projected Through Responsibility to Protect,' *Global Change, Peace&Security*, 405–424.

Rashid S. (2013): 'Preventive Diplomacy, Mediation and the Responsibility to Protect in Libya: a Missed Opportunity for Canada?' *Canadian Foreign Policy Journal*, Vol. 19, No. 1, 39–52.

Rotfeld A.D. (2016): 'Porządek międzynarodowy: wartości vs. interesy i potencjały' in: Hausner J. (ed.), *Open Eyes Book*, Cracow: Fundacja Administracji i Gospodarki Publicznej, 43–67.

Schabas W. (2006): *Preventing Genocide and Mass Killing: The Challenge for the United Nations*, Minority Rights Group International.

Schabas W. (2007): 'Preventing the "Odious Scourge": The United Nations and the Prevention of Genocide,' *International Journal on Minority and Group Rights*, Vol. 14, 379–397.

Schmidt J. (2016): 'EU and UN Partnership in Light of the Responsibility to Protect' in: Chappel L., Mawdsley J., Petrov P. (eds.) *The EU, Strategy and Security Policy: Regional and Strategic Challenges*, London: Routlege, 139–144.

Sewall S., Raymond D., Chin S. (2010): *Mass Atrocity Response Operations: A Military Planning Handbook*, Army War College Carlisle Barracks PA Peacekeeping and Stability Operations Institute.

Stanton G.H. (2013): *The Ten Stages of Genocide*, http://www.genocidewatch.org/genocide/tenstagesofgenocide.html.

Stoel M. van der (1998): 'Zapobieganie konfliktom w sytuacjach związanych z kwestiami mniejszości narodowych,' *Sprawy Międzynarodowe*, No. 3, 59–74.

Sviatun O. (2014): 'The Role of Human Rights Clause in the EU Agreements with Third Countries' in: Jaskiernia J., *Uniwersalny i regionalny wymiar ochrony praw człowieka. Nowe wyzwania – nowe rozwiązania*, Vol. 1, Warsaw: Wydawnictwo Sejmowe, 643–653.

Sykuna S., Zajadło J. (2012): 'The Theory of Hard Cases and Humanitarian Intervention,' *Polish Review of International and European Law* 2012, No. 1, 11–60.

Toungara J.M. (2001): 'Ethnicity and Political Crisis in Côte d'Ivoire,' *Journal of Democracy*, Vol. 12, No 3, 63–72.

Verwimp P. (2006): 'Machetes and Firearms: The Organization of Massacres in Rwanda,' *Journal of Peace Research*, No. 43(1), 5–22.

Vincent R. J. (1982): 'Human Rights and Foreign Policy,' *Australian Outlook*, Vol. 36, No. 3, 1–5.

Waal A. de (2013): African Roles in the Libyan Conflict of 2011, *International Affairs*, Vol. 89, No. 2, 365–379.

Weiss T. (2011): 'RtoP Alive and Well After Libya,' *Ethics & International Affairs*, Vol. 25, 287–292.

Weissgerber R., Bierdziński S., Nawrocki M., Piłat Z. (2012): 'Operacja powietrzna "Zjednoczony Obrońca 2011",' *Przegląd Sił Powietrznych*, No. 3, 12–18.

Williams I. (2012): 'Applying "Responsibility to Protect" to Syria no Cakewalk,' *The Washington Report on Middle East Affairs*, Vol. 31, No. 4.

Williams P.D. (2007): 'From Non-Intervention to Non-Indifference: The Origins and Development of the African Union's Security Culture,' *African Affairs*, March 12, 253–279.

Zellner W., Evers F. and others (2014): *The Future of OSCE Field Operations (Options)*, OSCE Network of Think Tanks and Academic Institutions.

Zifcak, S. (2012) 'The Responsibility to Protect After Libya and Syria,' *Melbourne Journal of International Law*, No. 13(1), 59–93.

Documents, reports, statements

Aall P.R. (1996): *NGOs and Conflict Management. Responses to International Conflict Highlights From The Managing Chaos Conference*, United States Institute of Peace.

Code of Conduct Regarding Security Council Action Against Genocide, Crimes against Humanity or War Crimes, Accountability, Coherence and Transparency Group, New York, October, 23 2015.

Action Plan on Human Rights and Democracy (2015–2019) – Keeping Human Rights at the Heart of the EU agenda, JOIN(2015) 16 final, April 28, 2015, https://ec.europa.eu/anti-trafficking/sites/antitrafficking/files/joint_communication_on_human_rights_and_democracy_en.pdf.

Action Plan to Prevent Genocide, UN Secretary General Speech in Geneva, April 7, 2004, http://www.preventgenocide.org/prevent/UNdocs/KofiAnnansActionPlantoPreventGenocide7Apr2004.htm.

African Union, Communiqué of the 261st Meeting of the Peace and Security Council, PSC/PR/COM (CCLXI), February 23, 2011.

African Union, Communiqué of the 265th Meeting of the Peace and Security Council, PSC/PR/COM (CCLXI), March 10, 2011.

African Union Constitutive Act, Lomé, July 11, 2000, https://au.int/sites/default/files/pages/34873-file-constitutiveact_en.pdf.

African Union Ezulwini Consensus, Executive Council 7th Extraordinary Session, March 07–08, 2005, Addis Abeba, Etiopia, Ext/EX.CL/2(VII).

Agreement Establishing the Inter-Governmental Authority on Development (IGAD), Nairobi, March 21, 1996, http://www.ifrc.org/docs/idrl/N527EN.pdf.

Albright M., Cohen W. (2008), *Preventing Genocide: A Blueprint for US Policymakers, Genocide Prevention Task Force (GPTF)*, United States Holocaust Memorial Museum.

Annan K., *In Larger Freedom: Towards Development, Security and Human Rights for All*, Report of the Secretary-General, A/59/2005, March 21, 2005.

Annual Report 2015, The Latin American Network for Genocide and Mass Atrocity Prevention, https://www.stanleyfoundation.org/publications/other/LAN-ANNUALRPT2015ENGLISH.pdf

Annual Report 2016, The Latin American Network for Genocide and Mass Atrocity Prevention, https://www.stanleyfoundation.org/publications/other/LAN-ANNUALRPT2016ENGLISH.pdf

Arab Charter on Human Rights, League of Arab States, May 22, 2004, http://hrlibrary.umn.edu/instree/loas2005.html?msource=UNWDEC19001&tr=y&auid=3337655

ASEAN Charter, November 20, 2007, http://asean.org/wp-content/uploads/images/archive/publications/ASEAN-Charter.pdf

ASEAN Human Rights Declaration, November 18, 2012, http://www.asean.org/storage/images/ASEAN_RTK_2014/6_AHRD_Booklet.pdf

ASEAN Political-Security Community Blueprint, June 2009, http://asean.org/wp-content/uploads/archive/5187-18.pdf.

Budapest Centre for Mass Atrocities Prevention, *African Regional Communities and the Prevention of Mass Atrocities*, African Task Force on the Prevention of Mass Atrocities, Budapest 2016.

Budapest Centre for Mass Atrocities Prevention, *Capabilities of the Visegrad Group in preventing extremism*, Budapest 2017.

Budapest Centre for the International Prevention of Genocide and Mass Atrocities, *The EU and the Prevention of Mass Atrocities. An Assessment of Strengths and Weaknesses*, February 2013.

Carnegie Corporation of New York, *Preventing Deadly Conflict: Final Report*, 1997.

Chair statement, First International Meeting of Global Action Against Mass Atrocity Crimes, March 4–6, 2014, San José, Costa Rica, March 6, 2014.

Charter of the United Nations, June 26, 1945.

Claes J., 'Libya and the Responsibility to Protect,' March 1, 2011, United States Institute of Peace, https://www.usip.org/publications/2011/03/libya-and-responsibility-protect

Communication from the Commission to the European Parliament, the Council, the European Economic and Social Committee and the Committee of the Regions, *Proposal for a new European Consensus on Development Our World, Our Dignity, Our Future*, COM(2016) 740 final, Strasbourg, November 22, 2016.

Constitution of the Republic of Rwanda, 4 June 2003 r., https://www.parliament.gov.rw/fileadmin/Images2013/Rwandan_Constitution.pdf.

Côte d'Ivoire: "The War Is Not Yet Over", International Crisis Group Africa Report, No. 72, New York, November 28, 2003, https://www.crisisgroup.org/africa/west-africa/c%C3%B4te-divoire/cote-d-ivoire-war-not-yet-over.

Council for Security Cooperation in the Asia Pacific (CSCAP), Study Group on the Responsibility to Protect (RtoP), *Final Report*, 2011, http://www.cscap.org/uploads/docs/RtoP/CSCAP%20Study%20Group%20on%20RtoP%20-%20Final%20Report.pdf.

Council of Europe Parliamentary Assembly, Evaluation of the Prospects for a Political Solution of the Conflict in the Chechen Republic, Resolution 1315 (2003), http://assembly.coe.int/nw/xml/XRef/Xref-XML2HTML-en.asp?fileid=17075&lang=en.

Council's of Europe Parliamentary Assembly resolutions: 1315 (2003), 1323 (2003), 1402 (2004), 1403 (2004), 1678 (2004), 1679 (2004).

Dar-Es-Salaam Declaration on Peace, Security, Democracy and Development in the Great Lakes Region, International Conference on the Great Lakes Region, Dar-Es-Salaam 2004, https://peacemaker.un.org/sites/peacemaker.un.org/files/041120_DarEsSalaamDeclaration.pdf.

Declaration of the Latin American Network for Genocide and Mass Atrocity Prevention, Santiago, May 29, 2015, http://www.auschwitzinstitute.org/wp-content/uploads/2015/08/Network-Declaration-EN.pdf.

Declaration on Democracy, Political, Economic and Corporate Governance, July 08, 2002, http://www.commit4africa.org/sites/

default/files/NEPAD-Declaration-Democracy-Economic-Political-Corporate-Governance.pdf.

Decision No. 3/11, Elements of the Conflict Cycle, Related to Enhancing the OSCE's Capabilities in Early Warning, Early Action, Dialogue Facilitation and Mediation Support, and Post-Conflict Rehabilitation, MC.DEC/3/11, December 7, 2011, in: *Organization for Security and Co-operation in Europe, Eighteenth Meeting of the Ministerial Council*, 06–07.12.2011, Vilnius 2011, 11–16.

Department for International Development, Operational Plan 2011–2016: DFID Rwanda, London 2014, https://www.gov.uk/government/uploads/system/uploads/attachment_data/file/389305/Rwanda.pdf.

Des Forges A., *Leave None to Tell the Story. The Genocide in Rwanda*, Human Rights Watch Report, March 1999, https://www.hrw.org/reports/1999/rwanda/.

Diène D., Special Rapporteur on contemporary forms of racism, racial discrimination, xenophobia and related intolerance, Mission to Côte d'Ivoire, *Racism, Racial Discrimination, Xenophobia and All Forms of Discrimination*, E/CN.4/2004/18/Add.4, March 4, 2004.

Document of the Moscow Meeting of the Conference on the Human Dimension of the CSCE, October 3, 1991, in: *OSCE Human Dimension Commitments, A Reference Guide*, Warsaw 2001.

ECOWAS Conflict Prevention Framework, Regulation MSC/REG, January 1, 2008, https://www.right2info.org/resources/publications/instruments-and-standards/africa_ecowas-regulation_conflct-prevention.

ECOWAS Protocol on Non-aggression, April 22, 1978,

http://documentation.ecowas.int/download/en/legal_documents/protocols/Protocol%20on%20Non-aggression.pdf.

ECOWAS Protocol Relating to the Mechanism for Conflict Prevention, Management, Resolution, Peace-Keeping and Security, December 10, 1999, http://www.zif-berlin.org/fileadmin/uploads/analyse/dokumente/ECOWAS_Protocol_ConflictPrevention.pdf.

ECOWAS Protocol Relating to Mutual Assistance on Defence, May 29, 1981, http://documentation.ecowas.int/download/en/legal_documents/protocols/Protocol%20Relating%20to%20Mutual%20Assistance%20on%20Defence.pdf.

ECOWAS Revised Treaty, July 25, 1993, http://www.ecowas.int/wp-content/uploads/2015/01/Revised-treaty.pdf.

EU Council of the European Union, *Conclusions on Conflict Prevention*, 11820/11, June 20, 2011.

EU European Commission, *Proposal for a New European Consensus on Development our World, our Dignity, our Future*, Strasbourg, COM(2016) 740 final, November 22, 2016.

EU European Council, *Report on the Implementation of the European Security Strategy: Providing Security in a Changing World*, S407/08, Brussels, December 11, 2008.

EU European Parliament, *Report with a proposal for a European Parliament recommendation to the Council on the UN principle of the "Responsibility to Protect"*, A7-0130/2013, A7-0130/2013, March 27, 2013.

EU Gothenburg European Council Programme 2001, SN 200/1/01 REV 1, June 15–16, 2001.

EU Strategic Framework and Action Plan on Human Rights and Democracy, 11855/12 Luxembourg, June 25, 2012.

Federation of American Scientists, Military Analysis Network, *First Chechnya War - 1994–1996*, December 2, 2002

First Round of OSCE Talks Concluded in Grozny, *OSCE Newsletter* 1995, No. 2(5).

Feinstein L., Lindberg T., Report: Allies Against Atrocities: The Imperative for Transatlantic Cooperation to Prevent and Stop Mass Killings, March 2017, https://www.ushmm.org/m/pdfs/20170301-Allies-Against-Atrocities-March-2017-Report.pdf.

Foreign Affairs Council, Council Conclusions on Côte d'Ivoire, 3058th meeting, Brussels, 13.12.2010, http://www.consilium.europa.eu/uedocs/cms_data/docs/pressdata/EN/foraff/118442.pdf.

Founding Document, The Global Action Against Mass Atrocity Crimes, San Jose, March 04–06, 2014, http://static.gaamac.org/media/uploads/PDFs/gaamac_founding_document.pdf.

Framework Analysis for Atrocity Crimes. A Tool for Prevention, United Nations 2014.

Freedom House Reports, Côte d'Ivoire.

Global Action Against Mass Atrocity Crimes II Outcome Document, Manila, February 04, 2016, http://static.gaamac.org/media/uploads/PDFs/gaamac_ii_outcome_document_final.pdf.

Global Centre for the Responsibility to Protect, National R2P Focal Points Recommendations, *Policy Briefs*, July 26, 2012, https://www.globalr2p.org/publications/national-r2p-focal-points-recommendations/.

Global Centre for the Responsibility to Protect, Open statement on the situation in Côte d'Ivoire, December 17, 2010, https://reliefweb.int/report/côte-divoire/open-statement-situation-côte-divoire.

Gowan R., Woocher L., Solomon D., Preventing Mass Atrocities: An Essential Agenda for the Next UN Secretary-General, September 2016, https://www.ushmm.org/m/pdfs/Preventing-mass-atrocities.pdf.

Guterres A., *Implementing the Responsibility to Protect: Accountability for Prevention,* Report of the Secretary-General, A/71/1016-S/2017/556, August 10, 2017.

Guterres A., *Responsibility to Protect: From Early Warning to Early Action*, Report of the Secretary-General, (A/72/884-S/2018/525), June 1, 2018.

Guterres A., *Responsibility to Protect: Lessons Learned for Prevention*, Report of the Secretary-General, (A/73/898-S/2019/463), June 10, 2019.

Guterres A., *Prioritizing Prevention and Strengthening Response: Women and the Responsibility to Protect*, Report of the Secretary-General, (A/74/964 – S/2020/501), July 23 2020.

Helsinki Document 1992: The Challenges of Change, CSCE, Helsinki, July 10, 1992.

Höynck W. (1996): 'CSCE Missions in the Field as an Instrument of Preventive Diplomacy – Their Origin and Development' in: *From CSCE to OSCE: Statements and speeches of Dr. Wilhelm Höynck, Secretary General of the OSCE (1993–1996)*, OSCE, Vienna, 116–131.

Human Rights Watch World Reports, Rwanda.

Human Rights Watch World Reports, Libya.

Human Rights Watch, *Ivory Coast: Call for the Protection of Civilians and Respect of the Population's Fundamental Rights*, December 16, 2010, https://www.hrw.org/news/2010/12/16/ivory-coast-call-protection-civilians-and-respect-populations-fundamental-rights.

Human Rights Watch, *Côte D'Ivoire: Ensure Security, Protect Expression, Movement. Constitutional Council's Overrule of Election Results Raises Risk of Violence*, December 4, 2010, https://www.hrw.org/news/2010/12/04/cote-divoire-ensure-security-protect-expression-movement.

Human Rights Watch, *Dispatches: Rwanda Turns the Clock Back on Access to Justice* March 11, 2016, https://www.hrw.org/news/2016/03/11/dispatches-rwanda-turns-clock-back-access-justice.

Human Rights Watch, *Justice Compromised. The Legacy of Rwanda's Community-Based Gacaca Court*, May 31, 2011, https://www.hrw.org/report/2011/05/31/justice-compromised/legacy-rwandas-community-based-gacaca-courts.

Human Rights Watch, *War Crimes in Chechnya and the Response of the West*, February 29, 2000, https://www.hrw.org/news/2000/02/29/war-crimes-chechnya-and-response-west.

Human security reports.

International Conference on the Great Lakes Region, Pact on Security, Stability and Development in the Great Lake Region, Nairobi, December 15, 2006, https://ungreatlakes.unmissions.org/sites/default/files/icglr_pact_on_security_stability_and_development_for_the_glr.pdf.

International Conference on the Great Lakes Region, Protocol for the Prevention and the Punishment of the Crime of Genocide, War Crimes and Crimes Against Humanity and all Forms of Discrimination, Nairobi, November 21, 2006, http://www.icglr.org/images/LastPDF/Protocol_on_Crime_Prevention_and_Punishment_of_the_Crime_of_Geno.pdf

International Federation of Red Cross and Red Crescent Societies, *Community Early Warning Systems: Guiding Principles*, Geneva 2013, http://www.ifrc.org/PageFiles/103323/1227800-IFRC-CEWS-Guiding-Principles-EN.pdf.

Ki-moon B., *A Vital and Enduring Commitment: Implementing the Responsibility to Protect*, Report of the UN Secretary-General, A/69/981–S/2015/500, July 13, 2015.

Ki-moon B., *A Vital and Enduring Commitment: Implementing the Responsibility to Protect*, Report of the UN Secretary-General, A/70/999–S/2016/620, July 22, 2016.

Ki-moon B., *Early Warning, Assessment, and the Responsibility to Protect*, Report of the Secretary-General, A/65/864, July 14, 2010.

Ki-moon B., *Fulfilling our Collective Responsibility: International Assistance and the Responsibility to Protect*, Report of the Secretary-General, A/68/947S/2014/449, July 11, 2014.

Ki-moon B., *Implementing the Responsibility to Protect*, Report of the Secretary-General, A/63/677, January 12, 2009.

Ki-moon B., *Plan of Action to Prevent Extremism*, Report of the Secretary-General, A/70/674, January 15, 2016.

Ki-moon B., *State Responsibility and Prevention*, Report of the Secretary-General, A/67/929–S/2013/399, July 9, 2013.

Ki-moon B., *The Responsibility to Protect: Timely and Decisive Response*, Report of the Secretary-General, A/66/874–S/2012/578, July 25, 2012.

Ki-moon B., *The Role of Regional and Sub-regional Arrangements in Implementing the Responsibility to Protect*, Report of the Secretary-General, A/65/877-S/2011/393, July 12, 2011.

League of Arab States Council's resolution No, 7360, March 12, 2011.

Letter dated 12 July 2004 from the UN Secretary-General addressed to the President of the Security Council, S/2004/567.

Letter dated 31 August 2007 from the UN Secretary-General addressed to the President of the Security Council, S/2007/721.

Mudingu J., Girinka Programme Transforms Livelihoods, Reconciles Communities, http://rab.gov.rw/fileadmin/user_upload/documentss/article_about_Girinka.pdf.

NGOs and the prevention of mass atrocities crimes: A practical workshop for NGOs to develop and share strategies to implement the Responsibility to Protect in the Asia-Pacific Region, November 23–24, 2009, Outcome document, Oxfam Australia, March 16, 2010.

Official Records of the General Assembly, Sixty-third Session, Plenary Meetings 96th to 101st meetings, A/63/PV.96–101.

Organization of American States, Declaration of Bridgetown. The Multidimensional Approach to Hemispheric Security, Bridgetown, June 04, 2002, http://www.oas.org/xxxiiga/english/docs_en/docs_items/agcgdoc15_02.htm.

Organization of American States, Inter-American Commission on Human Rights, Report on citizen security and human rights, OAS Doc. OEA/Ser.L/V/II. Doc. 57, December 31, 2009,

Organization of American States, *Inter-American Democratic Charter*, Lima, September 11, 2001.

Organization of American States, *Plan of action*, Quebec, April 22, 2001.

Organization of American States, General Assembly resolutions No. 1080, OAS Doc. AG/RES. 1080 (XXI-0/91), 05.06.1991.

Organization of Islamic Cooperation, *Cairo Declaration on Human Rights in Islam,* August 5, 1990.

Organization for Security and Cooperation in Europe, *Handbook*, Vienna 1999.

Organization for Security and Cooperation in Europe, Internal Early Warning Guidelines, data SEC.GAL/52/12.

Organization for Security and Cooperation in Europe, Annual Report on OSCE Activities 1997 (1 November 2016 – 30 November 1997), http://www.osce.org/secretariat/14551?download=true.

Organization for Security and Cooperation in Europe, Annual Report on OSCE Activities 1999, (December 1998 – 31 October 1999), http://www.osce.org/secretariat/14539?download=true.

Organization for Security and Cooperation in Europe, Analysis of OSCE Long-Term Field Activities, prepared by the Research Assistants at the OSCE Parliamentary Assembly, International Secretariat in Copenhagen, June 1999.

Peace agreement between the Government of the Republic of Rwanda and the Rwandese Patriotic Front, January 9, 1993, http://www.incore.ulst.ac.uk/services/cds/agreements/pdf/rwan1.pdf.

Protocol of amendments to the Charter of the Organization of American States, Washington DC, December 14, 1992, http://www.oas.org/assembly2001/assembly/GAAssembly2000/Protocol%20of%20Washington.pdf.

Protocol of the Establishment of a Conflict Early Warning and Response Mechanism for IGAD Member States, January 9, 2002, https://www3.nd.edu/~ggoertz/rei/rei900/rei900.02tt1.pdf.

Protocol on Politics, Defense and Security Co-operation, Blantysa, August 14, 2001, http://www.sadc.int/files/3613/5292/8367/Protocol_on_Politics_Defence_and_Security20001.pdf.

Protocol relating to the establishment of the Peace and Security Council of the African Union, Durban, July 9, 2002, http://www.peaceau.org/uploads/psc-protocol-en.pdf.

Intervention of G.H. Stanton on the occasion of the opening of the Budapest Centre for the Prevention of Genocide, 10.2010, https://d0dbb2cb-698c-4513-aa47-eba3a335e06f.filesusr.com/ugd/e5b74f_cd65c6b605534d80b0ff6a6eca3011ba.pdf.

Speech by the Secretary General of the ICGLR Amb. Liberaty Mulamuly during the II Regional Forum in Arusha, 3–5 March 2010, dedicated to the prevention of genocide, https://www.icglr.org/images/LastPDF/GENOCIDE_PREVENTION_Mulamulapaper_2.pdf.

Statement by the UN Secretary-General Kofi Annan at the UN General Assembly in its 1999 session, UNIS/SG/2381, September 21, 1999.

Statement by the UN Secretary-General at the opening of the fifty-fourth session of the Commission on Human Rights, New York, March 26, 2004.

Report of the Office of the UN High Commissioner for Human Rights, *The Role of Prevention in the Promotion and Protection of Human Rights*, A/HRC/30/20, July 16, 2015.

Report of the High-Level Panel on Threats, Challenges and Change, *A More Secure World: Our Shared Responsibility, United Nations 2004.*

Report of the UN Secretary-General, *Implementing the Responsibility to Protect*, A/63/677, 12 January 2009.

Report of the UN Secretary-General, *Early Warning, Assessment, and the Responsibility to Protect*, A/65/864, 14 July 2010.

Report of the UN Secretary-General, *Preventive Diplomacy: Delivering Results*, https://www.un.org/undpa/sites/www.un.org.undpa/files/SG%20Report%20on%20Preventive%20Diplomacy.pdf.

Report of the UN Secretary-General *Prevention of Armed Conflict*, A/55/985–S/2001/574, July 7, 2001.

Report of the UN Secretary-*General pursuant to General Assembly resolution* No. 53/35, November 15, 1999,

Report by Mr. Alvaro Gil-Robles, Commissioner for Human Rights, on his visit to the Russian Federation (in particular Chechnya, Daghestan and Ingoushetia), 7–10 December 1999, CommDH(1999)1, 10.12.1999.

Report from the HCNM, *OSCE Newsletter*, May, 1999.

Report of the Eminent Persons Group on the ASEAN Charter, Association of South-East Asian Nations, December 2006, http://www.asean.org/wp-content/uploads/images/archive/19247.pdf.

Report of the Independent Civil Society Fact-Finding Mission to Libya, January, 2012.

Report of the Independent Inquiry into the Actions of the United Nations During the 1994 genocide in Rwanda, S/1999/1257, December 15, 1999.

Report of the International Commission of Inquiry on Côte d'Ivoire, A/HRC/17/48, July 1, 2011.

Report of the International Commission on Intervention and State Sovereignty, The Responsibility to Protect, December 2001, https://undocs.org/pdf?symbol=en/a/57/303.

Report of the Secretary-General's Panel of Experts on Accountability in Sri Lanka, March 03, 2011, https://www.securitycouncilreport.org/un-documents/document/poc-rep-on-account-in-sri-lanka.php.

Report of the Working Group, Human Rights Council, *Universal Periodic Review*, A/HRC/13/9, Geneva, January 04, 2010.

Southern African Development Community, Revised edition strategic indicative plan for the organ on politics, defense and security cooperation, Maputo, August 5, 2010, http://www.sadc.int/files/3213/7951/6823/03514_SADC_SIPO_English.pdf.

Rights Up Front' Detailed Action Plan, January 2014 (*updated*), https://interagencystandingcommittee.org/system/files/detailed_hruf_plan_of_action.pdf.

Rules of Procedure of the Inter-American Commission on Human Rights, www.oas.org/en/iachr/mandate/Basics/rulesiachr.asp.

Rules of Procedure of the Inter-American Court of Human Rights, www.corteidh.or.cr/reglamento/regla_ing.pdf.

Sammut D., Shields J., *An Assessment of the Work of the OSCE in the Caucasus*, Report for the OSCE Review Conference, Istanbul, November 08–10, 1999.

Report of the UN Secretary-General's Panel of Experts on Accountability in Sri Lanka, March 31, 2011.

Report of the High-Level Panel on the Resolution of the Crisis in Côte d'Ivoire, January, 31 2011.

Report of the Independent Inquiry into the Actions of the United Nations during the 1994 Genocide in Rwanda, December 15, 1999, S/1999/1257, https://www.securitycouncilreport.org/atf/cf/%7B65BFCF9B-6D27-4E9C-8CD3-CF6E4FF96FF9%7D/POC%20S19991257.pdf.

Statement attributed to the UN Secretary-General's Special Advisers on the Prevention of Genocide and the Responsibility to Protect on the Situation in Côte d'Ivoire, Geneva, January 19, 2011, https://www.un.org/en/genocideprevention/documents/media/statements/2011/English/2011-01-19-OSAPG,%20Special%20Advisers%20Statement%20on%20Cote%20d%27Ivoire,%2019%20Jan%202011.pdf.

Statement attributed to the UN Secretary-General's Special Advisers on the Prevention of Genocide and the Responsibility to Protect on the Situation in Côte d'Ivoire, Geneva, December 29, 2010,

https://www.un.org/en/genocideprevention/documents/media/statements/2010/English/2010-12-29-Special%20Advisers'%20Statement%20on%20Cote%20d'Ivoire,.pdf.

Statement by Mary Robinson, High Commissioner for Human Rights on the situation of human rights in Chechnya in the Russian Federation, UN Commission on Human Rights, Geneva, April 5, 2000, https://reliefweb.int/report/russian-federation/statement-mary-robinson-high-commissioner-human-rights-situation-human.

Statement by Navy Pillay, UN High Commissioner for Human Rights on the Situation of Human Rights in the Libyan Arab Jamahiriya, Human Rights Council, 15th Special Session, Geneva, February 25, 2011, https://reliefweb.int/report/libya/situation-human-rights-libyan-arab-jamahiriya-statement-navy-pillay-un-high.

Statement by UN Secretary-General Kofi Annan at the opening of the fifty-fourth session of the Commission on Human Rights, March 18, 1998, Press Release SG/SM/6487 HR/4355.

Statement by UN Special Advisor on RtoP Jennifer Welsh at the Thematic Discussion in the UN General Assembly on "Ten Years of the Responsibility to Protect: From Commitment to Implementation", February 26, 2016, http://

www.un.org/en/genocideprevention/documents/responsibility-to-protect/Doc.6_2016-02-26-PGA%20Event%20RtoP%20at%20Ten%20Welsh.pdf.

Statement on Situation of Migrant Workers in Libya, April 08, 2011, http://www.ohchr.org/EN/HRBodies/CERD/Pages/EarlyWarningProcedure.aspx

Summary of the Sixth Informal Interactive Dialogue of the UN General Assembly on the Responsibility to Protect, held on 8 September 2014, Global Centre for the Responsibility to Protect, September 2014, http://s156658.gridserver.com/media/files/summary-of-the-r2p-dialogue-2014.pdf.

The Auschwitz Institute for Peace and Reconciliation, Annual Reports, http://www.auschwitzinstitute.org/publications/#aipr

The Responsibility to Protect (RtoP) and Genocide Prevention in Africa, International Peace Institute, Report, June 2009, https://www.ipinst.org/wp-content/uploads/publications/rtopinafrica_epub.pdf.

Traynor I., 'UN Chief ends Futile Chechnya Trip,' *The Guardian*, April 4, 2000, https://www.theguardian.com/world/2000/apr/04/chechnya.unitednations

Treaty of the Southern African Development Community, Windhoec, August 17, 1992, http://www.sadc.int/files/9113/5292/9434/SADC_Treaty.pdf.

United Nations Committee against Torture, Convention against Torture and Other Cruel, Inhuman or Degrading Treatment or Punishment, General Comment No. 2, Implementation of article 2 by States parties, CAT/C/GC/2, January 24, 2008.

United Nations Committee on the Elimination of Racial Discrimination, Early Warning and Urgent Action Procedure, March 2, 2011, http://www.ohchr.org/EN/HRBodies/CERD/Pages/EarlyWarningProcedure.aspx

United Nations Committee on the Elimination of Racial Discrimination, Guidelines for he Early Warning and Urgent Action Procedures, Annual Report, A/62/18, August 2007.

United Nations Committee on the Elimination of Racial Discrimination, Prevention of Racial Discrimination, Including Early Warning and Urgent Procedures, Working Paper 1993, A/48/18, annex III.

United Nations Committee on the Elimination of Racial Discrimination, Concluding Observations on the Russian Federation, CERD/C/304/Add.43, March 30, 1998.

United Nations Committee on the Elimination of Racial Discrimination, Concluding Observations on the Rwanda, CERD/C/304/Add.97, March 06–24, 2000.

United Nations Committee on the Elimination of Racial Discrimination, *Declaration on the Prevention of Genocide*, CERD/C/66/1, March 11, 2005.

United Nations Committee on the Elimination of Racial Discrimination, Guidelines for the Early Warning and Urgent Action Procedures, Annual Report A/62/18, August 2007.

United Nations Human Rights Committee, Concluding Observations, Russian Federation, CCPR/CO/79/RUS, December 1, 2003.

United Nations Committee against Torture, Conclusions and Recommendations, Russian Federation, CAT/C/CR/28/4, June 6, 2002.

United Nations Committee on the Rights of the Child, Consideration of reports submitted by States parties under Article 44 of the Convention, concluding observations: Rwanda, CRC/C/15/Add.234, July 1, 2004.

United Nations Commissions on Human Rights resolutions: E/CN.4/RES/1994/31, E/CN.4/RES/1995/91, E/CN.4/RES/1998/69, E/CN.4/RES/2000/58, E/CN.4/RES/2001/24, E/CN.4/RES/2003/66, E/CN.4/RES/2005/62, E/CN.4/RES/2005/62.

United Nations Human Rights Committee, Concluding observations on the fourth periodic report of Rwanda, CCPR/C/RWA/CO/4, May 2, 2016.

United Nations Human Rights Committee, Ninety-fifth session, Consideration of reports submitted by States Parties Under Article 40 of the Covenant, Concluding Observations, Rwanda, CCPR/C/RWA/CO/3, New York, May 7, 2009.

United Nations Human Rights Council, Report of the Working Group: Libyan Arab Jamahiriya, *Universal Periodic Review*, A/HRC/16/15, Geneva, January 4, 2011.

United Nations Human Rights Council, Report of the Working Group: Rwanda, *Universal Periodic Review*, A/HRC/17/14, Geneva, March 14, 2011.

United Nations Human Rights Council, Report of the Working Group: Rwanda, *Universal Periodic Review*, A/HRC/31/8, Geneva, December 18, 2015.

United Nations Security Council resolutions: S/RES/688/1991, S/RES/827/1993, S/RES/912/1994, S/RES/918/1994, S/RES/935/1994, S/RES/955/1994, S/RES/965/1994, S/RES/978/1995, S/RES/997/1995, S/RES/1203/1998, S/RES/1291/2000, S/RES/1304/2000, S/RES/1366/2001, S/RES/1366/2001, S/RES/1572/2004, S/RES/1974/2006, S/RES/1706/2006, S/RES/1951/2010, S/RES/1962/2010, S/RES/1967/2011, S/RES/1970/2011, S/RES/1973/ 2011, S/RES/1974/2006, S/RES/1975/2011, S/RES/1975/2011, S/RES/1980/2011, S/RES/1996/2011, S/RES/2040/2012, S/RES/2109/2013, S/RES/2121/2013, S/RES/2134/2014, S/RES/2150/2014, S/RES/2171/2014, S/RES/2227/2015, S/RES/2228/2015, S/RES/2250/2015, S/RES/2296/2016.

United Nations Human Rights Council resolutions on R2P at the website of Global Centre for Responsibility to Protect, https://www.globalr2p.org/resources/un-human-rights-council-resolutions-referencing-r2p/.

United Nations Human Rights Council resolutions: A/HRC/RES/5/1, A/HRC/RES/7/25, A/HRC/RES/14/5, A/HRC/RES/S-15/1, A/HRC/RES/S-14/1, A/HRC/RES/22/L30, A/HRC/RES/24/16, A/HRC/RES/28/34, A/HRC/RES/28/34, A/HRC/RES/33/6, A/HRC/RES/33/19.

United Nations General Assembly resolutions: A/RES/46/182, A/RES/48/141, A/RES/60/251, A/RES60/251, A/RES63/308, A/RES/64/245, A/RES69/323.

United Nations General Assembly Suspends Libya from Human Rights Council, UN GA/11050, March 1, 2011, http://www.un.org/press/en/2011/ga11050.doc.htm.

UN General Assembly, 2005 World Summit Outcome, par. 138–140, http://www.un.org/en/preventgenocide/adviser/pdf/World%20Summit%20Outcome%20Document.pdf#page=30.

United Nations High Commissioner for Refugees, *UNHCR to Establish New Camp in Liberia for Refugees from Côte d'Ivoire*, December 31, 2010, http://www.unhcr.org/news/press/2010/12/4d1dd09b9/unhcr-establish-new-camp-liberia-refugees-cote-divoire.html.

United Nations Human Rights Council, Report of the Working Group, *Universal Periodic Review*, A/HRC/13/9, Geneva, 04.01.2010.

United Nation Human Rights Office of the High Commissioner, *Human Rights Indicators. A Guide to Measurement and Implementation*, New York – Geneva 2012.

United Nations Office on Genocide Prevention and the Responsibility to Protect, *Framework Analysis for Atrocity Crimes. A Tool for Prevention*, New York 2014.

United Nations Progress report of the Secretary-General on the United Nations Assistance Mission for Rwanda, S/1994/1133, October 6, 1994.

United Nations Progress report of the Secretary-General on the United Nations Operation in Côte d'Ivoire, S/2010/537, October 18, 2010.

United Nations, *Report of the Independent Inquiry into the Actions of the United Nations During the 1994 Genocide in Rwanda*, New York 1999, https://www.securitycouncilreport.org/atf/cf/%7B65BFCF9B-6D27-4E9C-8CD3-CF6E4FF96FF9%7D/POC%20S19991257.pdf.

United Nations, *The Fall of Srebrenica*, Report of the Secretary-General to the UN General Assembly, New York 1999, https://digitallibrary.un.org/record/372298.

Woocher L., *Developing a Strategy, Methods and Tools for Genocide Early Warning*, Office of the Special Adviser to the UN Secretary-General on the Prevention of Genocide, Center for International Conflict Resolution, Columbia University, New York, September 26, 2006.

Yeremenko I., Novikov. Y., *Rossiya i Chechnya (1990–1997 gody). Dokumenty svidetelstvuyut,* Vserossiyskoe obshchestvenno-politicheskoe dvizhenie „Dukhovnoe nasledie", Moscow 1997.

Index of Names

A

al-Bashir O. 127
al-Islam S. 193
al-Senussi A. 193
Aall P.R. 103, 104
Abdel-Elah Al-Khatib M. 190
Abdul-Khakim S. 144
Adams S. 188, 190
Ajello A. 157
Akayesu J.P. 162
Akhavan P. 45
Albright M. 130
Alebeek R. 124

van Alfredsson G. 125

Aning K. 72
Annan K. 9, 10, 24, 30, 33, 38, 43, 155
Arantes P.L. 78
Asher D.L. 128
Ashton C. 178
Atuobi S. 72
Axworthy L. 30

B

Babbitt E.F. 120
Bachmann K. 25
Badescu C. 90
Baechler G. 118
Baehr P.R. 101, 122
Bah A.B. 173
Baldwin C. 191
Bamba Y. 179
Bar J. 153, 169
Barnett M. 153
Barqueiro C. 116, 131
Barrs C.A. 103
Bartnicki A. 136
Bates R.H. 120
Beck Ch. 95
Bédié H.K. 173
Beeson M. 79
Beetham D. 92
Bellamy A.J. 76, 79, 80, 115–117, 129, 183
Ben-Naftali O. 26, 32
Bielecka M. 57
Bieńczyk-Missala A. 10, 25, 63, 64, 102, 118, 124, 126
Bierdziński S. 192
Biersteker T.J. 123
Bindig R. 143, 146
Bizimungu P. 153
Bloed A. 64, 140
Bmeki T. 183
Bobb S. 159
Borghard E.D. 197
Boutros-Ghali B. 157
Boyle F.A. 138
Brennan R.J. 159
Buchroithner M. 113
Buchsbaum T.M. 64
Burke-White W.W. 39

C

Caflish L. 125
Carter J. 85, 86, 158, 176
Cederroth S. 121
Chakravarty A. 163
Chalk F. 116, 131
Chappel L. 53
Chin S. 95, 130
Chirot D. 173
Claes J. 197

Clark P. 163
Clarke G. 80
Cochetel V. 140
Coghlan B. 159
Cohen R. 91
Cohen W. 130
Compaoré B. 176
Comras V.D. 122, 128
Cook N. 177
Cotler I. 30, 66, 67, 81, 129
Cronin P.M. 128

D
Dallaire L.R. 111, 131, 152
Danecki J. 185
Davies J.L. 115, 118
Davis R. 112, 152
Deng F. 44, 147, 179, 188
Des Forges A. 151, 153, 155
Diène D. 174
Dieng A. 44, 98
Dobriansky P.J. 87
Donnelly J. 87, 95
Doyle N. 80
Doyle S. 131
Drummond C. 79, 80
Drzewicki K. 88
Dudayev D. 135, 139
Dzisiów-Szuszczykiewicz A. 185

E
Eckert S.E. 123
Egerton F. 31, 72, 79, 80, 91
Emizet F.K. 159
Ertürk Y. 148
Evans G. 130
Evers F. 64

F
Fabius L. 33
Feil S. 152
Feinstein L. 106, 130
Finkel J. 94
Fiott D. 53
Flood P.J. 124
Flowers N. 102
Forsythe D.P. 87

G
Gaddafi M. 90, 93, 185–187, 189–196, 205
Gaeta P. 26, 32
Galis T. 96, 113, 122, 126, 128, 130
Gbagbo L. 173–179, 181–183
Gbagbo S. 182
Genser J. 30, 32, 66, 67, 81, 129
Geremek B. 142
Ghanea N. 125
Ghebali V.-I. 57
Gibbons P. 102
Gil-Robles A. 144, 145
Glanville L. 31
Goldstone J.A. 120
Goudé Ch.B. 182
Gowan R. 106
Griffin S. 117
Grimheden J. 125
Grochmalski P. 135
Grzebyk P. 31, 93, 102
Guéï R. 173
Guldimann T. 140
Gurr T.R. 115, 118, 120
Gyarmati I. 136

H
Habyarimana J. 151, 152
Hałaciński A. 62
Hamburg D.A. 112
Hammarberg Th. 145
Hampson F.J. 125
Harff B. 120
Hayman R. 168

Hehir A. 45, 90, 112, 113, 116, 197
Heidrich D. 25
Heintze H.J. 102
Helal M.S. 81, 129
Helsing J.W. 102
Henkin L. 25, 88
Higgins R. 85, 122
Hilaire Sobers O. 78
Hoeffler A. 129
Hollande F. 33
Houphouët-Boigny F. 173, 182
Howland T. 160
Höynck W. 61
Hultman L. 129
Hurlburt H.F. 137
Hussein S. 93

I

Ingabire V. 166
Insulza J.M. 76
Ipinyomi F. 173, 183

J

Jacob C. 115
Jaskiernia J. 55
Jones A. 143

K

Kadyrov R. 145, 148
Kagame P. 153, 155
Kalamanov V. 144
Kambanda J. 126, 162, 163
Karremans Th. 112
Kathman J. 129
Kayibanda G. 151
Keller H. 124
Ki-moon B. 36, 37, 39–43, 82, 94
Kilner J. 145
Kingah S. 76
Kinzer S. 153
Klaas B. 173
Knight W.A. 31, 72, 79, 80, 91
Kohlschutter A.V. 118
Korey W. 57
Kothari M. 125
Kovács L. 136
Ku J. 126
Kuźniar R. 57, 85, 86, 88, 89, 101, 138

L

Lavrov S. 144
Leaning J. 113
Lemkin R. 9, 26, 96, 108, 126
Lebed A. 138
Lillich R.B. 24, 89
Lindberg T. 106
Locatelli T. 104
Longman T. 155
Lopez G.A. 122, 123
Lord J.E. 102
Luck E.C. 37, 39, 44, 179, 188
Lupin A. 129
Lustik M. 120

M

Madej M. 10, 103
Maisonneuve M. 117
Majekodunmi B. 112, 152
Malknecht A. 94
Mallory C. 65
Margelow M. 193
Marshall M.G. 120
Maschadov A. 138
Matthews K. 116, 131
Mawdsley J. 53
Mbeki T. 177
McLoughlin S. 40, 115
Melvern L. 127
Mertus J.A. 102
Michałowska G. 66, 124

Miskel J.F. 111
Missala M. 136, 138
Modrzejewska-Leśniewska J. 136
Mosso D. 117
Mubarak H. 186
Mucha W. 115
Mudingu J. 154
Mulamula L. 73

N
Nambiar S. 31
Nawrocki M. 192
Ndiay B. 111
Neier A. 93
Neuenkirch M. 123
Neumeier F. 123
Ngoy P. 159
Nollkaemper A. 124
Norris J. 94
Norton R.J. 111
Nuruzzaman M. 197
Nyerere J. 158
Nzelibe J. 126

O
Obama B. 94
Odinge R. 177
Ogata S. 158
Ouattara A. 175–178, 180–183

P
Parzymies S. 57
Pattinson J. 90
Petrov P. 53
Piiparinen T. 89
Pillay N. 178, 188
Piłat Z. 192
Pischedda C. 197
Ponte C. del 162
Pradhan B. 113
Przełomiec M. 135, 138

R
Ramcharan B.G. 32, 36, 49, 52, 119, 125, 129
Rashid S. 119
Raymond D. 95, 128, 130
Razali Kassim Y. 90
Resnick D. 121
Reyntjens F. 159
Riera R. 96
Robinson M. 147
Rodley N.S. 123
Rosenberg Sh.P. 96, 113, 122, 126, 128, 130
Rotberg R.I. 37
Rotfeld A.D. 57
Rudahigwa M. 151

S
Sahnoun M. 130
Sammut D. 142
Schabas W. 32, 50
Schmidt J. 53
Schreiber H. 124
Seiwert E. 76
Serrano M. 120, 123
Sewall S. 95, 130
Shannon M. 129
Shelton D. 101, 123, 125
Shields J. 142
Skar H.O. 121
Slaughter A.M. 130
Smith R. 65
Smith-Hohn J. 112, 152
Solomon D. 106
Soro G. 173, 174
Stanton G.H. 105
Steenberghe R. van 102
Stefanopoulos A. 123
Steiner B.H. 120
Stoel M. van der 118
Straus S. 155, 166, 168, 170
Sulowski S. 185

Sviatun O. 55
Symonides J. 92
Szmigielski A. 55

T
Tarbel F. 186
Thakur R. 90
Toungara J.M. 174
Touré A.T. 158
Tourinho M. 123
Traynor I. 147
Tutu D. 158

U
Ugarte B.S. 32
Ulfelder J. 120
Ulfstein G. 124

V
Védrine H. 33
Verhofstadt G. 155
Verwimp P. 128
Vincent M. 53
Vincent R.J. 118
Vlasic M.V. 66

W
Waal A. 186, 189, 191, 193
Waldorf L. 155, 166, 168, 170
Walle N. van de 121
Warner D. 57
Weiss T.G. 120, 123, 197
Weissgerber R. 192
Welsh J. 39, 45
Wieruszewski R. 126
Wilks A. 121
Williams I. 197
Williams P.D. 68, 183
Wingfield-Hayes R. 145
Woocher L. 106, 112
Woodward M. 120

Z
Zajadło J. 129
Zayas A. de 125
Zellner W. 64
Zięba R. 57
Zifcak S. 197
Zins H. 151
Zorbas E. 166, 170
Zucker A. 96, 113, 122, 126, 128, 130
Zyberi G. 53, 65, 78, 102

Studies in Politics, Security and Society

Edited by Stanisław Sulowski

Vol. 1 Robert Wiszniowski (ed.): Challenges to Representative Democracy. A European Perspective. 2015.

Vol. 2 Jarosław Szymanek: Theory of Political Representation. 2015.

Vol. 3 Alojzy Z. Nowak (ed.): Global Financial Turbulence in the Euro Area. Polish Perspective. 2015.

Vol. 4 Jolanta Itrich-Drabarek: The Civil Service in Poland. Theory and Experience. 2015.

Vol. 5 Agnieszka Rothert: Power of Imagination. Education, Innovations and Democracy. 2016.

Vol. 6 Zbysław Dobrowolski: Combating Corruption and Other Organizational Pathologies. 2017.

Vol. 7 Vito Breda: The Objectivity of Judicial Decisions. A Comparative Analysis of Nine Jurisdictions. 2017.

Vol. 8 Anna Sroka: Accountability and democracy in Poland and Spain. 2017.

Vol. 9 Anna Sroka / Fanny Castro-Rial Garrone / Rubén Darío Torres Kumbrián (eds.): Radicalism and Terrorism in the 21st Century. Implications for Security. 2017.

Vol. 10 Filip Pierzchalski: Political Leadership in Morphogenetic Perspective. 2017.

Vol. 11 Alina Petra Marinescu: The Discursive Dimension of Employee Engagement and Disengagement. Accounts of keeping and leaving jobs in present-day Bucharest organizations. 2017.

Vol. 12 Jacek Giedrojć: Competition, Coordination, Social Order. Responsible Business, Civil Society, and Government in an Open Society. 2017.

Vol. 13 Filip Ilkowski: Capitalist Imperialism in Contemporary Theoretical Frameworks. 2017.

Vol. 14 Leszek Leszczyński / Adam Szot (eds.): Discretionary Power of Public Administration. Its Scope and Control. 2017.

Vol. 15 Tadeusz Klementewicz: Understanding Politics. Theory, Procedures, Narratives. 2017.

Vol. 16 Tomasz Bichta: Political Systems of the Former Yugoslavia. 2018.

Vol. 17 Miroslav Palárik / Alena Mikulášová / Martin Hetényi / Róbert Arpáš: The City and Region Against the Backdrop of Totalitarianism. 2018.

Vol. 18 Jolanta Itrich-Drabarek / Stanisław Mazur / Justyna Wiśniewska-Grzelak (eds.): The Transformations of the Civil Service in Poland in Comparison with International Experience. 2018.

Vol. 19 Jerzy Juchnowski / R. Jan Sielezin / Ewa Maj: The Image of "White" and "Red" Russia in the Polish Political Thought of the 19th and 20th Century. Analogies and Parallels. 2018.

Vol. 20 Roman Kuźniar: Europe in the International Order. 2018.

Vol. 21 Piotr Jaroszyński: Europe - the Clash of Civilisations. 2018.

Vol. 22 Stanisław Filipowicz: Truth and the Will to Illusion. 2018.

Vol. 23 Andrzej Szeptycki: Contemporary Relations between Poland and Ukraine. The "Strategic Partnership" and the Limits Thereof. 2019.

Vol. 24 Sylwester Gardocki / Rafał Ożarowski / Rafał Ulatowski (eds.): The Islamic World in International Relations. 2019.

Vol. 25 Jacek Zaleśny (ed.): Constitutional Courts in Post-Soviet States. Between the Model of a State of Law and Its Local Application. 2019.

Vol. 26 Andrzej Antoszewski / Przemysław Żukiewicz / Mateusz Zieliński / Katarzyna. Domagała: Formation of Government Coalition in Westminster Democracies. Towards a Network Approach. 2020.

Vol. 27 Joanna Osiejewicz: Global Governance of Oil and Gas Resources in the International Legal Perspective. 2020.

Vol. 28 Anita Oberda-Monkiewicz: Poland-Mexico towards a Strategic Partnership. 2020.

Vol. 29 Bartosz Czepil / Wojciech Opioła: Ethnic diversity and local governance quality. The case of Opole Province in Poland. 2020.

Vol. 30 Adam Szymański / Jakub Wódka / Wojciech Ufel / Amanda Dziubińska: Between Fair and Rigged. Elections as a Key Determinant of the 'Borderline Political Regime' - Turkey in Comparative Perspective. 2020.

Vol. 31 Tomasz Grzegorz Grosse (ed.): Fuel for Dominance. On the Economic Bases of Geopolitical Supremacy. 2020.

Vol. 32 Dariusz Jarosz / Maria Pasztor: From Subjection to Independence. Post-World War II Polish-Italian Relations. 2020.

Vol. 33 Paweł Sekuła: Chernobyl Liquidators. The Unknown Story. With the Testimony of the President of Latvia. 2020.

Vol. 34 Kamil Glinka (ed.): Urban Policy System in Strategic Perspective: From V4 to Ukraine. 2020.

Vol. 35 Paweł Lesiński: At the Origins of German Liberalism: the State in the Thought of Robert von Mohl. 2020.

Vol. 36 Jana Popovicsová (ed): Reflexions about a Cultural and Social Phenomenon: Identity. 2020.

Vol. 37 Agnes Bernek: Geopolitics of Central and Eastern Europe in the 21st Century. From the Buffer Zone to the Gateway Zone. 2021.

Vol. 38 Marek Antoni Musioł: The European Union as a Post-Lisbon Regional Security Complex. 2021.

Vol. 39 Alina Petra Marinescu: Manipulation in the Disclosure of the *Securitate* Files. The Case of Mona Muscă. 2021.

Vol. 40 Jiří Zákravský: Cycling Diplomacy. Undemocratic Regimes and Professional-Road Cycling Teams Sponsorship. 2021.

Vol. 41 Mirosław Karwat / Filip Pierzchalski / Marcin Tobiasz (eds.): Constituents of Political Theory. Selected Articles of the Warsaw School of Political Theory. 2021.

Vol. 42 Angieszka Bieńczyk-Missala: Preventing Mass Human-Rights Violations and Atrocity Crimes. 2021.

Printed by
CPI books GmbH, Leck